DISCARDED

Issues in Public-Utility Pricing and Regulation

Issues in Public-Utility Pricing and Regulation

Edited by
Michael A. Crew
Rutgers University

LexingtonBooks
D.C. Heath and Company
Lexington, Massachusetts
Toronto

Library of Congress Cataloging in Publication Data

Main entry under title:

Issues in public-utility pricing and regulation.

"Result of two seminars held at Rutgers University, Newark on October 26, 1979 and March 28, 1980, entitled respectively 'The Demand for and Pricing of Public Utility Services,' and 'Current Issues and Problems in Public Utility Regulation.'"
Bibliography: p.
Includes index.
1. Public utilities—Congresses. 2. Public utilities—Rates—Congresses. I. Crew, Michael A.
HD2763.I87   351.87   79-6033
ISBN 0-669-03606-4

Copyright © 1980 By D.C. Heath and Company

All rights reserved. No part of this publication may be reproduced or transmitted in any form or by any means, electronic or mechanical, including photocopy, recording, or any information storage or retrieval system, without permission in writing from the publisher.

Published simultaneously in Canada

Printed in the United States of America

International Standard Book Number: 0-669-03606-4

Library of Congress Catalog Card Number: 79-6033

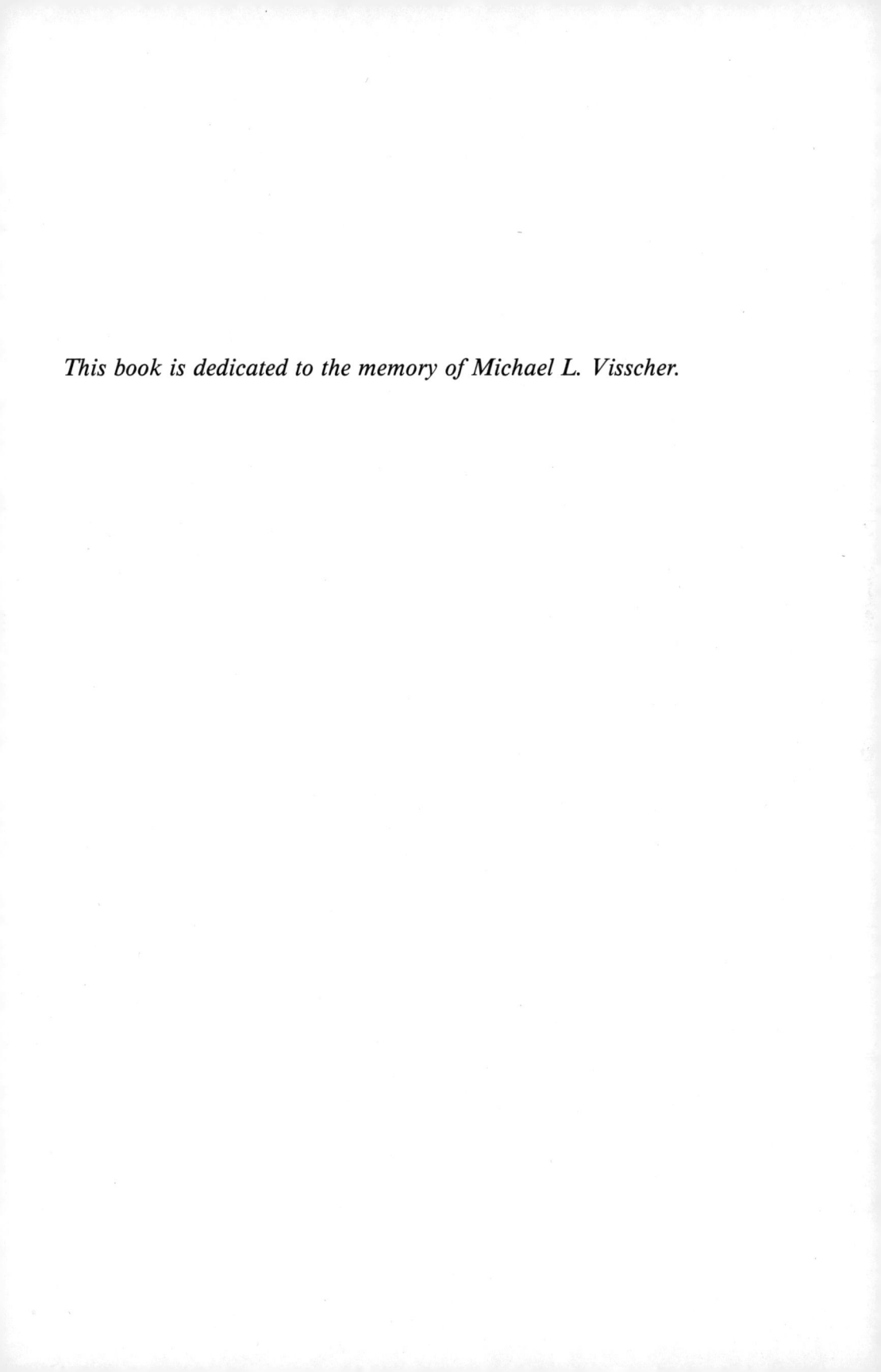

This book is dedicated to the memory of Michael L. Visscher.

Contents

	Preface and Acknowledgments	ix
Chapter 1	Introduction to Issues in Public-Utility Pricing and Regulation *Michael A. Crew*	1
Chapter 2	Hope against *Hope* *Roger Sherman*	7
Chapter 3	Regulatory Pricing Procedures and Economic Incentives *David P. Baron* and *Robert A. Taggart, Jr.*	27
Chapter 4	Public-Utility Regulation and Reliability with Applications to Electric Utilities *Michael A. Crew* and *Paul R. Kleindorfer*	51
Chapter 5	Fuel-Adjustment Clauses and Profit Risk *Frank A. Scott, Jr.*	77
Chapter 6	The Demand for Telecommunications: A Nontechnical Exposition *Lester D. Taylor*	93
Chapter 7	Alternative Measured-Service Structures for Local Telephone Service *Bridger M. Mitchell*	107
Chapter 8	Spatial Considerations in Public-Utility Pricing *Robert E. Dansby*	125
Chapter 9	Implementing Time-of-Day Pricing of Electricity: Some Current Challenges and Activities *J. Robert Malko* and *Ahmad Faruqui*	145
Chapter 10	Demand for Electricity by Time of Day: An Evaluation of Experimental Results *Wallace Hendricks* and *Roger Koenker*	165
Chapter 11	Measuring the Potential Impacts from Lifeline Pricing of Electricity and Natural-Gas Services *Dennis Ray* and *Rodney Stevenson*	183

References	209
Seminar Speakers and Discussants	223
About the Editor	225

Preface and Acknowledgments

This book is a result of two seminars held at Rutgers University, Newark, New Jersey, on October 26, 1979, and March 28, 1980, entitled, respectively, "The Demand for and Pricing of Public-Utility Services" and "Current Issues and Problems in Public-Utility Regulation." Two previous seminars in the same series resulted in *Problems in Public Utility Economics and Regulation*, published by Lexington Books in 1979.

Like the previous seminars, the current seminars received financial support from the leading New Jersey utilities. I thank Elizabethtown Gas Company, New Jersey Bell, Public Service Electric and Gas Company, and South Jersey Gas Company for their continued support of the seminars in 1979 and 1980. In addition, I thank Jersey Central Power and Light Company for its support of the seminars during 1979 and Atlantic City Electric Company, New Jersey Natural Gas Company, and United Telephone Company of New Jersey for their support in 1980. The support went far beyond financial assistance. Company managers freely gave their time and advice and on several occasions provided information about their industries. Their wise counsel was especially useful to me in striving to achieve clarity of exposition both at the seminars and in the chapters of this book. I especially thank George Baulig, Bert Blewitt, Lawrence Codey, Russ Fleming, Theodore Holliday, Douglas Huggard, Edward Jones, Don Marione, William Miners, Paul Preis, and George Wickard.

I also thank Fred Grygiel, Chief Public Utility Economist of the New Jersey Board of Public Utilities. In addition to his contribution as a seminar discussant, he has been a frequent source of ideas and information for use in the seminars. His knowledge of regulatory processes has proved invaluable to Paul R. Kleindorfer and me in our efforts to apply our work to the real world.

My thanks are owed to the distinguished speakers and discussants listed at the end of the book, for their cooperation in making the seminars and this book possible. From this group, I especially thank my long-time collaborator, Paul R. Kleindorfer, for the help and encouragement he has given me with this book.

I am most grateful to Laurel Gould and Florine Hunt of the Public Service Electric and Gas Company's library for their patient assistance on several occasions. Similarly, the secretarial assistance of Pat Rotonda, Ellen Seneca, and Adele Weiss was essential to the completion of this book.

Finally, I thank Horace J. De Podwin, dean of the Rutgers University School of Management, for his interest in the project. By his introductory remarks he ensured that our seminars got off to a good start. In addition, he saw that resources of the school were made available for the project.

The usual disclaimers are applicable. None of the persons named above are responsible for any errors. The views expressed are the views of the authors and not of the sponsoring companies.

**Issues in
Public-Utility
Pricing and
Regulation**

1

Introduction to Issues in Public-Utility Pricing and Regulation

Michael A. Crew

This book discusses some of the major issues which currently face utilities and which are likely to linger for several years to come. Indeed, belief in the durability of these problems provides an important justification for many of the chapters contained in this book. The treatment is selective rather than comprehensive, dealing with only a particular class of problems. The problems covered in this book owe their origin to the early 1970s, which marked the end of what, during the 1950s and 1960s, had been something of a golden age for utilities and regulators, notable for its stability, smooth-running and apparently unobtrusive regulation, falling relative fuel prices, rapid technological advancement and falling relative utility prices. Utilities and regulators had few problems. Voices of criticism were few and far between and had little impact during this period, including the now-famous contribution of Averch and Johnson (1962), which raised the possibility that regulation, as practiced, might lead to inefficiencies in terms of the capital-labor mix employed by utilities.

With a change in the fortunes of utilities and regulators, increased academic, political, and legal interest in the problems of utilities was created. This change in fortune was brought about by a number of factors, such as increased inflation, increasing relative fuel prices, and probably a reduction in the rate of technological progress and productivity growth, at least in energy utilities. Strains were placed on the regulatory process in a number of ways. With inflation and increased relative fuel prices, utilities were forced into more frequent rate hearings in order to attempt to maintain their revenues in real terms. This placed an added burden on the regulatory process and placed many regulators in a difficult dilemma: Either the utilities could be allowed to recoup their added costs resulting from inflation, or they could be denied these reimbursements in whole or in part. The former alternative would be unpopular with rate payers, and the latter would cause the utilities problems in replacing their plant and financing expansion. Regulators sought solutions to these problems by instituting arrangements such as fuel-adjustment clauses, which enabled utilities to be compensated by means of higher rates for increases in their fuel costs without recourse to the traditional formal and, possibly lengthy, rate proceedings. Such devices, without doubt, took some of the pressure of fuel increases off regulators and companies, though not without cost.

The question of what to do in response to the problems currently faced by utilities and regulators is the main theme of this book. Of necessity, the approach is rather selective, focusing on three main topics: making regulation more efficient, implications for demand and pricing in utilities, and questions of fairness and equity.

Approaches to More Efficient Regulation

In many ways, the flaws in the current procedures for rate-of-return regulation are more apparent in inflationary times. The frequency with which rate hearings have to be called highlights the cumbersome nature of legal processes in dealing with such problems. Rate cases are expensive in terms of the cost of management time, expensive lawyers, expert witnesses, and delay. Moreover, on occasion, the process may appear unresponsive or irrelevant to the problems faced by utilities and their customers. Indeed, the regulatory process itself, to the extent that it takes away talented managerial resources from the other problems of the company, such as the need to improve productivity and technology, might be regarded as counterproductive. Given the problems of recent years and the increased frequency of rate cases, this may be a nontrivial problem. Along similar lines, the price paid in X-inefficiency[1] of using regulation, as outlined by Sheshinski (1971), may take on added significance when utilities are faced with the problems of the last few years, and there may be an added impetus and desire on the part of the regulators and companies to address the issue of making regulation more efficient. Chapters 2 through 5 accordingly address a number of ways of making the regulatory process more efficient.

In chapter 2, Sherman discusses some of the inefficiencies resulting from rate-of-return regulation. He briefly outlines the legal background to regulation, beginning with *Munn* v. *Illinois* and culminating in *FPC* v. *Hope Natural Gas*. The latter provides the basis for current rate-of-return regulation. Sherman examines some of the effects of the process on the incentives for efficiency within the regulated firm. His findings in this regard are negative, pointing to incentives for operating inefficiency, discriminatory pricing, and an excessive amount of risk from demand changes being borne by consumers. In addition, he argues that the risks faced by the regulated firm arise, to a considerable extent, from the behavior of regulatory agencies themselves. He does, however, offer the prospect of improvement based on cost and output targets which he demonstrates reduce the potential for inefficiency. In addition, his proposal of reducing the discretionary power of regulators lessens the scope for regulation itself being a principal source of risk for the regulated firm.

In chapter 3 Baron and Taggart and in chapter 4 Crew and Kleindorfer

Introduction to Issues

examine the nature of regulation with stochastic demand. The stochastic demand requires models more complicated than the traditional deterministic models developed by Averch and Johnson. This, in turn, leads to a complicated redefinition of the Averch-Johnson effect. The analysis results in a number of important new questions being raised about the regulatory process. These concern such complexities as the interaction of the firm and the regulator, the extent to which regulation takes place within a rational expectations framework, or, as Baron and Taggart see it, the extent to which regulation is sophisticated or naive. Other issues include the extent to which the company is allowed to exceed the rate-of-return constraint. In turn, this raises the question as to the appropriate nature of the rate-of-return constraint under uncertainty.

In addition to examining theoretical issues, in chapter 4 Crew and Kleindorfer also attempt to perform some empirical work. They aim to test the relationship between reserve margins (roughly, the excess of capacity over peak demand) and rate of return. An earlier paper by Crew and Kleindorfer (1979a) hypothesized that reserve margin is inversely related to rate of return. This hypothesis, as well as various technological effects, is tested with published data on the 100 largest electric utilities.

In chapter 5, Scott examines the effects of fuel-adjustment clauses on the regulatory process. The *raison d'être* for fuel-adjustment clauses is the need to protect company earnings in times of rapid increase in relative fuel prices. Scott examines the extent to which these clauses are successful in stabilizing earnings in such circumstances and their effect on resource allocation. By compensating the firm for fuel-price increases in inflationary times, regulators not only might reduce the variance of company earnings, but also might encourage substitution of fuel for other inputs. This seems to be yet another possibility for the "tar baby" effect.[2]

Implications for Demand and Pricing in Public Utilities

The problems facing utilities create the need for more research in the area of pricing and demand by public-utility economics. In the case of electric utilities, this arises from the need to apply peak-load pricing policies. In the case of telephone utilities, competition and technological advances resulting in reduced metering costs make the possibility of substituting local measured-service rates for a flat rate a particularly important consideration. Chapters 6 through 10 are accordingly concerned with theoretical and practical policy issues in pricing and demand.

In chapters 6 and 7, Taylor and Mitchell are concerned with the framework underlying some problems in moving from a flat rate to measured-service pricing of local telephone calls. Taylor provides a highly readable, nontechnical introduction to the nature of telephone demand, the extent to which demand is affected by such considerations as the relative prices of access to the network and use of the network. While his aim is to provide a simple introduction, he also points the reader in the direction of other determinants of telephone demand, such as the value of time. Mitchell examines some of the practical considerations in implementing local measured service, in particular the implications of offering optional measured and flat-rate services.

In chapter 8 Dansby is concerned with a relatively undeveloped area, spatial economics and public utilities. His theoretical framework enables him to examine the question of efficient pricing in an idealized network where production and consumption are located separately and connected by a transmission network. He examines the role of his models in electric-power systems. In addition, he demonstrates the light his model can shed on some aspects of telephone tariffs, namely, the option of extended-area service (roughly, the ability to extend the geographic area covered by flat-rate service). His analysis of this problem is particularly important in the light of the current interest in the issue of local measured service.

In chapter 9, Malko and Faruqui and in chapter 10 Hendricks and Koenker examine some of the problems involved in conducting experiments with innovative rates, which are the forerunner to the adoption of peak-load pricing and advanced-load management techniques. Malko and Faruqui draw from their highly relevant experience at the Electric Power Research Institute in the "Electric Utility Rate Design Study." They deal with a number of important issues, such as the implications of the Public Utility Regulatory Policies Act (PURPA) of 1978 and methods of planning and evaluating different load-management strategies. They also survey some of the results of recent rate-design experiments, including various estimates of elasticities.

In chapter 10, Hendricks and Koenker in some respects are concerned with the very basic foundations underlying rate-design experiments and attempts to measure electric demand. They provide an important survey and critique of the various methodologies employed in recent studies.

Fairness, Equity, and Efficiency

Traditionally, economists have taken the view that problems of income distribution could be better dealt with by using macroeconomic instruments, such as subsidies and taxes, rather than through the essentially micoeconomic controls of public-utility regulation.[3] Thus in chapter 11, Ray and Stevenson have displayed a certain amount of courage in examining some of the economic consequences of the introduction of lifeline rates. As they note,

Introduction to Issues

these can take several forms. One example might be a simple increasing block tariff. Another might be a rate targeted at some particular group(s) of consumers.

Chapter 11 is based on Ray's and Stevenson's study of lifeline rates for the New Mexico Public Service Commission. It does not aim to provide a complete analysis of the welfare consequences of incorporating lifeline rates. Thus, it does not deal with the effects on efficiency, such as the effects of the deviations from marginal cost that are implied. Nor does it deal with the efficiency of lifeline rates when compared with alternative redistribution devices. The approach is much more limited, comparing the effects on various classes of customers of a number of lifeline proposals. It represents a first step by economists in examining the consequences of lifeline rates.

Notes

1. Liebenstein (1966) first used the term *X-efficiency* to describe the technical efficiency in the sense of output being produced at least cost. Thus the Averch-Johnson effect, where as a result of regulation the firm employs a higher capital-labor ratio than the one that minimizes cost, is an example of X-inefficiency.

2. The idea of the "tar baby" effect derives from a situation where regulation reveals or creates another problem for which the solution appears to be more regulation. For a good discussion, see McKie (1970, p. 9).

3. Of course, this is apparent with the now-traditional use of the social welfare function $W = TR + S - TC$, where TR = total revenue, S = consumer's surplus, and TC = total cost. This function concentrates on efficiency being neutral as to who gains or who loses. For details, see Williamson (1966, 1968) and Crew and Kleindorfer (1979c).

2

Hope against *Hope*

Roger Sherman

Introduction

A public-utility company looks very much like any other private business firm. It commercially advertises its products and services, offers regular employment opportunities, and has its share values fluctuate in daily stock market reports, just like the ABC Manufacturing Company. The seemingly minor difference is that profit for the public utility is set by a regulatory agency, presumably to mimic a competitive market process, rather than by the genuine interplay of many producers in a competitive market. But because profit is set through a quasi-judicial regulatory process, guided largely by a Supreme Court decision more than thirty-five years ago in the *Hope Natural Gas* case, the public utility really differs strikingly from an unregulated business firm. Indeed, when regulation under *Hope* guidelines sets the firm's rate of return, incentives within the firm are distorted. Besides causing waste, inefficiency, and excessively discriminatory pricing, such regulation also introduces new uncertainties which both consumers and investors must bear. Perhaps these consequences should not be surprising, for regulation by Supreme Court guidance is a judicial process which focuses on issues of equity rather than efficiency. As a result, public-utility regulation according to Court guidelines never even faced many important economic questions.

Hope for improving efficiency and risk bearing in regulated public utilities lies in supplanting the *Hope* rate-of-return guidelines with broader principles. Much analysis of the regulated firm exists as a basis for such modification, although the question of risk bearing has received remarkably little attention. The next section contains a brief description of rate-of-return regulation under the *Hope* guidelines and identifies major problems. The third section describes in greater detail four unintended and undesirable consequences of regulation according to *Hope* guidelines. The fourth section contains proposals for change in regulatory practice intended to remedy these problems. A different form of profit constraint, to be applied to a past test period, is designed to correct inefficiencies in choices of both inputs and outputs. Consistent procedures are urged for estimating the cost of capital, so that commissions' actions will become more predictable. Also introduced are cost and output targets, which afford something like cost and volume variance analysis from managerial accounting, as a basis for judging when a hearing to consider new rates is in order. Such a procedure can help to retain risk bearing by shareholders rather than shift risks to consumers. The last section is a summary.

Rate-of-Return Regulation according to *Hope*

Public regulation of private monopoly in the United States began a hundred years ago with *Munn* v. *Illinois*, a Supreme Court decision which endorsed intervention by a state government to limit prices set by a private firm.[1] Although the legislature, rather than the courts, was called on to prescribe prices under that decision, the Court later gave detailed guidance. In its 1898 *Smyth* v. *Ames* decision, specific factors were to determine allowable profit to investors in what came to be known as the "fair return on fair value" guidelines.[2] The many factors suggested in this guideline were not related to one another by any tidy logic, however. So when courts paid attention to them all, the decisions inevitably were inconsistent.

Of course, the task of setting rates of return was ambitious. In the two decades between the *Munn* v. *Illinois* decision and *Smyth* v. *Ames*, the price level had moved steadily downward. Confusion was caused by this decline in the values of capital investments, for regulatory commissions were unsure whether investors in regulated utilities should absorb nominal capital losses. Immediately after *Smyth* v. *Ames*, the price level began to rise, starting an inflationary trend that has continued with only minor interruptions to the present. This rising price-level trend brought new arguments from the regulated firms, which now sought profits related to the higher, replacement, costs of their assets rather than original costs. Neither commissions nor courts were consistent in their responses to this valuation question.[3]

The watershed *Hope Natural Gas* case, which guides present rate-of-return regulation, came in 1944.[4] That decision freed regulatory commissions from considering the many factors that could determine a fair return on fair value according to *Smyth* v. *Ames*; and attention was focused instead on the final result of a regulatory decision. The *Hope* decision set out broad guidelines for choosing the rate of return. It also specified a basis for asset values that rested on their costs. Less attention was to be devoted to valuing assets that rested on their costs. Less attention was to be devoted to valuing assets under the *Hope* guidelines because their value was seen potentially to depend in a circular way on the earnings allowed. Thus the *Hope* decision attempted to break the pattern of circular reasoning which was inherent in the *Smyth* v. *Ames* "fair value" goal. The key to breaking that circularity came from tying allowed profit to a *cost* basis for asset value and proposing a rule for setting the rate of return on such an asset value.

Asset cost might be reckoned in either original cost or current-replacement-cost terms. Replacement cost differs from original cost because of changes in the value of the dollar, which in recent years would raise the replacement cost resulting from inflation, and improvements in technology, which might lower the replacement cost of achieving a certain output level compared with older methods. In setting the rate of return, debt in the firm's capital structure was to be treated separately from equity. The actual historical interest rate on debt was to be counted as the allowed rate of return to the portion of the rate base financed by debt.[5] Two broad standards were articulated for setting the rate of return to equity: the "comparable earnings" standard and the "capital attraction" standard. The latter was to ensure financial soundness, and it called for a rate of return that was "sufficient to assure confidence in the financial integrity of the enterprise, so as to maintain its credit and to attract capital."[6] The comparable earnings standard, which also was to be applied to only the equity portion of capital, called for returns to be set equal to those earned currently by other firms that faced comparable risks.[7]

After the *Hope* decision, regulatory commissions were by no means uniform in their actions. In following the *Hope* precedent, a regulatory commission would narrow the range of its considerations, but the rate-of-return guidelines still left enough room for local interpretation that methods of application could differ substantially from jurisdiction to jurisdiction. By nominally adhering to the *Hope* guidelines, however, a commission was able to remain somewhat independent of judicial review. Original cost became widely used as a basis for asset valuation. The rate of return on the debt portion of the firm's capital structure usually was set at a level sufficient to meet the interest rate on existing debt, and a similar practice has been followed with respect to preferred stock.[8] The main question that has been debated in rate hearings since *Hope* is the rate of return to be allowed on the remaining, *equity*, portion of capital. To quote from an analysis of practices made by Thompson and Thatcher (1973, p. 148):

> The contractual feature of return to bondholders and preferred stockholders reduces argument on the return accruing to these investors to minor significance. However, in economic literature and in regulatory cases substantial debate centers on the determination of the rate of return to be granted common stockholders.

The variety of arguments used by expert witnesses to support equity rates of return remains as great today as in the first years after the *Hope* decision.[9] Sometimes the past experience of shareholders of the regulated firm—such as earnings-price ratio or as dividends-price ratio plus growth in share value—is offered as a guide in setting a return that can attract capital and thereby qualify as a rate of return to allow on equity. The comparable-earnings standard recently has been urged more often, too, sometimes in the form of a premium above a riskless rate of return to adjust for estimated risk and sometimes by reference to the return earned by a firm or group of firms deemed to face comparable risk. Such a wide range of possible arguments has often led to bitter disagreement in adversary rate hearings.

While so much effort has gone into arguments about a rate of return on the equity of public utilities, possible effects of this regulatory process on incentives within the utilities have been almost ignored. Yet these effects are serious. With profit set largely through legalistic debate which focused on equity returns rather than, say, on the level of costs, the pressure for efficiency was muted. Moreover, inefficiency might invite a proposal by the firm for a rate increase rather than genuine corrective action.

The many possible grounds available (through precedent) for asset valuation and rate-of-return determination also have given more scope to the regulatory agency in its decision making. And regulators could exercise discretion because the profit they decided was well within the maximum profit that could be wrung from the firm's monopoly position. But since regulators tended to be unpredictable, uncertainties about their decisions could overshadow inherent business risk as an influence on the value of ownership shares in the firm. And since performance is seldom well evaluated, shareholders of an inefficient firm may receive a return that meets the *Hope* guidelines because of prices higher than those which an efficient firm would require. The excessive prices are paid, of course, by consumers. In an unregulated competitive market, however, the shareholders would suffer from inefficient firm performance, because the firm would have to meet competitive prices to make sales to consumers. Thus it is possible that the incentives which shareholders of unregulated firms have to seek efficient management are attentuated when rate-of-return regulation is applied.

Even when rate-of-return regulated firms faithfully seek profit for shareholders, their incentives are distorted away from efficiency. With allowed profit tied to capital value through rate of return, a new incentive may be created to increase the use of capital as a means of increasing allowed profit. As a result, capital will not be joined with other inputs most efficiently in production. And monopolistic tendencies to discriminate in price, which can serve this profit-seeking aim, are not restrained by rate-of-return regulation either. Moreover, as Crew and Kleindorfer have recently emphasized (1979b), managers within the regulated public utility have a greater opportunity to pursue their own interests, and efficiency may suffer as a consequence.

Thus if somehow it could be correctly done, setting a rate of return on asset cost as a basis for profit under the *Hope* guidelines still distorts and weakens incentives within the regulated firm. And setting a rate of return by the comparable-earnings and capital-attraction standards can seldom be

Hope against *Hope*

based on any compelling economic rationale. The unique U.S. privately owned public utility regulated by the rate-of-return constraint according to *Hope* guidelines can therefore be portrayed, admittedly in caricature, as follows:

1. Input efficiency in the firm is perverted.
2. Prices of the firm's services are discriminatory, so output quantities are inefficient.
3. The regulatory agency is the source of much of the firm's financial risk.
4. Most risk of demand change or loss of operating efficiency is borne by consumers.

Although these bold statements sound foolishly extreme, there is an element of truth in each of them.

Unintended Consequences of Regulation under *Hope*

Let us now turn from this general discussion to specify four problems of present-day regulation. We state these problems here and provide remedies for them in the next section.

Input Inefficiency

Legal debates from *Munn* v. *Illinois* to *FPC* v. *Hope Natural Gas* focused almost exclusively on how to set a profit level for the firm, as if that could be done and all other aspects of the market process would continue unaffected. We noted that in unregulated firms shareholders entitled to the residual difference between revenues and costs, the amount we call profit, will exert pressure for efficient operation. When profit is determined by a different mechanism, dependent not on operating efficiency but rather on debate involving comparisons with the earnings of other firms or in other times, the incentive for efficiency will be muted. For now the firm can merely add allowed profit to its costs in order to determine prices.

Even if the management of the firm is faithful to the shareholders' interest in profit, there is still a problem for efficiency under rate-of-return regulation. Whereas the ordinary firm seeks only profit, the rate-of-return regulated firm has two goals. One goal is to earn profit and the other is to be allowed to keep it. If allowed profit depends on the level of one input, as it depends on capital under rate-of-return regulation, then the firm will use more of that input. Capital is valuable not only for its productive contribution to output but also for the increase it will bring in the amount of profit the firm is allowed to earn.

The resulting bias toward more-than-efficient quantities of capital in producing any level of output is called the Averch-Johnson (1962) bias, in honor of the two economists who first described it in detail. As shown by Peles and Stein (1976) and by Crew and Kleindorfer in chapter 4 of this book, under uncertainty the question of bias can be much more complicated; nevertheless, evidence thus far has tended to support the higher-capital Averch-Johnson bias.[10]

The Averch-Johnson analysis greatly simplifies the regulatory setting to one where the firm is continuously held exactly to an allowed rate of return s which exceeds capital cost r. Suppose a single product x that is sold at price p has total cost $wV + rK$, where K is capital (measured in numeraire value) and V represents all other inputs, with r and w the capital and other-inputs prices. The firm's problem is to maximize

$$L(V, K, \lambda) = px - wV - rK - \lambda(px - wV - sK) \quad (2.1)$$

From the necessary conditions for a maximum of L, Averch and Johnson showed that

$$-\frac{\partial V}{\partial K} = \frac{r - \lambda(s - r)/(1 - \lambda)}{w} < \frac{r}{w} \quad (2.2)$$

which means the firm adopts an inefficient mixture of inputs. Inputs are chosen as if capital were cheaper, at $r - \lambda(s - r)/(1 - \lambda)$, than its true cost of r (as long as $s > r$, which implies $0 < \lambda < 1$).

Output Inefficiency

When the regulated firm offers more than one product or service, the question arises of whether it will choose to produce them in an efficient mixture, through efficient relative prices. Sherman and Visscher (1979) have emphasized that the rate-of-return regulated firm will be influenced by demand elasticities and marginal capital intensities of its outputs in ways that conflict with efficient pricing. To show this, let us take an especially simple example of two products with independent demands where x_1 requires no capital in its production and x_2 does require capital. We also assume constant productivity of all other inputs, so V of the previous problem now is $\Sigma_{i=1}^{2} v_i x_i$, where v_i represents the amount of V needed per unit of x_i. Thus, the regulated firm faces the problem ($i = 1, 2$)

$$G(x_1, x_2, \mu) = \Sigma p_i x_i - w\Sigma v_i x_i - rK_2 - \mu(\Sigma p_i x_i - w\Sigma v_i x_i - sK_2) \quad (2.3)$$

Necessary conditions for a maximum yield the two prices

$$p_1 = \frac{wv_1}{1 - 1/\eta_1} \tag{2.4}$$

and

$$p_2 = \frac{wv_2 + [r - \mu(s - r)/(1 - \mu)]\partial K_2/\partial x_2}{1 - 1/\eta_2} \tag{2.5}$$

where η_1 and η_2 are own-price elasticities of demand. Price p_1 is obviously a profit-maximizing monopoly price, with regulation having no effect whatever. Price p_2 is a monopoly price modified by the subtraction from marginal cost of an amount $\mu(s - r)(\partial K_2/\partial x_2)/(1 - \mu)$. Since this amount is positive, the price of x_2 is reduced from the monopoly level. But demand elasticity influences price, just as it would for an unregulated monopolist. Thus, although demand elasticity acts to lower the firm's view of its marginal capital cost, rate-of-return regulation does nothing to inhibit the price-discrimination tendency in an unregulated monopoly.

Regulatory Action as a Source of Risk

Having the regulatory commission contribute to uncertainty is undesirable. Some uncertainty, such as that owing to whether demand is strong or whether management is effective, is usefully borne by investors who are willing to bear it, for if they bear the consequences, they will have greater incentive to oversee management performance. But uncertainty due to regulatory action that is independent of demand or management performance is not so constructive. It adds to investor risk and perhaps consumer risk, and because investors will want higher returns for bearing more risk, it will raise the cost to consumers. Risk from uncertainty about regulatory-commission decisions also complicates the valuation problem in capital markets, as Gordon and McCallum (1972) have shown.

Under the ordinary functioning of competitive markets, a return on all the assets of the entire firm will be based on current conditions, because the decisions of new entrants determine returns in competitive markets and new entrants always face current conditions. Of course, traditionally bonds have been issued in nominal terms, but since overall returns depend on current conditions, shareholders of unregulated firms will either gain or lose when historically agreed-upon interest rates are below or above current ones. The *Hope* guideline for allowing returns to regulated utilities avoids such a spillover effect to shareholders of any change in interest rate by applying a current return to only the equity portion of assets. Unfortunately, this procedure interferes with the ordinary valuation process, for it can make the capital structure of the regulated firm influence its allowed rate of return.[11] Since the ordinary theory of firm valuation is not entirely applicable, the decision of a regulatory commission is more difficult to predict.

The aim of the Court in allowing the historical rather than the current interest rate as the rate of return on debt capital has been rationalized as an attempt to avoid creating what might be deemed windfall gains or losses to shareholders.[12] This clearly was one concern of Justice Brandeis when he urged in his concurring minority opinion in the *Southwestern Bell* case[13] that returns be applied to the original cost of assets in order to free regulation from "the confusing metaphysics of reproduction cost" which flourished under the fair-value guideline.[14] Justice Douglas, in the majority opinion in the *Hope* case, sought to avoid complete reliance on setting a fixed return at some initial starting date when capital was first committed to the firm, as Brandeis had recommended, and called instead for treating debt that way but for estimating a *current* return to equity by comparable-earnings and capital-attraction standards. Thus the major modification that was contained in *Hope* probably was intended to avoid what seemed like windfall gains and losses for shareholders due to price-level changes. Nevertheless, it also had the effect of separating debt and equity returns into nominal (for debt) and real (for equity) categories, creating a hybrid mixture to which ordinary valuation theory may not apply.

Thus, a regulated firm's value may turn not on the inherent business risk of the entire enterprise, which could be reflected by the fortunes of monopoly in an unregulated state, but rather on how the regulatory agency will choose from contending arguments in setting a return for holders of equity. This is uncertainty about s in the models examined above. No one market result is forced on the regulators' attention in determining s because the market cannot value shares as it would in the absence of regulation. And as long as regulators are allowing returns well below the full monopoly levels, their decisions can be quite removed from the business risk inherent in the monopoly position. That is why the main uncertainties shareholders face may be the uncertainties of regulatory-agency decision.

Risks Borne by Consumers

The process followed in setting an allowed rate of return can affect risk bearing crucially. After a rate of return to equity is decided, that rate typically is combined with the historical rate of return to debt and preferred stock into a weighted average as the overall rate of return to be allowed on all assets of the firm. The weights given to debt, preferred stock, and equity rates of return usually reflect their importance in the book-value capital structure of the firm, in part because the total asset base of a regulated firm in most states is taken from the book, or original cost, value of assets deemed properly a part of the regulated firm. Then the firm adds to its own estimate of total cost a profit allowance that will yield the allowed rate of return on assets and sets prices to cover the sum of total cost and profit.

Consider what will happen if demand falls below the level anticipated by the firm when prices were set or if the firm is operated less efficiently than expected so its costs rise. The firm almost certainly will turn to the agency that regulates it and ask for higher prices, so that its allowed rate of return can be preserved. Regulatory agencies sometimes make modest efforts to evaluate efficiency but seldom are able to do it well; and although there may be some delay before action, the delay called "regulatory lag," price increases can be expected. As a result, those placed to oversee the operating efficiency of the firm—the shareholders—are robbed of the incentive to do it; resort can be made to the regulatory authority to draw on monopoly power for revenues instead. Without strong interests of shareholder as residual claimants to discipline them, managers have greater opportunity to pursue their personal interests in place of efficiency. And, of course, the effects of unexpected demand shifts or even of deteriorating cost control can be borne by consumers through price changes rather than by the presumed risk bearers, the shareholders of the firm.

Hope against *Hope*

Suggestions are now presented to overcome these drawbacks of rate-of-return regulation as imposed under *Hope* guidelines. There are four proposals in all, one to deal with each problem that has been diagnosed: (1) Shift from use of the actual measured investment rate base to another, constructed as a *target* amount of investment related to actual output levels. (2) Use a past test period, with past output levels (rather than the future test periods that have recently come into use), in determining a target allowed profit. (3) Adopt any of several proposals that have been made to improve the process for setting a rate of return, so that uncertainty about the process might be reduced. (4) Allow the target profit to rise or fall with output or performance, so that it can be compared with actual profit to help in deciding at any time whether a new rate hearing should be scheduled. Such a target will help in identifying effects of unanticipated demand shifts or performance changes which shareholders, rather than consumers, should absorb.

Input Inefficiency

Consider as a rate base for a single-product firm the firm's output, rather than its actual capital. For example, some specified fraction α times a price of capital s plus the fraction $1 - \alpha$ times a price of other inputs w would create an allowed cost per unit of output.[15] That is, allowed profit might simply be set so that $px = [\alpha s + (1 - \alpha)w]x$, or so $[\alpha s + (1 - \alpha)w]x - wV - rK$ would equal allowed profit. The determination of α here should be based on an analysis of other public utilities in the same industry, with appropriate adjustments made for differences in the utilities' situations. For example, electric utilities face differences in fuels available, methods of construction (mainly weather-protection needs, which vary according to climate), and demand patterns. With a standard created from other firms for the input mix, one firm would no longer be able to influence allowed profit through its own capital input choices.

A modification to the problem posed in equation 2.1, introducing a profit allowance based on output, leads to the new problem for the regulated firm:

$$L'(V, K, \psi) = px - wV - rK - \psi\{px - [\alpha s + (1 - \alpha)w]x\} \quad (2.6)$$

In addition to the constraint, necessary conditions for a maximum of equation 2.6 are

$$\left(p + x \frac{\partial p}{\partial x}\right) \frac{\partial x}{\partial V} (1 - \psi) - w + \psi[\alpha s + (1 - \alpha)w] \frac{\partial x}{\partial V} = 0 \quad (2.7)$$

and

$$\left(p + x \frac{\partial p}{\partial x}\right) \frac{\partial x}{\partial K} (1 - \psi) - r + \psi[\alpha s + (1 - \alpha)w] \frac{\partial x}{\partial K} = 0 \quad (2.8)$$

Solving for $-\partial V/\partial K$ as before, we obtain

$$-\frac{\partial V}{\partial K} = \frac{r}{w} \quad (2.9)$$

which indicates that no Averch-Johnson technical input inefficiency is present. That the Averch-Johnson bias can be avoided by allowing profit per unit output, rather than per unit capital, was first shown by Bailey and Malone (1970).

The adoption of such an output basis for profit regulation will not prevent output inefficiency in a multiproduct firm, however. If the constraint in equation 2.3 is replaced by a constraint that allows profit $p_i - \alpha_i s - (1 - \alpha_i)w$ per unit of output i, the resulting problem is

Hope against *Hope*

$$G'(x_1, x_2, \gamma) = \Sigma p_i x_i - w\Sigma v_i x_i - rK_2 - \gamma[\Sigma p_i x_i - s\Sigma \alpha_i x_i$$
$$- w\Sigma(1 - \alpha_i)x_i] \quad (2.10)$$

Necessary conditions for a maximum to this problem yield prices

$$p_1 = \frac{w[v_1 - \gamma(1 - \alpha_1)]/(1 - \gamma)}{1 - 1/\eta_1} \quad (2.11)$$

and $p_2 =$

$$\frac{\{w[v_2 - \gamma(1 - \alpha_2)] + r\, \partial K_2/\partial x_2 - \gamma s \alpha_2\}/(1 - \gamma)}{1 - 1/\eta_2}$$
$$(2.12)$$

While these pricing rules may appear as improvements over those in equations 2.4 and 2.5, they will still lead to inefficient outputs. It is true that as a basis for price, marginal cost will now tend to be understated for x_1 because of the $\gamma(1 - \alpha_1)/(1 - \gamma)$ term, and the marginal cost for x_2 will be understated for both inputs.[16] The prices are not ideal because demand elasticity in the denominator still has its full effect as an influence in marking up these implicit marginal costs to determine final prices.

Output Inefficiency

Now consider the alteration of the problem G' in equation 2.10 to reflect the use of a past test period. By using a past test period we make the allowed total revenue, which appears in the constraint, depend on outputs from the past test period $\bar{x}_i$ rather than on unknown future x_i. Thus, expanding to the multiproduct firm, we form the slightly altered problem G'':

$$G''(x_1, x_2, \gamma') = \Sigma p_i x_i - w\Sigma v_i x_i - rK_2 + \gamma'\{\Sigma p_i \bar{x}_i - [s\Sigma \alpha_i + w\Sigma(1 - \alpha_i)]\bar{x}_i\} \quad (2.13)$$

Necessary conditions for this problem are

$$\frac{\partial G''}{\partial x_1} = p_1 + x_1 \frac{\partial p_1}{\partial x_1} - wv_1 - \gamma' \bar{x}_1 \frac{\partial p_1}{\partial x_1} = 0$$

and

$$\frac{\partial G''}{\partial x_2} = p_2 + x_2 \frac{\partial p_2}{\partial x_2} - wv_2 - r\frac{\partial K_2}{\partial x_2} - \gamma' \bar{x}_2 \frac{\partial p_2}{\partial x_2} = 0$$

which yield prices

$$p_1 = \frac{wv_1}{1 + (1 - \gamma'\bar{x}_1/x_1)(1/\eta_1)} \qquad (2.14)$$

and
$$p_2 = \frac{wv_2 + r\,\partial K_2/\partial x_2}{1 + (1 - \gamma'\bar{x}_2/x_2)(1/\eta_2)} \qquad (2.15)$$

The pricing rules in equations 2.14 and 2.15 are improvements over equations 2.11 and 2.12 because equations 2.14 and 2.15 permit an adjustment which reduces the effect of demand elasticity on price in each case. These pricing rules also avoid the understatement of marginal cost which typified the rules given in equations 2.11 and 2.12. It is easy to show that the input efficiency condition in equation 2.9 will still be satisfied at a solution to the modified Averch-Johnson problem in equation 2.6 after x in the constraint is replaced by the given past value $\bar{x}$.

It is also possible to construct a social-welfare function to be maximized subject to the constraint based on previous period outputs $\bar{x}_i$ that appears in equation 2.13. Social welfare can reasonably be represented by the sum of consumer plus producer surplus in the problem

$$\sum_i \int_0^{x_i} p_i(q_i)\,dq_i - w\sum v_i x_i - rK_2 - \phi\{\sum p_i x_i - [s\sum \alpha_i + w\sum(1 - \alpha_i)]\bar{x}_i\} \qquad (2.16)$$

where $p_i(x_i)$ is the inverse demand function for the ith product. Necessary conditions for maximizing the Lagrangian problem in equation 2.16 yield second-best welfare-maximizing prices

$$p_1 = \frac{wv_1}{1 - \phi\bar{x}_1/(\eta_1 x_1)} \qquad (2.17)$$

and
$$p_2 = \frac{wv_2 + r\,\partial K_2/\partial x_2}{1 - \phi\bar{x}_2/(\eta_2 x_2)} \qquad (2.18)$$

The solution prices in equations 2.14 and 2.15 would be the same as those in 2.17 and 2.18 if cost and demand functions were the same and if

$$\frac{\gamma'\bar{x}_1}{x_1} - 1 = \frac{\phi\bar{x}_1}{x_1}$$

and
$$\frac{\gamma' \bar{x}_2}{x_2} - 1 = \frac{\phi \bar{x}_2}{x_2}$$

The solution prices for equations 2.13 and 2.16 are similar in form in that the terms shown as equal immediately above serve in the respective problems to reduce the influence of demand elasticity. By regulatory choices of s and α_i which affect γ', the prices chosen in turn by the firm facing equation 2.13 can be made approximately equal to constrained welfare-maximizing prices given in equations 2.17 and 2.18.[17] The latter prices rely on demand elasticity only enough to meet the budget constraint, and otherwise would have prices equal to marginal costs.

When outputs from a past test period are used in the allowed profit constraint, to avoid the discriminatory-pricing incentive, a problem may arise if outputs grow or decline continuously. Persistent growth would penalize the firm unless $\alpha + (1 - \alpha)$ were adjusted to exceed 1, to moderate any effect caused by the x_i tending to exceed $\bar{x}_i$. The problem would be more serious as the test periods were longer.[18]

Regulatory Action as a Source of Risk

A constraint geared to previous outputs, as in equation 2.13 or 2.16, which seems able to avoid the most serious distortions due to rate-of-return regulation, still requires some choice for the allowed return s. Greater investor uncertainty about that choice may raise the cost of capital r. The reason for this connection is that as any security's return is less reliably known, investors place less value on it, or equivalently they want a higher rate of return for holding it. Thus a regulated public utility's profit is affected not only by the level at which the allowed return is set, but also by the uncertainty surrounding its setting.

Several proposals already exist to make simpler and clearer the determination of the allowed return s. Those proposals which are closest to present practice have suggested sensible ways to estimate a current return to equity, which would then be followed routinely to make decisions more predictable. Gelhaus and Wilson (1968) argued for the use of the earnings-price ratio as the cost of equity capital, largely on the ground that when allowed returns equal the earnings-price ratio, they also will equal the cost of capital. More recently the Federal Power Commission (FPC) suggested systematic use of the discounted-cash-flow method of valuation, which determines the cost of capital as the rate which discounts all future dividends by taking into account their expected rate of growth, so their present value equals share price.[19] Both proposals call for announcement of the procedure to be used by the regulatory commission, to give investors a basis for forming expectations about future regulatory decisions.

Either original cost or current replacement cost could be used as a basis for asset value on which to allow this rate of return, for the difference between these bases has been shown by Gordon (1977) to be reconcilable. This means that the choice of asset valuation method need not produce vastly different results, although more risks will be borne by investors if no adjustment is made for price-level change. After converting returns in jurisdictions that use these two different asset costs to a comparable basis, however, Peterson (1976) found that "fair value" jurisdictions, which do make a price-level adjustment that might lower shareholder risk, actually allow *higher* rates of return. Moreover, Keran (1976) has shown that public-utility equities behave very much like bonds which offer nominal rather than real returns. Thus, the regulation of public-utility equity returns seems to follow historical influences, perhaps because original cost jurisdictions are more common, and does not mirror current real returns in comparable unregulated industries.

More extreme proposals call for reliance on historical returns to equity as well as debt, as originally proposed by Justice Brandeis.[20] Here the equity would be offered a particular return and, once having agreed to it, would henceforth receive that return, much like the fixed return commonly awarded to preferred stock. By adjusting the return automatically for changes in the price level, thereby reducing risk to investors from price-level change, some reduction in cost of capital can be obtained to benefit consumers, as Gordon (1977) has shown. Of course, the Keran (1976) evidence indicated that equity shareholders in regulated firms have received nominal returns rather than real returns, so some vestige of this Brandeis proposal seems to be having effect even if presently it is unintended.

Either proposal, to determine a real return or a nominal return to equity, might reasonably be adopted because uncertainty about regulatory behavior almost certainly could be reduced as a result. The question of which proposal to choose seems less important than making a choice of procedure, so whichever is closer to a commission's present practice might be chosen. We remark briefly in the next section about how they will affect risk bearing, especially by the consumer, but that does not appear crucial to the choice between them.

Risks Borne by Consumers

Let us focus on risks caused by the stochastic nature of demand. Consider continuous regulation under two alternative policies, the *Hope* guideline which, in simplified form, allows profit equal to $(s - r)K$ versus the alternative introduced above which allows a profit of $[\alpha s + (1 - \alpha)w]x - wV - rK$. With s and r both constant and K constant for given expected demand, the variance of $(s - r)K$ would be zero because any fluctuation in demand would be met with an immediate price adjustment to maintain $(s - r)K$. On the other hand, the variance of $[\alpha s + (1 - \alpha)w]x - wV - rK$, which we call target profit, would not be zero. If demand for output is $D(p,u)$, where u is an additive random variable having mean of zero and variance σ_u^2, the variance of target profit $[\alpha s + (1 - \alpha)w]x - wV - rK$ for fixed price would equal $[\alpha s + (1 - \alpha)w]^2 \sigma_x^2$. This result of demand uncertainty would be felt by shareholders rather than by consumers through price changes. And since these are precisely the financial risks shareholders ordinarily bear, there is no reason to shift them to consumers by making price changes.

Of course, the *target* profit we describe here is not the same as the *allowed* profit, based on past or average $\bar{x}_i$ and to be decided in a rate hearing, as described above. The target profit based on current outputs is a fluctuating target that can be used at any time to evaluate whether a rate case really is warranted. This target profit will give essentially the profit to be expected at any output level actually realized, even though, on average, the return would be at the allowed level s. If the fluctuating x_i fall and cause a low profit, the shareholders will no longer be able to plead for a rate increase because the target profit they would receive with these low x_i will show they should expect to receive low profit. Similarly, shareholders could keep higher profit warranted by unexpected increases in the x_i that raised target profit.

This same type of argument can be applied to cost fluctuations as well as demand fluctuations. Since α reflects a target level of performance, any inferior or superior performance can result in less or more profit being earned by the firm. By comparing actual cost with target cost, an evaluation of cause is possible, however, so the firm and its shareholders might retain profit due to good performance. Proper analysis of cost performance would require skillful design of input price-adjustment clauses, as Scott (1979) has described.

Whether a performance incentive can be constructed in this setting is crucial to the success of the modifications proposed here. Unless α can depend on some comparison with other firms, in particular, the improvement over present practice will be limited. If managers can have their own performance, good or bad, influence the basis for earned profit α, then clearly their incentive for efficiency will be much reduced. We offer little help here in determining a standard to determine α, which could depend on quite sophisticated methods. Finding such a basis for reward appears essential, though, for introducing incentive, including that of risk bearing, in public utilities.[21]

With regulatory lag, a return based on the $\bar{x}_i$ or K might appear to yield the same profit and the same variance of profit, because on average $\Sigma \alpha_i \bar{x}_i$ will tend to equal K and there is no price adjustment during the lag period. However, in setting $\Sigma \alpha_i \bar{x}_i$, the regulatory authority will influence the firm's capital decision differently than it currently does in setting an allowed return; in setting $\Sigma \alpha_i \bar{x}_i$, it does not accept whatever K is chosen by the firm. Thus K and $\Sigma \alpha_i \bar{x}_i$ may not be the same in later periods even if $\Sigma \alpha_i \bar{x}_i$ is first determined by reference to past values of K.[22] Moreover, when its allowed profit is determined by $\Sigma \alpha_i \bar{x}_i$, the firm has incentive to conserve capital, since more capital does not directly raise allowed profit. That is why the $px - [\alpha s + (1 - \alpha)w]x$ form of constraint eliminates the Averch-Johnson input bias and motivates peak-load pricing. Without the extra service capacity motivated by the Averch-Johnson bias, some penalties might be considered in advance for denying service to consumers, for that event may become more likely.

In this discussion essentially we assumed that a current rate of return is allowed in a manner that maintains $s - r$ roughly constant. If a historical return were adhered to instead, as Justice Brandeis urged, then s would remain constant at $\bar{s}$ despite fluctuations in r. Under stable expected-demand conditions an allowed profit based on $(\bar{s} - r)K$ would then have a variance equal to $K^2 \sigma_r^2$, with σ_r^2 the variance of r. The variance of profit to investors could also be greater with $\bar{s}$ constant when profit was allowed according to $[\alpha s + (1 - \alpha)w]x - wV - rK$, if x and r moved in opposite directions. Since investors would demand a higher return for bearing such added risk, the consumers would then tend to face higher prices. However, the greater predictability of regulatory-commission action might still reduce risk from that source and thereby lower the cost of capital. And a price-level adjustment in the allowed return could go quite far in removing great discrepancies between s and r. Thus, although it can lead to different sources of risk, the *ex ante* determination of s is not necessarily inferior to the use of a current estimate of s for allowing profit to the firm.

It is conceivable that one of the methods noted in the previous subsection for determining the current cost of capital could be applied on an almost-continuous basis. Then some capital cost-adjustment clause might introduce changes in allowed rate of return for possible price adjustments. Sophisticated analysis of cost deviations due to changes in output quantities or in performance would be needed first, however, so that other influences could also be interpreted and evaluated before price adjustments were put into effect.

Summary

Four problems of rate-of-return regulation according to *Hope* guidelines have been emphasized here: (1) input efficiency is distorted; (2) output prices are discriminatory; (3) the regulatory agency creates risk; and (4) consumers bear some financial risks, which moderates shareholders' oversight and weakens management incentives for efficiency. If past rather than future test periods are used, the discriminatory pricing can be limited. And if a target-cost standard is constructed from output rather than capital alone, the Averch-Johnson (1962) input bias toward capital can be avoided. Consistent procedures for estimating the cost of capital can go far toward reducing the risk which a regulatory commission creates by being unpredictable in its decisions. Finally, an output-based cost target also can give a fluctuating guide to help evaluate whether a request for rate changes should be given a hearing, at the same time allowing shareholders to bear financial risks which presently may be shifted to consumers.

The output-based cost standard still requires considerable refinement, but all the other suggestions made here can be implemented quite easily. If franchised monopoly regulation is to continue, serious inadequacies in present practice based on the *Hope Natural Gas* decision need to be corrected. Hope for improvement can be found in the output-based target cost or in any similar scheme that can realign incentives currently being distorted in regulated firms. Proposals have been analyzed here in a static framework which represents uncertainty in only a very simple form, and the real world will be much more complicated than this. It is hoped nevertheless that these proposals can provide a basis for overcoming the serious weaknesses to be found in *Hope* guidelines.

Notes

1. Munn v. Illinois, 94 U.S. 133 (1877). This case did not mark the beginning of all price regulation, of course. For instance, common carriers had been allowed to charge only "a reasonable sum" at common law.

2. Smyth v. Ames, 169 U.S. 466 (1898).

3. For a good example of this inconsistency, see three important cases decided in 1923: Southwestern Bell Telephone Co. v. Public Service Commission, 262 U.S. 276 (1923); Bluefield Waterworks and Improvement Co. v. Public Service Commission, 262 U.S. 679 (1923); and Georgia Railway and Power Co. v. Railway Commission, 262 U.S. 625 (1923). The *Bluefield* and *Southwestern Bell* cases favored reproduction cost while *Georgia Railway* endorsed original cost for valuing the asset rate base.

4. Federal Power Commission v. Hope Natural Gas Co., 320 U.S. 591 (1944). An analysis of the effects of this decision is available in Leventhal (1965).

5. Using a historically agreed-upon rate of return as the allowed return has been argued generally by Justice Brandeis in his opinion (joined by

Justice Holmes) in the *Southwestern Bell* case. See Southwestern Bell Tel. Co. v. Public Service Commission, 262 U.S. 276 (1923). For analysis of his proposal see Sherman (1977*a*).

6. FPC v. Hope Natural Gas Co., 320 U.S. 591 (1944), p. 603.

7. Id., p. 603.

8. There were some adjustments from actual interest rates. See Leventhal (1965, p. 994). The general problem of price-level change and the use of historical versus replacement costs of assets are typically discussed along with the use of a historical basis for debt cost. For an early treatment, see Bauer (1925). An elaborate discussion is available in Bonbright (1948), Morton (1952), Clemens (1954), Thatcher (1954), and Morehouse (1955); for recent analysis see Leland (1974).

9. A description of major arguments is available in Gelhaus and Wilson (1968). See also Thompson and Thatcher (1973). A brief history of rate-of-return regulation is available in Sherman (1974).

10. For a recent test and a review of other tests, see Jones (1978) and Petersen (1975). The theory is discussed in Crew and Kleindorfer (1979*b*).

11. The now-classical paper by Modigliani and Miller (1958) demonstrated under restrictive assumptions that a firm's market value could not depend on its capital structure. That this argument need not hold for regulated firms is shown in Sherman (1977*b*).

12. See Clemens (1954), Morehouse (1955), or Sherman (1977*a*). Since the historical return is the one actually paid to bondholders, allowing a current return would affect only shareholders (and, of course, consumers) who would absorb any difference between historical and current interest obligations.

13. Missouri *ex rel.* Southwestern Bell Tel. Co. v. Public Service Commission, 262 U.S. 276 (1923).

14. The point and the quoted phrase are from Morton (1952, p. 121). It is clear that in his *Southwestern Bell* opinion Brandeis was concerned about the large returns shareholders could enjoy when the price level increased but debtholders had not anticipated the increase; returns also could turn out to be very low, however, as he noted.

15. It is possible that input price-adjustment clauses might also be included, as noted in the subsection "Risks Borne by Consumers." Only by combining all costs into a single target cost per unit of x, however, can the firm be induced to make economically efficient choices between capital and other inputs.

16. The marginal cost of capital might actually be overstated after division by $1 - \gamma$.

17. This efficient pricing result is similar to that achieved by Vogelsang and Finsinger (1979). The method essentially applies to pricing the incentive argument that Scott (1979) made with respect to fuel-adjustment clauses.

Such an argument is presented more generally by Baron and Taggart in chapter 3.

18. For discussion of the advantages of a longer lag period and ways to enhance it through fuel-adjustment clauses, see Scott (1979).

19. See FPC Docket No. RM 77-1, Notice of Proposed Statement of Policy, *Just and Reasonable Rate of Return on Equity for Natural Gas Pipeline Companies and Public Utilities*, October 15, 1976. For an early discussion of this general method for setting allowed return, see Morton (1952).

20. Brandeis' proposal came in his dissent in Southwestern Bell Tel. Co. v. Public Service Commission, 262 U.S. 276 (1923). A more practical version of the proposal was worked out by Bauer (1966). See also Sherman (1977a).

21. The alternative of bidding for monopoly franchise rights on the basis of low price to consumers creates a very good efficiency incentive, as Demsetz (1968) argued. Crain and Ekelund (1976) have discussed the origin and nature of that proposal. But serious weaknesses in its practical use have been shown by Williamson (1976).

22. No automatic connection between future α and current K should be presumed, however. If the firm expects in future that $\alpha = K/x$, it can affect α through its K decisions, and some Averch-Johnson bias will result. In order to prevent the firm being regulated from influencing α through its own capital choices, a better basis for setting α will be found in the input decisions by other firms, suitably adjusted for their differing circumstances.

3 Regulatory Pricing Procedures and Economic Incentives

David P. Baron and
Robert A. Taggart, Jr.

Introduction

In principle, economic regulation is intended to promote social welfare by intervening in markets that, because of some imperfection, do not yield the competitive outcome. In practice, however, the regulator's ability to replace the market outcome in an imperfect market by a more efficient outcome is subject to important limitations.

First, the objectives of regulatory agencies may not be consistent with economic-efficiency criteria. Owen and Braeutigam (1978), for example, have argued that regulatory processes are often intended to insulate consumers and firms from market forces and that such processes may be supported even if efficiency losses are known to result from their use. In addition, norms such as fairness and public participation may be important components of regulatory objectives and may impose requirements on the process by which regulators administer their legislative mandate. It may be necessary, for instance, for price-setting procedures to be highly structured and easily understood by all interested parties, even if this limits the regulator's flexibility in achieving economic efficiency.

A second limitation on the regulator's ability to promote efficiency results from the information she or he possesses. It may be quite costly for the regulator to obtain as much information about a firm as its managers possess, and this may impose further simplification and structure on the price-setting process.

As a result of these limitations, the regulated firm may have an opportunity to behave strategically in order to further its own goals. The purpose of this chapter is not to question the objectives of regulation, but instead to investigate the incentives for strategic behavior created by regulatory pricing procedures. The basic viewpoint taken here is that the informational limitations on the regulator and the procedures used to satisfy the process requirements of regulation can create incentives for firms to alter their

---

The authors would like to thank Raymond De Bondt for his helpful comments. This research was supported in part by National Science Foundation Grant No. SOC 77-07251.

production and financing decisions in an attempt to influence the regulated prices and enhance their profits.

If a regulator uses a pricing procedure based on a firm's inputs or costs, for example, the firm may have an incentive to bias its choice of inputs in order to affect the regulated price. This general class of incentive problems is illustrated first through a reinterpretation of the Averch-Johnson (AJ) (1962) model that focuses on the relationship between the regulator's pricing rule and the capital stock chosen by the firm.[1] After this reinterpretation, the case of regulatory price adjustments in response to factor price changes is considered in the context of both fuel-adjustment clauses and a revenue-requirements approach in which a rate adjustment is made through an administrative rate review triggered by a factor price change. Fully distributed cost procedures are also considered in order to investigate the incentives that can be created by those procedures for a multiproduct firm. Finally, the effect of capital-structure decisions on the output price of a regulated firm are investigated to determine the incentives which are created by regulatory pricing responses to capital-structure decisions.

A Simple Model of Rate-of-Return Regulation

In this section a simple model is used to illustrate the manner in which regulatory pricing procedures can create incentives for strategic behavior on the part of a firm. The specific procedure analyzed is that in which the regulator sets a single-product firm's output price equal to average operating cost plus an allowed return on its rate base. Under a "naive" application of this approach, the regulator allows the firm's actual input choice to affect the price, and the firm's consequent ability to exploit the regulator's pricing procedure is shown to create an incentive for inefficient production. The Averch-Johnson overcapitalization effect may be interpreted as resulting from this type of naive regulation. This incentive problem may be eliminated through a more "sophisticated" application of the same pricing approach, but such sophistication is shown to place a heavy informational requirement on the regulator. As further discussed in the next section, naive regulation thus may arise in the first place because the regulator has less information than do the managers of the firm about its operations.

The Setting

In order to provide a basis for the discussion in the next section, the model is formulated to incorporate uncertainty and to allow for consideration of dynamic aspects of pricing, although those aspects are not dealt with explicitly in this section. The length of each period in the model's multi-period context is to be interpreted as the time required for the firm to change its capital stock; this might correspond, for example, to the delivery time for new capital equipment. At the beginning of period n, the regulator sets a price p_n, and the firm chooses a capital stock K_n, given the regulated price. The regulator sets p_n so that the firm is "expected" *ex ante* to earn a fair rate of return during the period. This pricing procedure may be thought of as representing a future test-year approach, whereby costs are estimated over a future period and price is set each period to yield an "expected" fair return based on those cost estimates.

Realized, or *ex post*, profits depend on the level of demand, which the firm is assumed to be obligated to supply by adjusting its variable factor inputs given its capital stock K_n. The demand $q_n(p_n, \theta_n)$ is negatively related to price but also depends on the state of nature θ_n, where θ_n is not revealed until after p_n and K_n have been set. Both the price and the capital stock are assumed to be fixed for the duration of the period. Because of the uncertainty and the inflexibility of price and capital within a period, the firm may earn *ex post* more or less than the *ex ante* fair rate of return.

Once θ_n is revealed, both the firm and the regulator have new information, and an administrative rate review is assumed to be initiated in order to determine the regulated price for the next test period. The firm then chooses its capital stock for that test period, and the process repeats itself. To avoid unnecessary complication, however, it is assumed that the firm invests a positive amount in each period, because, for example, expected demand is growing or depreciated capital is replaced. Consequently, the firm can be viewed as acquiring the capital stock in period n that it deems optimal for that period regardless of its previous capital stock or its expectations of the optimal capital stock in the future. The analysis can thus focus on regulation and production for a single period, since because of the envelope theorem the periods are linked only by information about future states of the world contained in present and past states. Accordingly, all time subscripts can be dropped.

Within each period the firm is obligated by the regulatory authority to satisfy whatever demand occurs, and the production function is assumed to be such that an *ex post* labor input L is used in conjunction with the capital stock K chosen *ex ante* to produce the required output. The production function is expressed as $f(K, L)$, and for a given capital stock the required labor input $L = L(q, K)$, satisfies

$$q = q(p, \theta) = f(K, L(q, K)) \tag{3.1}$$

The standard assumptions are made about the marginal productivities of the factors:[2]

$$\frac{\partial q}{\partial K} > 0 \quad \frac{\partial q}{\partial L} > 0 \quad \frac{\partial^2 q}{\partial K^2} < 0 \quad \frac{\partial^2 q}{\partial L^2} < 0 \quad \frac{\partial^2 q}{\partial K \, \partial L} > 0$$

Given K, the properties of $L(q, K)$ are derivable from those of the production function.[3] The *ex post* profit $\pi(p, K, \theta)$ is a function of p, K, and θ and can be expressed as

$$\pi(p, K, \theta) = pq(p, \theta) - wL(q, K) \qquad (3.2)$$

where w is the wage rate.

The firm's capital stock is assumed to be financed by equity investors who trade its equity securities in a market that is complete within a period. That is, a price ρ (θ) exists at the beginning of each period for a dollar of return to be delivered if and only if the state θ occurs.[4]

The present value of a dollar of return if θ occurs will be denoted by ρ $(\theta)/r$, where r is the gross ($r > 1$) risk-free interest rate, and investors use these state prices to evaluate the firm's *ex post* profit levels. At a securities-market equilibrium, the market value of the firm is given by[5]

$$V = \int \rho(\theta)\pi(p,K,\theta)d\theta/r \qquad (3.3)$$

Since $\int \rho(\theta)\, d\theta = 1$, the $\rho(\theta)$ can be interpreted as market "probabilities," and in turn V may be thought of as the market "expected" present value $E(\pi(p, K, \theta))$ of the firm's *ex post* profits. The function V is assumed to be strictly concave in K.

Naive Regulation and the Averch-Johnson Model

The regulator in this model faces two problems. First, he or she must decide how a given allowed rate of return can be translated into a pricing rule. Second, the regulator must decide how to respond when the firm changes its capital stock. The first problem may be dealt with by monitoring the relationship between the firm's market value V and the replacement value of its capital stock K. The implicit rationale for an allowed-return constraint is to prevent excess profits, and since the *ex ante* value of any excess profits is measured by $V - K$, the regulator can restrict those profits by fixing the value of a parameter s and then setting the firm's output price so that $V = sK$.[6] From equation 3.3 this pricing rule implies

$$\frac{\int \rho(\theta)\pi(p,K,\theta)\, d\theta}{K} = rs \qquad (3.4)$$

Regulatory Pricing/Economic Incentives

The left side of equation 3.4 can be interpreted as the firm's market "expected" rate of return on invested capital and the right side as an allowed return (expressed as a percentage s of the cost of capital). Thus for a regulated price that sets $V = sK$, the firm's market "expected" rate of return is equal to the allowed rate of return, and for the special case where $s = 1$, the allowed return is equal to r, the cost of capital.

Furthermore, substituting equation 3.2 into equation 3.4 and solving for p yield

$$p = \frac{rsk + w \int \rho(\theta) L(q,K) \, d\theta}{\int \rho(\theta) q(p,\theta) \, d\theta} \tag{3.5}$$

Thus setting the price so that $V = sK$ is also equivalent to setting the price equal to average expected operating cost plus an allowed return to capital per unit of expected output.

How the regulator deals with the second problem, the response to changes in the firm's capital stock, determines whether regulation is naive or sophisticated. In the naive case, the regulator responds passively to the firm's input decisions and adjusts the price so that the firm can "expect" to earn the allowed return on whatever capital stock it chooses. But in this case the firm's choice of its capital stock will be predicated on the stock's impact on the regulated price, and hence an incentive for strategic behavior is present.

The firm's optimal capital stock is that which maximizes the net present value $V - K$. Under a naive regulatory pricing procedure, the firm will wish to increase its capital stock a long as

$$\frac{d(V - K)}{dK} = \frac{\partial V}{\partial K} - 1 + \frac{\partial V}{\partial p} \frac{dp}{dK} \tag{3.6}$$

is positive, where dp/dK reflects the regulatory pricing response to the firm's choice of capital stock. The regulated price will vary with K along the constraint $V = sK$, so differentiating this constraint yields

$$\frac{\partial V}{\partial K} + \frac{\partial V}{\partial p} \frac{dp}{dK} = s$$

and substituting into equation 3.6 yields

$$\frac{d(V - K)}{dK} = s - 1 \tag{3.7}$$

The following proposition results.

Proposition 1: For $s > 1$ the firm will increase its capital stock to the point where a further increment in K can no longer yield an increase of s in the value of the firm.[7] The optimal capital stock is thus the greatest K such that the firm earns its allowed rate of return.

The efficiency of the optimal capital stock under naive regulation can be analyzed by comparing this model with the AJ model, in which the firm sets its own price and may choose any price-capital stock combination that satisfies the allowed-rate-of-return constraint. In the context of the model developed here, the AJ firm maximizes $V - K$ with respect to p and K, subject to the constraint $V < sK$. By letting λ_N be a Lagrangian multiplier and by assuming that the constraint is binding at the optimal (p_N, K_N), the necessary optimality conditions are

$$\frac{\partial V}{\partial K} - 1 - \lambda_N \left(\frac{\partial V}{\partial K} - s \right) = 0 \qquad (3.8)$$

$$\frac{\partial V}{\partial p} (1 - \lambda_N) = 0 \qquad (3.9)$$

$$V - sK_N = 0 \qquad (3.10)$$

Since $0 < \lambda_N < 1$ when $s > 1$,[8] equation 3.8 may be rewritten as

$$\frac{\partial V}{\partial K} = 1 + \lambda_N \frac{1 - s}{1 - \lambda_N}$$

Then, evaluating $\partial V / \partial K$ yields

$$-\int \rho(\theta) \frac{\partial L}{\partial K} d\theta = \frac{r}{w} + \lambda_N r \frac{1 - s}{1 - \lambda_N} \qquad (3.11)$$

The left side of equation 3.11 is the *ex ante* marginal rate of substitution (MRS) between labor and capital. Since $0 < \lambda_N < 1$, the MRS is less than the factor price ratio for $s > 1$ and overcapitalization results.

The firm's optimal capital stock in this AJ formulation of the model can be shown to be the optimal capital stock under naive regulation. The firm facing naive regulation is unconstrained in its choice of K, but the regulator chooses the price p in order to provide the allowed return for the capital stock chosen by the firm. Since the firm knows the regulator's decision rule, it can

Regulatory Pricing/Economic Incentives

predict the price that will be set for any capital stock it chooses. An example of such a predictable price-setting rule is the "revenue requirement" approach described by Robichek (1978) that is followed by many regulatory commissions. The total revenue required by the firm in order to earn the allowed return is the sum of the allowed return applied to the firm's actual capital stock and an estimate of labor and other operating costs. The regulator can then set the price by dividing the revenue requirement by an estimate of total output. As long as the regulator follows some predictable price-setting rule such as this, the firm has an incentive to manipulate its capital stock so as to achieve any price consistent with the regulatory constraint $V = sK$, and thus the decision problem of the firm under naive regulation is identical to that of the firm in the AJ model. Since the feasible set is the same in both cases, the solutions must be the same. This establishes proposition 2.

Proposition 2: The optimal capital stock and regulated price under naive regulation, in which price is set in response to K to yield $V = sK$, are the same as in the optimal solution to the Averch-Johnson model. Thus, overcapitalization results relative to the firm's market expected output when $s > 1$.

Sophisticated Regulation

Under sophisticated regulation, on the other hand, the output price is based on some ideal capital stock, and this price is not changed even if the firm chooses a capital stock different from the ideal. Output price and total revenue are thus exogenous to the firm, and the incentive for strategic behavior is eliminated. The firm will best serve its shareholders by choosing the capital stock that maximizes $V - K$, with p taken as fixed, and thus the optimal K in this case satisfies

$$-\int \rho(\theta) \frac{\partial L}{\partial K} d\theta = \frac{r}{w} \qquad (3.12)$$

That is, the firm chooses its capital stock so as to equate the *ex ante* marginal rate of substitution of capital for labor with the factor price ratio, and hence the following counterpart of Leland's (1974) result obtains.

Proposition 3: The firm's optimal input combination under sophisticated regulation is *ex ante* efficient.

The only condition necessary for this result is that the firm treat the output price as beyond its control. Technical efficiency thus holds for any price, as long as it is neither so high nor so low as to drive the firm out of business. This does not imply that the regulator may choose a price arbitrarily, however, since she or he also faces an allowed-return objective. For any given value of s, then, the regulator must simultaneously solve equations 3.4 and 3.12 for the efficient capital stock and the output price consistent with $V = sK$. Eliminating r first from equations 3.4 and 3.12 yields

$$p_S = \frac{\int \rho(\theta) w L(q,K) \, d\theta}{\int \rho(\theta) q(p,\theta) \, d\theta} \left[1 - s \, \frac{K \int \rho(\theta)(\partial L/\partial K) \, d\theta}{\int \rho(\theta) L(q,K) \, d\theta} \right]$$

$$= w \, \frac{E(L)}{E(q)} (1 - s\eta) \qquad (3.13)$$

where $E(L)$ is the market expected labor requirement, $E(q)$ is expected output, and η is the elasticity of the "expected" labor requirement with respect to the capital stock. The sophisticated regulator can then set price according to equation 3.13 for any allowed return rs and thereby induce the firm to choose an efficient capital stock.

Since equation 3.13 depends on K, the regulator must be able to determine the efficient capital stock in order to set the price properly. That is, the regulator must solve equations 3.4 and 3.12 simultaneously so that p_S will be predicated on a particular value of K that the firm will then be induced to choose once p_S is announced. To set the sophisticated price, the regulator must know the firm's production function and expected demand curve—in short, he or she must know as much about the firm's operations as do the firm's own managers. These informational requirements are discussed further in the concluding section.

A Comparison of Naive and Sophisticated Regulation

Both naive and sophisticated regulation, then, can occur in the context of allowed rate-of-return pricing procedures, but the latter results in *ex ante* technical efficiency, whereas the former does not. To further characterize the difference between the two, suppose that a firm facing naive regulation starts out at the point (p_S, K_S) that a sophisticated regulator would have chosen for the same allowed return rs. From equation 3.8, the optimal capital stock K_N for the firm facing naive regulation is that which satisfies $\partial V/\partial K = 1 + \lambda_N (1 - s)/(1 - \lambda_N)$, where $0 < \lambda_N < 1$. But since $\partial V/\partial K = 1$ at (p_S, K_S), $\partial V/\partial K$ is too large for K_S to be optimal, and by the concavity of V the firm will wish to increase K. As the firm increases K, the naive regulator responds by changing p along the constraint $V = sK$. Differentiating this constraint with respect to K yields

$$\frac{\partial V}{\partial K} + \frac{\partial V}{\partial p}\frac{dp}{dK} = s$$

or

$$\frac{dp}{dK} = \frac{s - \partial V/\partial K}{\partial V/\partial p}$$

Since $\partial V/\partial K = 1$ and $\partial V/\partial p > 0$ at (p_S, K_S), the naive regulator will increase the price as the firm increases its capital stock. These results are summarized in proposition 4.

Proposition 4: Starting from the sophisticated regulatory solution, the firm under naive regulation increases its capital stock, which induces the regulator to increase the regulated price. The optimal solution with naive regulation thus entails a higher price and a greater capital stock than with sophisticated regulation.

It is shown in appendix 3A that both naive regulation and sophisticated regulation result in a larger capital stock, lower price, and greater expected

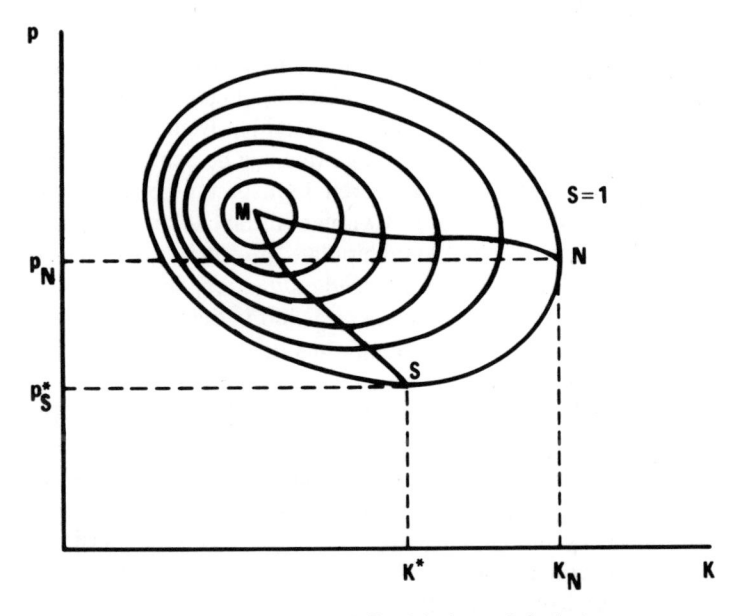

Figure 3-1 Naive and Sophisticated Solutions

output than an unconstrained monopolist would choose as long as $s < s_M$, where rs_M is the monopolist's expected rate of return. If the regulated firm is viewed as operating on a hill in $(V - K, p, K)$-space, then an allowed return $rs < rs_M$ forces the firm to move down the hill from the summit at which the monopolist would operate.[9] As indicated in the contour diagram in figure 3-1, firms facing sophisticated and naive regulation move down different sides of this hill. The concentric contours in Figure 3-1 represent intersections of the $V - K$ hill with the constraint plane $V = sK$, and the outer contours correspond to successively lower values of s. The firm facing naive regulation moves down the line MN, the locus of maximum capital stocks consistent with each value of s,[10] while the firm facing sophisticated regulation moves down the line MS, the locus of efficient capital stocks consistent with each value of s. As s approaches unity, there is no reason to expect the firm under naive regulation to move closer to the efficient locus, and at $s = 1$ this firm would be indifferent among any of the (p, K) combinations for which $V = K$. The firm under sophisticated regulation, by contrast, would be indifferent between going into business or not at $s = 1$, but if it did go into business, it would prefer K^* in figure 3-1 to all other values of K.

Price Adjustments in Response to Factor Price Changes

An implicit assumption in the model in the last section is that the price adjustment made under naive regulation is instantaneous. In practice, price adjustments in response to changes in the rate base of a firm typically take place in the context of a time-consuming administrative rate-review proceeding involving staff evaluations and public hearings. A number of models, including those by Bailey and Coleman (1971), Baumol and Klevorick (1970), and Davis (1973), assume that a price can be achieved as a result of a change in input proportions in an Averch-Johnson type of model only after a lag. In a multiperiod context, a firm with an initial capital-labor ratio could easily be thwarted in its attempt to manipulate the output price by adopting a regulatory policy in which price is changed only in response to an exogenous event such as a change in a factor price or a shift in demand. The analysis of efficiency in a multiperiod model should thus be conducted in the context of administrative rate reviews triggered by exogenous forces.

Adjustments in output prices made in response to a change in factor prices take place either through an administrative rate-review proceeding or, to avoid the delays associated with such proceedings, according to a formula such as a fuel-adjustment clause or a comprehensive adjustment mechanism such as that used by the New Mexico Public Service Commission (1975). Both types of procedures can result in incentive problems although they are of a different nature from that considered in the previous section. The use of a fuel-adjustment clause, such as those based on the change in the average cost of fuel, creates two types of incentive problems. First, if the factor price of fuel is anticipated to increase at some time in the future, Baron and De Bondt (1979) show that a utility will have an incentive to choose too high a fuel-capital ratio in order to obtain a greater price adjustment when the factor price actually does change.[11] Second, a fuel-adjustment clause could create an incentive to purchase an inefficient fuel supply in order to obtain a higher price. While in the context of their model Baron and DeBondt show that this latter incentive is not present if the firm has nondecreasing returns to scale and the adjusted price is at least as great as the marginal cost, public concern with this possibility suggests that in a more realistic model such an incentive may be present [see Baron and De Bondt (1979) for a discussion].[12]

The principal alternative to an automatic adjustment mechanism is a price adjustment determined in the context of an administrative rate-review proceeding. One basis on which the price adjustment could be made in this context is a revenue-requirements procedure in which the price is adjusted so that total revenue equals the total cost plus the allowed return on the utilized rate base. When an increase in the factor price of fuel is anticipated and it is known that the output price will be adjusted according to this revenue-requirements procedure after a review period of known length, a firm is able to affect the magnitude of the output price adjustment through its choice of a fuel-capital ratio. A model of this type has been analyzed by Baron and De Bondt (1980) who show that there exists an allowed rate of return such that for lower allowed rates the firm has an incentive to undercapitalize while for higher allowed rates the firm overcapitalizes. The incentive problem in this context arises because the factor price change initiates an administrative rate review that the firm cannot initiate through its own actions. The output price adjustment involves both a price increase to offset the factor price increase and an opportunity for the firm to increase its value by increasing its rate base and hence its total allowed return. The first effect insulates the firm from the cost impact of the factor price change, except during the processing period associated with the proceedings, and hence creates an incentive for the firm to choose too great a fuel-capital ratio. The second effect is analogous to the Averch-Johnson effect and provides an incentive for the firm to substitute capital for fuel and hence to choose too low a fuel-capital ratio. For low values of the allowed rate of return, the first effect dominates and the firm undercapitalizes; for higher rates of return, the second effect dominates and the firm overcapitalizes.

By requiring that an administrative rate review be initiated by only a factor price change or a shift in demand, a regulatory authority can avoid the incentive problems that result from a firm-initiated rate review. If, however, the procedure used to adjust the output price depends on endogenous measures, as in the revenue-requirements approach, the anticipation of a factor price change creates an incentive problem that can result in either undercapitalization or overcapitalization, depending on the allowed rate of return. To avoid this incentive problem, it is necessary to make the output-price adjustment a function of exogenous parameters only, as in the sophisticated regulation of the previous section. The informational requirements for such a regulatory procedure are substantial, however, as in sophisticated regulation. For example, a procedure in which the output price for an electric utility were to be increased by the increase in the fuel cost per kilowatt hour of electricity would yield the allowed rate of return only if the technology exhibited constant returns to scale. If the firm had increasing returns to scale, such an adjustment formula would not yield the allowed rate of return because of demand-elasticity effects. To adjust the output price so that the firm earns the allowed rate of return in this case requires knowledge of the demand and cost functions of the firm.

Fully Distributed Costs

Although the allocation of fixed or common costs has no role in the pursuit of social-welfare objectives when the surplus of each consumer is given equal weight, some regulatory commissions, particularly the Federal Communications Commission, have supported the use of fully distributed costs. One reason for this support may be a consequence of opposition to marginal-cost pricing principals and their implementation in terms of Ramsey prices.[13] This opposition apparently results from perceived difficulties in verifying marginal costs, which market forces will not be able to do under regulation, while cost allocations based on accounting data are readily verifiable even if any such allocation is necessarily arbitrary. The support of fully distributed cost procedures also may be due to a desire to provide benefits to one customer class over another without consideration of demand elasticities. Another explanation for this type of pricing procedure is that, although the allocations are arbitrary, they give an image of fairness and a concern for equity. Furthermore, if prices are set equal to fully distributed costs, the regulator may feel comfortable in ignoring demand elasticities, even though without information on elasticities the regulator would have no idea if the prices so determined would yield the allowed return.

Since fully distributed costs are arbitrary by definition, there is no reason to focus on any particular method of allocation. Braeutigam (1979), for example, has considered the welfare losses relative to Ramsey prices of prices determined by common-cost allocations based on gross revenues, attributable costs, and relative outputs. With any allocation method that creates a dependence of price on the decisions of the firm, incentive problems are created.

The incentive problems may be present at one of two levels. First, if the firm can influence the choice of an allocation rule, it will have an incentive to support a rule which allocates more of the common costs to services with inelastic demands and less to services with elastic demands. Second, given a cost-allocation procedure prescribed by the regulatory authority, the firm may have some latitude for strategic behavior. For example, consider a fully distributed cost-pricing procedure with the allocation of common costs based on the total quantity of the output of all the services produced. In choosing its outputs, the firm will evaluate a change in output in terms that will be different from the price because the allocated cost and hence the price depend on the output. Given the restrictions imposed by the demand relationships, outputs will be adjusted until the difference between marginal revenue and marginal cost for each service is equal. If the fully distributed cost procedure is used in the context of revenue-requirements regulation and if the revenue requirement is expressed as a function of the rate base, the firm will adjust its output so as to obtain the largest rate base consistent with the allowed rate of return.[14]

To implement a fully distributed cost-pricing procedure that does not create an incentive problem, the regulator must set the price equal to the estimated marginal cost plus an estimate of the average allocated cost for each service. For this to yield the revenue requirement, however, the regulator needs to know essentially everything that the firm knows about demand and cost, as in the sophisticated regulation of the second section.

The Firm's Capital Structure

The incentive problems described in the preceding sections are all based on the regulated firm's production decisions. Similar problems can arise in the context of the firm's financing decisions, and, as in the cases above, a necessary condition for the presence of an incentive problem is the regulator's use of a price rule which depends predictably on the firm's financing choices.

If the firm has bondholders as well as shareholders, then a regulator with an allowed-return objective will attempt to set the price so that the firm's expected revenue is sufficient to compensate both classes of securityholders for the risks they bear. Under the revenue-requirements procedure described by Robichek (1978), for example, the regulator calculates the average (or "embedded") interest rate on the firm's debt, solicits expert testimony on the rate of return required by shareholders (the "cost of equity"), multiplies each percentage rate by the corresponding book value of funds actually raised from that source, and then sets the price so that the firm's revenue can be expected to cover the total dollar magnitude of these capital costs.

Sherman (1977b) has argued that this procedure is plagued by two problems which may, in turn, give the firm an incentive to manipulate its capital structure. First, since the embedded interest cost reflects the actual coupon rates paid by the firm on its outstanding debt, mistakes by the regulator in setting the allowed return are more likely to occur in the cost-of-equity component. Thus, if a firm about to enter a rate proceeding has reason to believe that the regulator will set the allowed return to equity too high, then the firm has an incentive to increase the equity component of its capital structure in the hope of obtaining a higher output price.

Second, since the allowed returns to debt and equity are set separately, Sherman argues that it is common for regulators to lose sight of their interrelationship. Since the financial risk borne by shareholders is an increasing function of the debt-equity ratio, a substitution of equity for debt by the firm reduces this risk and thus lowers the rate of return required by shareholders. Indeed in the perfect capital-market world with no taxes, as described by Modigliani and Miller (1958), the required return to equity adjusts to any change in capital structure so as to just keep the overall, or weighted-average, cost of capital constant. If the allowed return to shareholders is intended to reflect their required return, then it, too, should be adjusted to changes in the firm's capital structure. But if the allowed return to equity is unaffected by the firm's financing proportions, as Sherman argues, then a firm about to enter a rate proceeding has an incentive to increase the equity proportion of total funds raised. By doing so, it increases the component of its capital structure having the higher allowed return, and if this allowed return remains fixed, the weighted-average allowed-return to capital must necessarily increase. This, in turn, results in a higher price being set in the rate proceeding.

In the presence of corporate taxes, this incentive to substitute equity for debt may be enhanced. If the regulator attempts to pass through to consumers any tax saving from debt by lowering the price, the disparity between the effective allowed returns to debt and equity will be widened further, and a substitution of equity for debt will result in an even larger increase in the output price than in the no-tax case.

A number of state regulatory commissions have shown an awareness of this incentive problem and have even used a version of sophisticated regulation to combat it. It is not uncommon in rate proceedings for prices to be set on the basis of a hypothetical capital structure containing a larger debt proportion than the firm has actually employed.[15] By implicitly crediting the firm with more tax savings than it is actually achieving, the regulator sets a lower price than he or she would set on the basis of the firm's actual structure. If the firm, in turn, perceives that the output price depends on exogenous factors only, it will have no incentive to manipulate its financing and will adopt whatever capital structure is optimal from a private standpoint.

Two problems are still inherent in this regulatory procedure, however. The first is proper compensation for the firm's securityholders. Any price that depends on only exogenous factors will eliminate the firm's incentive to manipulate its capital structure, but not all such prices will exactly give the firm's securityholders their required rates of return. If the regulator implicitly credits the firm with greater tax savings from debt than is privately optimal (say, because the threat of bankruptcy would be too great at that level of debt), then the price will be too low to yield the required returns to all securityholders at the capital structure which the firm would like to adopt. In turn, this may induce the firm to manipulate its operating decisions in an attempt to have the price raised. Thus the true sophisticated regulator must be able to predict the firm's optimal capital structure in advance and then set a price that will yield the required rate of return at that capital structure. As in the previous examples, then, the regulator must have as much knowledge about the workings of the firm as its managers in order to set the price properly.

The second problem is that the firm's privately optimal capital structure may not be socially optimal. It is not clear from a social standpoint, for example, whether regulators should be forcing firms to take advantage of tax savings from debt, since this results in lower federal-tax receipts and is thus an implicit attempt to subsidize local consumers at the expense of taxpayers generally [see Litzenberger and Sosin (1979)]. Furthermore, externalities may result from the bankruptcy of a public utility, and the regulator may wish to take added precautions against this possibility. In order to determine a socially optimal capital structure, however, the regulator may require even greater knowledge than that possessed by the firm's managers, and in order to induce the firm to adopt such a capital structure, the regulator may need to resort to direct decree.

Discussion

The procedures that regulatory authorities utilize to set prices, if not based solely on exogenous factors and on estimated or ideal factor inputs, thus can create an incentive for a firm to take strategic actions to further its own interests. This strategic behavior results in welfare losses through either prices that diverge from the regulatory ideal or technical inefficiency or both. To avoid these welfare losses, the authority must know as much as the firm does about demand, technology, and costs. Development of the expertise necessary for the authority to have such information is undoubtedly prohibitively costly, and so the search for improved regulatory pricing procedures must be subject to the limitation that the firm has information not possessed by the regulator. For example, in the context of the revenue-requirements model in the section entitled "A Simple Model of Rate-of-Return Regulation," the firm knows its technology while the regulator does not, and hence the regulator cannot determine *ex post* if the firm produced efficiently.

One approach that has been used by authorities to deal with the informational problems inherent in regulation is to expand their scope of control. For example, in the context of revenue-requirements regulation of electric utilities, regulators have been granted the authority to approve or disapprove the choice of technology, construction programs, and the sale of new securities, presumably as a means of reducing the opportunities a utility has to engage in strategic behavior. While a regulator's authority may be expanded in this manner, it is not at all evident that the informational gap between the regulator and the regulated firm is overcome by these extended powers; nor is it evident that they result in more efficient production and financing decisions.

A quite different approach to dealing with the informational limitations is to design regulatory procedures so that the firm has the incentive to truthfully reveal its private information to the regulatory authority. Then, recognizing that the authority will receive that information, the regulator can design the best pricing procedure subject to only the incentive-compatibility restriction that that procedure induce the firm to truthfully reveal its private information. As considered in Baron and De Bondt (1980), this type of procedure could be applicable to the design of a fuel-adjustment clause to deal with the potential incentive that a firm might have to choose an inefficient fuel supply when the regulator does not know the factor prices of available fuel supplies. Relative to the case in which the regulator knows everything that the firm knows, this approach results in welfare losses and hence can be optimal only in a second-best sense.

Baron and Myerson (1979) have also taken this approach for the case in which the regulator does not know a parameter of the firm's cost function, and they have shown that the optimal procedure can be characterized in closed form when a subsidy can be used to eliminate the natural incentive to misreport cost. This type of regulatory procedure has the property that once the firm reports its cost (truthfully), a price is set and the firm operates without further regulation. These results are limited because in the Baron and Myerson model the firm makes no decision other than to report a value for its cost parameter, and hence the model does not involve any choice of technology or financial structure. When the latter decisions are incorporated into the model, the incentive problem becomes intertwined with the problems caused by private information.

In practice, regulation is a long-term process that involves verification, monitoring, and auditing to diminish the informational gap between the regulatory authority and the regulated firm and to limit the incentives for strategic behavior. For example, in the context of revenue-requirements regulation, when a firm files a tariff revision as a consequence of a divergence between its earned rate of return and its allowed rate of return, the regulatory commission will initiate a public proceeding which not only gives the commission staff the opportunity to review the firm's cost and operating procedures, but also gives intervenors a similar opportunity. Such a proceeding not only diminishes the informational gap, but also reduces any incentive that the firm may have to misrepresent its costs or the demand for its services. Furthermore, the authority may be able to monitor on an ongoing basis the major operating decisions of a firm as well as the factor prices it faces in order to limit the incentive, for example, to strategically choose its technology. In addition, a regulatory authority can audit on an *ex post* basis the performance of a firm to determine the factor inputs, for example, chosen by the firm. Also, most regulatory commissions are granted the authority to penalize a firm by disallowing costs or elements of the rate base if decisions taken by the firm are judged to be inappropriate. The possibility of detecting inappropriate actions through auditing and imposing penalties provides a potentially important incentive to a firm to act in accord with regulatory objectives. The use of verification and auditing in regulatory pricing has been considered by Baron (1980).

Perhaps the most important means of reducing the informational gap between a regulatory authority and a regulated firm is the ability to observe past performance and to use those observations to adjust regulatory procedures. For example, Vogelsang and Finsinger (1979) have considered a regulatory model in which the authority observes only the total cost incurred by the firm in the previous period in addition to the market-observable prices and quantities and uses those observations to modify its regulatory policy for the next period.[16] For a firm that maximizes its profit each period, this simple procedure results in the limit in the Ramsey prices. This result offers considerable hope that the ongoing relationship between a regulated firm and a regulatory authority can be used both to diminish the natural informational gap inherent in regulation and to reduce the incentive problems present in many regulatory pricing procedures.

Notes

1. The AJ model is used here because of its familiarity even though it does not describe regulatory procedures.

2. Although it is assumed that the production function is twice differentiable, less well-behaved functions are also compatible with the analysis. There may be an absolute capacity limit $\bar{q}(K)$ for any given capital stock, for example, in which case the firm must be restricted to choose K such that $\bar{q}(K) \geq q(p, \theta_{max})$, the maximum demand that might occur in that period.

3. Specifically, it can be shown that $\partial L/\partial q > 0$, $\partial L/\partial K < 0$, $\partial^2 L/\partial q^2 > 0$, $\partial^2 L/\partial K^2 > 0$, and $\partial^2 L/(\partial q\, \partial K) < 0$.

4. The securities market is not complete across periods, however, so an investor cannot make trades at the beginning of period n conditional on period $n + 1$ states.

5. The use of securities-market valuation frees the results from dependence on the specific characteristics of investors or of the managers of firms. The complete market assumption used to obtain this V is not as restrictive as it may appear. If the required labor function in equation 3.1 is such that $q(p,\theta)$ may be factored out in some way, then equation 3.3 can be used to solve for a "market certainty equivalent" of the uncertain output, $\int \rho(\theta) q(p,\theta)\, d\theta / r$, in terms of market-observable information. In that event, investors will agree on the value of the firm even if the state prices $\rho(\theta)/r$ differ among investors. The advantage of the complete market assumption is that it allows the analysis to proceed with a minimum of restrictions on the production function.

6. The restriction is binding only if $s < s_M$ where $s_M - 1$ is the level of rents, relative to K_M, that would be achieved by an unregulated monopolist. Also, $s \geq 1$ if the firm is to go into business.

7. An optimal K exists because the properties of the production function imply that $V - K$ is strictly concave in K. To facilitate comparison with the firm's decisions in the AJ and unregulated monopoly cases, it will also be assumed that $V - K$ is strictly concave in p. This requires that $2\, \partial q/\partial p - w(\partial^2 L/\partial q^2)(\partial q/\partial p)^2 - w(\partial L/\partial q)(\partial^2 q/\partial p^2)$ be negative.

8. The proof that $0 < \lambda_N < 1$ follows the one employed by Baumol and Klevorick (1970) for the AJ model.

9. A similar hill in (π, K, L)-space is depicted and analyzed by Zajac (1970), Baumol and Klevorick (1970), and Bailey (1973).

10. The (p, K) pairs consistent with any value of s are defined by $V = sK$. Differentiating implicitly yields $dK/dp = (\partial V/\partial p)/(\partial V/\partial K - s) = 0$ at any equilibrium point for the firm under naive regulation. Furthermore, $d^2K/dp^2 = -(\partial^2 V/\partial p^2)/(\partial V/\partial K - s) < 0$ at any equilibrium point, so K_N is the maximum K consistent with $V - sK$.

11. Stewart (1979) has considered a model in which an electric utility chooses capacity and the heat rate of a generating plant. His empirical results indicate that the plants studied were less fuel-efficient than predicted. The presence of fuel-adjustment clauses and anticipated increases in the relative price of fuel would explain such an observation.

12. Baron and De Bondt (1980) consider the problem of designing fuel-adjustment mechanisms that will mitigate the incentive to bias the choice of technology and deal with the potential incentive to choose an inefficient fuel supply.

13. See the FCC ruling, Docket No. 18128 (1976).

14. Baumol, Fischer, and Raa (1979) have shown that under rate-of-return regulation, fully distributed cost prices can be socially inefficient. However, they did not consider the firm's choice of outputs in response to a fully distributed pricing rule.

15. Regulators have even attempted to overcome more complicated capital-structure manipulations by firms. It is not uncommon in telecommunications, for example [see Nichols (1955)], for a number of operating subsidiaries to have lower debt ratios than their holding-company parent. The apparent hope by the firm is that in setting local rates, the parent company's cost of equity capital will be applied to the subsidiary's higher equity proportion, thus resulting in a higher price than if both units had identical capital structures. In such cases, however, regulators frequently have used the parent company's capital-structure proportions in order to set the price.

16. In their model, the environment of the firm is assumed to be stable.

Appendix 3A

Effects of Reducing s on Price, Capital Stock, and Expected Output under Sophisticated Regulation

Totally differentiating $V(p_S, K(p_S)) = sK$, where p_S is the price set by the sophisticated regulator, yields

$$\frac{\partial V}{\partial K}\frac{dK}{dp_S}dp_S + \frac{\partial V}{\partial p_S}dp_S = \frac{dK}{dp_S}dp_S + K\,ds$$

and the change in the regulated price, given a change in s, is

$$\frac{dp_S}{ds} = \frac{K}{(dK/dp_S)(\partial V/\partial K - s) + \partial V/\partial p_S} \qquad (3A.1)$$

The relationship F between K and p_S is implicitly defined by equation 3.12, rewritten as

$$F(K,p_S) \equiv -\int \rho(\theta)w\,\frac{\partial L}{\partial K}\,d\theta - r = 0$$

so that

$$\frac{dK}{dp_S} = -\frac{\partial F/\partial p_S}{\partial F/\partial K}$$

The denominator, $\partial F/\partial K$, is negative by the assumed properties of the production function; and the numerator, $\partial F/\partial p_S$, is negative, since expected demand increases with price. Thus a decrease in the regulated price increases the firm's optimal capital stock. Also, since the firm maximizes $V - K$, $\partial V/\partial K = 1$ at the optimal capital stock, and the term $(dK/dp_S)(\partial V/\partial K - s)$ in equation 3A.1 is positive for $s > 1$. To determine the sign of the dp_S/ds, it remains to evaluate $\partial V/\partial p_S$ at the optimal capital stock.

An unregulated monopolist raises the price until $\partial V/\partial p = 0$, so that $dp_S/ds > 0$ for $s = s_M$. For values of s marginally below s_M, therefore, $p_S < p_M$ and the firm's maximum attainable value of $V - K$ must be below the monopolist's $V - K$. If we view the firm as constrained by regulation to set the output price p equal to p_S, then formally its problem is max

$\{L = V - K - \mu(p - p_S)\}$, where μ is a Lagrangian multiplier, and the first order optimality conditions are

$$\frac{\partial L}{\partial K} = \frac{\partial V}{\partial K} - 1 = 0 \tag{3A.2}$$

$$\frac{\partial L}{\partial p} = \frac{\partial V}{\partial p} - \mu = 0 \tag{3A.3}$$

$$\frac{\partial L}{\partial \mu} = p - p_S = 0 \tag{3A.4}$$

The multiplier μ represents the change in the maximum attainable value of $V - K$ given an increase in the constrained price p_S. This must be positive for the value of p_S under consideration, because an increase in the regulated price would allow the firm to move along its expansion path (according to equation 3A.2) back toward the monopoly solution. From equations 3A.3 and 3A.1, then, $dp_S/ds > 0$ for values of s marginally below s_M. Furthermore, $d(V - K)/dp_S = \partial V/\partial p_S + (\partial V/\partial K - 1)(dK/dp_S) = \partial V/\partial p_S$ along the expansion path, so as s is lowered further, p goes down and the maximum attainable value of $V - K$ is lowered further. Thus the argument above can be repeated for all s such that $1 < s < s_M$, and as s is reduced in this range, the regulated price is reduced, the firm's "expected" output increases, and the optimal capital stock increases.

Effects of Reducing s under Naive Regulation

Bailey (1973) has shown that

$$\frac{dK}{ds} = \frac{K(-\lambda_N)}{1 - s}$$

in the context of the AJ model. The identical result is obtained for the naive regulation model by totally differentiating $V - sK$ with respect to s and noting that p is a function of K under naive regulation. Since $0 < \lambda_N < 1$, $dK/ds < 0$ for $s > 1$.

To evaluate the change in price, totally differentiate equation 3.9 with respect to K, p and s to obtain

$$\frac{\partial^2 V}{\partial p^2} \frac{dp}{ds} + \frac{\partial^2 V}{\partial p \, \partial K} \frac{dK}{ds} = 0$$

# Regulatory Pricing/Economic Incentives

Here V is assumed to be strictly concave in p, and $\partial^2 V/(\partial p\, \partial K)$ is negative from the assumed properties of the production function. Price is thus an increasing function of s, which, in conjunction with $dK/ds < 0$, establishes that as s is reduced in the range of $1 < s < s_M$, the firm's optimal capital stock increases, the regulated price goes down, and the firm's expected output increases.

4

Public-Utility Regulation and Reliability with Applications to Electric Utilities

Michael A. Crew and
Paul R. Kleindorfer

Interest in the problem of rate-of-return regulation of a monopoly with stochastic demand is of rather recent origin, namely, Peles and Stein (1976), Perrakis (1976a, 1976b), Baron and Taggart (1977, 1978), Vogelsang and Neuefeind (1979, Chapter 3), Rau (1979), and Crew and Kleindorfer (1978, 1979a, 1979b). We note in the first section that there has been a considerable amount of disagreement as to not only what are the consequences of such regulation but also what is an appropriate framework for analyzing the problem. These disagreements, we argue, stem from widely divergent assumptions concerning three related isues: how reliability of supply is determined, how rate-of-return regulation under uncertainty is interpreted and enforced, and the nature of the adjustment process between regulators and firms.

Our first task is to attempt to clarify the situation to date by developing a general framework for the problem which we use to give perspective to the above contributions. We illustrate the direction that the general framework may take us by studying a simple case of a fixed-proportions technology in the second section. In the third section we examine some empirical results in the light of the earlier framework. Finally, we discuss some implications and future directions of this research.

Rate-of-Return Regulation with Stochastic Demand

Regulation of monopoly under stochastic demand (or stochastic supply) is inherently more complicated than regulation with deterministic demand, as pioneered by Averch and Johnson (1962). Aside from the obvious complications of the need to define the nature of the demand uncertainty—for example, whether it enters the demand function in an additive or a multi-

---

We would like to thank our discussants Robert Taggart and Ingo Vogelsang for their stimulating comments. In addition, thanks are due Murti Bhavaraju, John Blackstone, and Charles Hoffman for their advice on industry practices and problems and to Abba Krieger for advice on statistical problems. Thanks are also due to Uday Apte and Daniel Weaver for able research and computational assistance.

plicative way—certain fundamental questions about the nature of regulation under uncertainty arise which we now address.

The first of these is reliability, the extent to which demand will be met. Where capacity is fixed, as in the case of the traditional Boiteux-Steiner technology, in the diverse technology used in Crew and Kleindorfer (1976), or in the capacity-limited neoclassical technology introduced by Marino (1978), the possibility of demand exceeding capacity has to be faced. It seems clear that current technologies in transportation, electricity, gas, and water supply and telecommunications use technologies for which capacity is a long-term factor which, once set, implies some fixed limits on short-run output. Thus, the question of reliability and excess demand is rather important for public utilities.

The theory of welfare-optimal reliability is now reasonably well developed.[1] The same cannot be said for the theory of reliability under rate-of-return regulation. Indeed, except for Crew and Kleindorfer (1978, 1979a), the issue has been largely ignored. For example, Perrakis (1976a, 1976b), Peles and Stein (1976), Baron and Taggart (1978), and chapter 3 avoid the problems posed by reliability by assuming that demand must always be met in full, either through variations in short-run factors or in (*ex post*) output prices.[2]

Another fundamental issue concerns the nature of the regulatory constraint. Under deterministic demand, it is a straightforward upper bound which profits must not exceed. Under risk, the issue is more complicated. For instance, does the regulator set an inequality constraint *ex ante* and then *ex post* confiscate all or part of the firm's actual profit above the allowed level? Or does the regulator set *ex ante* a proportion that the firm may retain of any excess profits? In general, the issues concerning the rate-of-return constraint under risk may be summarized by the following questions: How often can it be violated and by how much? What are the consequences of violating it? To our knowledge, these questions have not been dealt with adequately in the literature to date.

The interaction between the regulator and the regulated firm has been ignored except by Barron and Taggart (1977, 1978). As in a duopoly situation, the consequences are different, depending on the assumptions each party makes regarding the other's behavior. Thus the question of the extent to which the parties operate within a rational-expectations framework clearly arises, much the same way as in simple duopoly theory the results depend on expectations about the other party's behavior. Although we do not explore such issues here, it seems likely that the effects of regulation under stochastic demand will be sensitive to such considerations.

To deal with the problems described above, we propose the formal framework described below. We assume that a rate-of-return regulated firm enjoys a monopoly in its output market and aims to maximize expected

Applications to Electric Utilities

profit. The regulator aims in his regulatory actions to maximize expected welfare, defined as the sum of producer and consumer surpluses. Before proceeding to state the problem formally, we define the following quantities:

Π = $\Pi(K, L(K, p, u), p, u)$ = profit = $p \cdot \min[D(p, \tilde{u}), F(K, \mathcal{L})] - w\mathcal{L} - rK$
$\bar{\Pi}$ = expected profit (net of regulatory actions)
p = price
K = physical quantity of capital
L = physical quantity of labor
$\mathcal{L}$ = $\mathcal{L}(K, p, \tilde{u})$ = short-run labor response as a function of K, p, and $\tilde{u}$
F = $F(K, L)$ = output, where F is a quasi-concave neoclassical production function with positive marginal products
D = $D(p, \tilde{u})$ = demand function
$\tilde{u}$ = random variable
g = probability density function of $\tilde{u}$
G = cumulative distribution function of $\tilde{u}$ where $G(u) = \Pr\{\tilde{u} \leq u\}$
T = $\{u \mid \Pi(K, \mathcal{L}, p, u) \leq (s - r)K\}$
T' = $\sim T$
s = rate of return on capital allowed by regulator
w = cost per unit of labor (wage rate)
h = price of physical unit of capital (henceforth = 1)
hr = r = cost of physical unit of capital
H = set of feasible $\mathcal{L}$'s
η, γ, α = regulatory parameters between 0 and 1 discussed below
$\bar{W}$ = expected value of welfare (regulator's social-welfare function)

Using the above notation, we can now state a general behavioral model for the rate-of-return regulated firm under uncertainty. The firm is assumed to choose capital K and a labor-response function $\mathcal{L}(K, p, u)$ *ex ante*. The firm or the regulator may set the price, as we discuss below.

The firm's problem is to determine K, $\mathcal{L}(\cdot)$, and possibly p so as to maximize

$$\bar{\Pi} = \int_{u \in T} \Pi \, dG(u) + \int_{u \in T'} [\eta \Pi + (1 - \eta)(s - r)K[\, dG(u) \quad (4.1)$$

subject to

$$\Pr\{\Pi(K, \mathcal{L}, p, \tilde{u}) > (s - r)K\} \leq \gamma \text{ (rate-of-return constraint)} \quad (4.2)$$

$$\Pr\{D(p, \tilde{u}) \leq F[K, \mathcal{L}(K, p, u)]\} \geq \alpha \quad \text{(reliability constraint)} \quad (4.3)$$

$$\mathcal{L}(\cdot) \in H \quad (4.4)$$

We discuss the import of the regulatory parameters $\{\eta, \gamma, \alpha\}$ and constraints 4.2 to 4.4 below. In solving its problem, the regulator is required to fix values of either $\{\eta, \gamma, \alpha, s\}$ or $\{\eta, \gamma, \alpha, s, p\}$. In each case, it must set the relevant values before K and L are observed. The regulator's problem is: to

$$\text{Maximize } \bar{W} \quad \text{subject to constraints 4.2 to 4.4} \quad (4.5)$$

Let us consider the problem in greater detail. The objective function 4.1 represents expected profits, with a slight twist introduced by Peles and Stein (1976). If $u \in T$, so that actual returns on capital do not exceed the allowed rate, the firm's profits are assumed to equal actual profits. If, however, $u \in T'$ and actual returns exceed the allow rate [that is, $\Pi(K, \mathcal{L}, p, u) > (s - r)K$], the firm (plans under the expectation that it) is allowed to keep only a certain fraction η of its actual profits above the allowed level $(s - r)K$. In this case, its profits are given by

$$\hat{\Pi} = (s - r)K + \eta [\Pi(K, \mathcal{L}, p, u) - (s - r)K] \quad (4.6)$$

as given in the second integral in equation 4.1.

We call η the incentive parameter since it represents the proportion of profits in excess of the allowed rate of return which the regulator allows the firm to retain when the rate-of-return constraint is violated. The parameter γ in constraint 4.2 is the probability with which the firm must meet the rate-of-return constraint. The reliability parameter α in constraint 4.3 is simply the probability that capacity will be sufficient to meet demand.

Constraint 4.4 restricts the firm's short-run labor response function to the class H. To illustrate, suppose the production function F is of the class described by Marino (1978), so that there is an increasing function $h(K)$ which specifies the maximum output obtainable from a capital input K,

$$h(K) = \max\{F(K, L) \mid L \geq 0\} \quad (4.7)$$

One class of functions H would specify $\mathcal{L}(\cdot)$ so that the firm meets demand to the extent that its capacity allows. That is, $\mathcal{L}(K, p, u)$ would be defined as the solution to

$$F[K, \mathcal{L}(K, p, u)] = \min\{D(p, u), h(K)\} \quad (4.8)$$

An alternative class of response functions H would be those representing a

Applications to Electric Utilities

short-run, *ex post*, profit-maximizing response to a given K, p, and u. For the capital-limited technology given in equation 4.7, the response function in equation 4.8 is *ex post* profit-maximizing as long as $p > w$.

The general issue of concern here is that H, like constraints 4.2 and 4.3, must be established and understood *ex ante* if rate-of-return regulation is to be well defined. The institutional incentives and procedures by which the regulator establishes 4.1 to 4.4 as a framework within which the firm believes itself to be operating is obviously important, but a matter which we do not explore further here.

The final matter of importance in this model is how price is set. Where the firm sets the price, it may do so either *ex ante* or *ex post*—that is, $p = p$ or $p = P(K, u)$, respectively. When the regulator sets the price, it is assumed done *ex ante*. For the case of the regulator setting the price *ex post*, he or she would either have to allow a market-clearing price or have some deliberate arrangement for setting the price above or below the market clearing price. Were the regulator allowed the market clearing price, he would, in effect, be giving up his right to regulate price. If he chose a price above or below the market clearing price, it would be deliberately requiring either rationing or excess capacity. In neither instance do compelling arguments in favor of such behavior occur to us. In the case of the firm's setting the price, Perrakis (1976*a*), Peles and Stein (1976), and Rau (1979) all set the price *ex post*. Crew and Kleindorfer (1979*a*) and Perrakis (1979*b*), however, have the firm setting the price *ex ante*, while Baron and Taggart (1978) have the regulator set the price. Despite arguments to support the firm's setting the price *ex post*, we feel that the balance of the arguments is in favor of a model in which price is set *ex ante*, that is, before demand is revealed.[3] However, this does not imply that when p and K are set *ex ante*, they are necessarily set at the same time. Indeed, in practice, after K has been set, the price may be changed and yet still be set before demand is revealed.

Summarizing the above discussion, we may note the following cases that typify the problem faced by the firm and the regulator, using the framework of equations 4.1 to 4.5:

Case A: Here p, K, and $\mathcal{L}$ are all determined by the firm, with $(\eta, \alpha, \gamma, s)$ set by the regulator. In general, the price could be set *ex ante* or *ex post*, permitting a subdivision of this case into case A(1) where p is *ex ante* and case A(2) where p is *ex post*.[4]

Case B: Here K and $\mathcal{L}$ are determined by the firm with $(p, \eta, \alpha, \gamma, s)$ set by the regulators.

For the remainder of this chapter, we restrict attention to case A(1). As in Baron and Taggart's "naive" case (chapter 3), however, case B may be viewed as equivalent to case A(1) when price and capital are set simultaneously and when constraints 4.2 to 4.4 determine a unique price p for each level of capital input K.

Some implications of these cases are examined for a fixed-proportion technology in the next section. However, before doing so, let us briefly comment on the nature of the Averch-Johnson (AJ) effect under uncertainty. If the AJ effect under uncertainty is simply taken to mean the same as the AJ effect under certainty, then by following Baumol and Klevorick (1970), an AJ effect means producing the regulated output at a higher capital-labor ratio for the same level of output. However, under uncertainty, simple application of this definition presents a problem, because of the question of reliability. Two identical *ex post* outputs may result from *ex ante* plans (that is, p, K, and $\mathcal{L}$) of quite different character, and in particular from plans entailing different *ex ante* reliability levels, and as we will see shortly, reliability is a key aspect of the AJ effect under uncertainty.

To define the AJ effect first, for given p, define $\{\bar{K}(p), \mathcal{L}(\bar{K}(p), p, u)\}$ as the solution to the following expected-cost minimization problem:

$$\min_{[K, \mathcal{L}]} E\{w\mathcal{L}(K, p, \tilde{u}) + rK\} \quad \text{subject to constraints 4.3 and 4.4} \quad (4.9)$$

Now by asuming demand and technology and all primitive random variables have been prespecified, an AJ effect may be said to exist if, for a given price and level of *ex ante* reliability[5] α, the distribution of $K/\mathcal{L}(K, p, \tilde{u})$ is everywhere to the right of the distribution of $\bar{K}(p)/\bar{\mathcal{L}}(\bar{K}(p), p, \tilde{u})$ with that same level of reliability. This is equivalent to saying that the K/L ratio chosen by the regulated monopolist will be greater than or equal to that chosen by the expected-cost-minimizing monopolist with reliability constrained, whatever the *ex post* demand level turns out to be.[6]

To illustrate the above, consider the case of a fixed-proportions technology of the Boiteux-Steiner type, where $F(K, L) = \min\{K, L\}$. If we let H be the set of response functions $\mathcal{L}$ which maximize *ex post* profits, then as noted above, $\mathcal{L}$ is of the form of equation 4.8 as long as $p > w$. Thus in this case

$$\mathcal{L}(K, p, u) = \min\{D(p, u), K\} \quad (4.10)$$

and profits can be written as

$$\Pi[K, \mathcal{L}(K, p, u), p, u] = (p - w) \min\{D(p, u), K\} - rK \quad (4.11)$$

Now it is easy to see for this case that the solution $\{\bar{K}(p), \bar{\mathcal{L}}(\cdot)\}$ to 4.9 is given by equation 4.1 with $\bar{K}(p)$ determined as the smallest K satisfying the

Applications to Electric Utilities

reliability constraint 4.3, at the reliability level achieved by the regulated monopolist. From this, for the fixed-proportions technology and H as specified, we see that the only case in which an AJ effect will occur is when the same level of reliability achieved by the regulated monopolist can be achieved with less capital. This will happen, in particular, when the regulated monopolist sets the capital stock at a level higher than that required to achieve a reliability level of unity. A class of examples of this sort of behavior is given in Crew and Kleindorfer (1978, 1979a) for bounded demand distributions.

When capital stock is greater than that required for 100 percent reliability, a pure AJ effect is present because, for reliability unchanged, the K-variable-factor ratio increases. This should be distinguished from the more complicated situation where the demand distribution is not truncated at the upper end. In this case, reliability can always be increased by increasing capacity. However, in this case, the absence of an AJ effect, as defined above, does not mean that an efficient point has been reached, because a tradeoff still remains between reliability and additional capacity.[7] Where reliability is very high, a small increase in reliability can be achieved only at the high cost of a large amount of capacity. In such cases, the inefficiency may be partitioned into two parts—the AJ effect (stemming from the higher K/L ratio induced by rate-of-return regulation) and a "gold plating on reliability" effect which derives from an amount of reliability excessive in relation to the benefits provided.

In the theory of the regulated firm under certainty, say, as presented by Baumol and Klevorick (1970), comparative statics reveals that K/L, K, and $F(K, L)$ (that is, output) all increase as s is decreased below the unregulated monopoly level. As Sheshinski (1971) points out, this gives rise to a tradeoff in setting s between consumer welfare gains due to increased output and the welfare losses due to increasing production inefficiency (as measured by the difference between K/L and r/w). A corresponding tradeoff would arise in the stochastic case, provided that K, the distributions of $K / \mathcal{L}(\cdot, \tilde{u})$ and of $F(K, \mathcal{L}(\cdot, \tilde{u}))$, and reliability all increase as s is decreased below the unregulated level.[8] If valid, these properties would imply a tradeoff between increased and more reliable output and the costs of providing it. In the stochastic case, however, a more complex informational and regulatory process must be orchestrated to coordinate reliability and rate-of-return regulation.

A Fixed-Proportions Technology

To provide some insights into the implications of the above model, we analyze in this section the case where technology is fixed proportions, so that short-run marginal cost is w per unit and capacity cost is r per unit. We assume throughout that p and K are set by the firm *ex ante*. Using equations 4.10 and 4.11, we may formulate the firm's problem as follows:

$$\underset{p,K}{\text{maximize }} \bar{\Pi} = \left\{ \int_{u \in T} [(p-w)\min\{D(p,u), K\} - rK] \, dG(u) \right.$$

$$\left. + \int_{u \in T'} \{(s-r)K + \eta[(p-w)\min\{D(p,u), K\} - sK]\} \, dG(u) \right\} \quad (4.12)$$

subject to

$$\Pr\{T'\} = \Pr\{(p-w)\min\{D(p,\tilde{u}), K\} > sK\} \leq \gamma \quad (4.13)$$

$$\Pr\{D(p,\tilde{u}) \leq K\} \geq \alpha \quad (4.14)$$

We are concerned here with the comparative-statics results indicated at the end of the last section. Specifically, we wish to show that K (which is both capital stock and maximum output), $K/\mathcal{L}(\cdot, \tilde{u})$, and reliability all increase as s is decreased below the unregulated level. We are also interested in shedding light on the effects of the regulatory parameters η, γ, and α. We deal explicitly with only the case where demand uncertainty is of the multiplicative form

$$D(p, \tilde{u}) = \tilde{u}X(p), \quad \tilde{u} > 0, \quad E(\tilde{u}) = 1, \quad X'(p) < 0 \quad (4.15)$$

But we indicate corresponding results for additive uncertainty:

$$D(p, \tilde{u}) = X(p) + \tilde{u} \quad E(\tilde{u}) = 0 \quad X'(p) < 0 \quad (4.16)$$

To begin our analysis, we simplify the expression 4.12 by characterizing the set $T = \{u | (p-w) \min\{D(p,u), K\} \leq sK\}$. To this end, we assume that s is small enough so that $p - w \geq s$ at the optimal price p. If $p - w < s$, then for every realization of $\tilde{u}$ we have

$$(p-w)\min\{D(p,u), K\} - sK \leq (p-w-s)K < 0 \quad (4.17)$$

which implies that the allowed rate of return s will not be earned for any realization of demand.

Applications to Electric Utilities

Now we assumed $p - w \geq s$, so that the set T is given by[9]

$$T = \{u(p - w)D(p, u) \leq sK\} \qquad (4.18)$$

The set T' in 4.13 is just the complement of T. It is useful to partition T' into the sets T_1' and T_2' respectively, where demand is less than or equal to capacity and where it exceeds capacity,

$$T_1' = \{u \in T' \mid D(p, u) \leq K[; \qquad T_2' = \{u \in T' \mid D(p, u) > K] \qquad (4.19)$$

From here on we concentrate on the multiplicative case, 4.15. First we define the quantities M and N as

$$M = \frac{sK}{(p - w)X(p)} \qquad N = \frac{K}{X(p)} \qquad (4.20)$$

Using these with equations 4.15 and 4.18 to 4.19, we may express T, T_1', and T_2' as

$$T = \{u \mid 0 \leq u \leq M\} \qquad T_1' = \{u \mid M \leq u \leq N\} \qquad T_2' = \{u \mid u > N\} \qquad (4.21)$$

Finally, using these and the cumulative distribution function[10] (cdf) G of $\tilde{u}$, we may reformulate the problem in 4.12 to 4.14 as follows:

$$\text{maximize } \bar{\Pi} = \int_0^M [(p - w)uX(p) - rK]dG(u)$$

$$+ \int_M^N \{(s - r)K + \eta[(p - w)uX(p) - sK]\} \, dG(u)$$

$$+ \int_N^\infty [(s - r)K + \eta(p - w - s)K] \, dG(u) \qquad (4.22)$$

subject to

$$\Pr\{T'\} = 1 - \Pr\{T\} = 1 - G(M) \leq \gamma \qquad (4.23)$$

$$\Pr\{\tilde{u}X(p) \leq K\} = G(N) \geq \alpha \qquad (4.24)$$

Define the monotonic increasing function $A:[0, 1] \to R$ by $A(y) = \inf \{x \mid G(x) \geq y\}$. We may also express equations 4.23 and 4.24 in the forms

$$A(1 - \gamma)(p - w)X(p) \leq sK \qquad (4.25)$$

$$A(\alpha)X(p) \leq K \qquad (4.26)$$

We wish to determine the comparative statics of the solution to equations 4.22 to 4.24. These are illustrated graphically in figure 4–1. There we show the isoreliability loci labeled α_1, α_2 with $\alpha_1 < \alpha_2$. These are just the solutions to $A(\alpha) X (p) = K$ (see constraint 4.26). We also show the isoprobability loci labeled γ_1, γ_2 where $\gamma_1 < \gamma_2$. These are the solutions to $A(1 - \gamma)(p - w)X(p) = sK$. Note from 4.25 that an increase in γ (the probability that the rate-of-return constraint can be violated) has the same effect as an increase in s.[11] Thus, the effects of varying α, γ, and s on the feasible policy region determined by equations 4.23 and 4.24 are clear. The hatched region in figure 4–1 shows the feasible region for (γ_1, α_2), that is, the set of prices and levels of capacity satisfying the regulatory constraints.

In figure 4–2 we show the feasible region for a given α and two values of γ. We also show isoprofit lines for the firm for a given value of η and s. The point (p^0, K^0) is the unconstrained solution to maximizing $\bar{\Pi}$ in equation 4.1. As shown, the optimal regulated solution when γ_i obtains is (p^i, K^i). As γ is

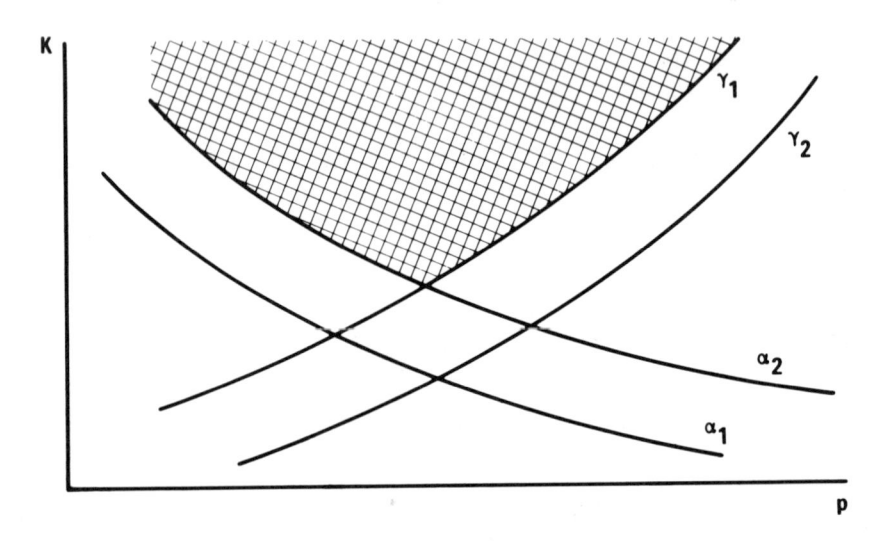

Figure 4–1 The Feasible Constraint Region

Applications to Electric Utilities

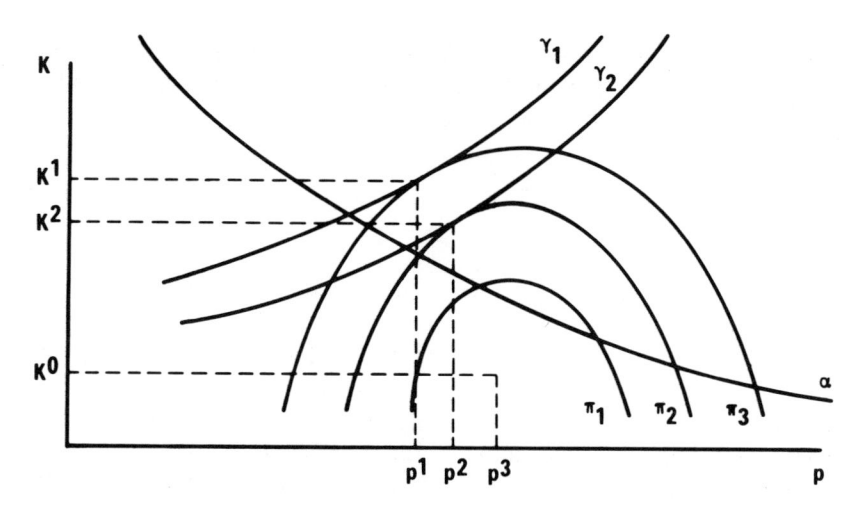

Figure 4-2 Comparative Statics of γ

decreased, the price decreases and K increases. This graphical analysis has its problems in dealing with variations in s when $\eta < 1$, since then the point (p^0, K^0) and the isoprofit contours depend on both s and η (see equation 4.1). Of course, when $\eta = 1$, (p^0, K^0) is just the unregulated profit-maximizing solution. To provide general results, we clearly need a more formal analysis. We are concerned here with the comparative statics with respect to s only, though we illustrate the comparative statics with respect to η, γ and α by numerical examples. For s, we provide a comlete analysis in appendix 4A, the main result of which is the following theorem for the multiplicative case, 4.15. Corresponding results for the additive case, 4.16, follow from the development in Crew and Kleindorfer (1979a).[12]

Theorem 1: If the expected net revenue function $R(p) = (p - w) X(p)$ is concave, then the solution $(\hat{K}, \hat{p})$ to equations 4.22 to 4.24 is such that $\hat{K}$ and $\hat{N} = \hat{K} / X(\hat{p})$ are decreasing functions of s when s is below the unregulated monopoly level. This implies that reliability and the entire distribution of $\hat{K}/\mathcal{L}(\hat{K}, \hat{p}, \tilde{u})$ shift to the right as s is decreased.

The reader should note that $d\hat{N}/ds < 0$ clearly implies that reliability $G(\hat{N})$ increases as s decreases. Note also that if both $\hat{K}$ and $\hat{N} = \hat{K}/X(\hat{p})$ increase, then, for every u, so $\hat{K}/\min\{uX(\hat{p}), \hat{K}\} = \hat{K}/\mathcal{L}(\hat{K}, \hat{p}, u)$ must increase or remain the same. Thus, for the fixed-proportions technology and demand in additive or multiplicative form, the tradeoff described in the previous section among reliability, output, and production efficiency does obtain.

To further explore the issues here, a computer model was constructed to solve equations 4.22 to 4.24 via direct search. Table 4–1 gives selected results for a problem with linear demands, uniform disturbances, and no reliability constraint. The problem data were

$$g(u) = \begin{cases} 1 & \text{for } u \in \{0.5, 1.5\} \\ 0 & \text{else} \end{cases} \quad (4.27)$$

$$X(p) = 100 - 3p \quad w = 5 \quad r = 10 \quad (4.28)$$

$$\alpha = 0 \quad \gamma = 0.5 \quad s \text{ and } \eta \text{ as indicated} \quad (4.29)$$

From these illustrative results we see the results of theorem 1 confirmed and the following other comparative statics results: $d\hat{p}/ds > 0$, $d\hat{p}/d\eta > 0$, $d\hat{K}/d\eta < 0$, $dG(\hat{N})/d\eta > 0$, and $[d(\hat{K})/\mathcal{L}(\hat{K}, \hat{p}, u)]/d\eta > 0$. Whether

Table 4–1
Results for Equations 4.27 to 4.29

η	s	$\hat{p}$	$\hat{K}$	$G(\hat{N})$ = Reliability
0.0	11.5	19.17	52.36	0.615
0.5		21.77	50.58	0.730
1.0		21.79	50.56	0.732
0.0	12.0	19.17	50.17	0.590
0.5		22.01	48.03	0.710
1.0		22.24	47.82	0.720
0.0	12.5	19.17	48.17	0.565
0.5		22.35	45.74	0.695
1.0		22.63	45.29	0.705
0.0	13.0	19.17	46.31	0.545
0.5		22.54	43.69	0.675
1.0		22.96	42.99	0.690
0.0	13.5	19.17	44.60	0.525
0.5		22.69	41.84	0.655
1.0		23.24	40.90	0.675
0.0	14.0	19.17	43.01	0.505
0.5		22.80	40.17	0.635
1.0		23.49	39.00	0.660
0.0	14.5	19.50	41.50	0.500
0.5		22.89	38.65	0.615
1.0		23.70	37.27	0.645
0.0	15.0	20.00	40.00	0.500
0.5		22.96	37.26	0.600
1.0		24.04	35.69	0.630

Applications to Electric Utilities

these results hold more generally, and for the case of additive uncertainty, is not known. The readers will note, however, that the effects of decreasing η, while similar to s as it relates to K, decrease reliability. This is as one would expect since as η decreases, the firm receives fewer of the benefits from high demands since profits are expropriated whenever they exceed the allowed level. Thus, η and s seem to work in opposite directions as relates to reliability. This might be used to advantage in fine-tuning the reliability response of the regulated firm under uncertainty.

Empirical Results

We now review the potential significance of the above analysis by performing some elementary econometric analysis and briefly review practice in the electric-utility industry. We are mainly concerned with the effects of regulation on AJ effects and reliability and particularly the testing of some of our own hypotheses in this regard.

The empirical research which we have undertaken does not take into account the effects of changes in all the parameters, η, α, γ, and s, because of lack of information. However, we have data on s, and we know that the companies themselves and not the regulators set α. We therefore restrict ourselves to testing the hypothesis generated by our theory that an AJ effect is present to the extent that reserve margin, a surrogate for system reliability defined below, increases as the allowed rate of return is reduced. We tested this by means of a set of cross-sectional time-series data derived from published sources as described in appendix 4B. They covered a period from 1971 to 1978, and consisted of the following:

S_E = reported rate of return on equity
S = reported rate of return on total assets[13]
L = load factor (a measure of utilization of a system)[14]
I = imports of power from other systems, in megawatthours
E = exports of power to other systems, in megawatthours
N = proportion of nuclear capacity
H = proportion of hydro capacity
C = proportion of fossil capacity
G = proportion of internal-combustion capacity, in megawatts
A = average plant size
R = reserve margin = $\dfrac{\text{capacity} - \text{peak}^{15}}{\text{capacity}}$

We performed various regressions on the pooled data after eliminating five of the observations because of problems of missing individual pieces of data that could not be readily obtained or verified. We considered carefully whether pooling the data was appropriate in this case. Structurally, there are several reasons to expect stability across companies over time: All the companies are subject in principle to the same method of regulation; they are all investor-owned with presumably similar motivations, and they cooperate extensively through power interchanges, reliability councils, and industry research and study groups. However, we did check this statistically as well as the hypothesis of stability of regression coefficients, and the usual qualifications with respect to pooling across companies apply here. Indeed, as it turns out, there are statistically significant differences across companies as relates to the magnitude of various factors affecting reserve margin.[16] Because we were concerned with mean effects, and also for reasons of data limitations, we saw no alternative to pooling the data, however.

The regressions were run in two groups. One group of thirty-nine companies consisted of combination gas and electric companies, and the other group consisted of the remaining electric companies. The regression equation had the following general form (all variables are measured in the current period t, except for s which was lagged k periods):

$$R_t = f(S_{t-k}, L_t, I_t, E_t, N_t, H_t, C_t, G_t, A_t)$$

On a priori grounds, we have no reason to hypothesize a definite sign for some of the variables. For example, the sign of L (load factor) might be positive or negative. On the one hand, we might expect the reserve margin to have to be increased if the load factor is increased because it results in the plant being run more intensively and therefore being more likely to break down. However, because of the methods used in system planning for reliability, it is possible that load factors could increase over a large range without the reserve margin being affected. Without going into detail, we know that systems are planned to meet demand within a given probability, which is usually very high. Whether demands can be met depends on several factors, among the most significant being the peak and the probability of outage of the plants. If the probability of outage of a plant is treated as a constant invariant to its rate of utilization, increases in base load are not going to raise significantly the probability of outage that is derived. More importantly, those systems that simply plan for reliability based on some percentage reserve margin over peak will not change their reserve margin at all if the load factor increases.[17] Thus, on a priori grounds, we cannot hypothesize a sign for the load factor.

Similarly, for the various types of capacity it may not be possible on a priori grounds to argue for a particular sign. We discuss elsewhere [in Crew and Kleindorfer (1980)] the effects of regulation on a diverse (multiple-plant-type) technology. Our analysis indicates that while base-load capacity may be no less under regulation, peak-load capacity might be greater or less under

Applications to Electric Utilities

regulation. This might lead us to argue for positive signs on hydro and nuclear, but not to hypothesize signs for internal combustion and fossil fuels. However, technological influences might play a dominating role in the problem. For example, the case of hydro, in view of its reliability (low probability of outage when required to meet a peak), might mean that reserve margins can be reduced.

On the other variables we can hypothesize definite signs. Based on our theory, we would clearly argue that rate of return and reserve margin are negatively related. We would argue in general that imports and reserve margin are positively related, and the opposite for exports. On grounds of indivisibility, we would argue that average plant size and reserve margin are positively related. The greater proportion of capacity provided by an individual plant, the larger reserve needed by the system to overcome the risk of that plant's going down.

We proceeded to test these hypotheses by means of a series of stepwise, ordinary-least-squares (OLS) regressions on the two groups of companies. For the combination gas and electric companies we obtained little of significance. This may be because the companies integrate their gas and electricity activities in such a way that AJ effects and reliability effects on the electricity side are no longer determinate. Possible ways in which this might happen are considerable. For example, some combination companies might use their gas operations to sell gas air conditioning rather than electric. This might have the effect of reducing both reserve margins, which are required, and load factors. In addition, gas shortages were faced during this period of various magnitude across these companies, perhaps making it difficult to identify what was happening in such companies.

The results for the thirty-nine electric-only utilities are reported in table 4-2. Since neither return on equity nor return on total assets is significant, we find no support for the hypothesis of our theory that reserve margin and allowed rate of return are inversely related.[18] The results show a clear dominance by other factors over the rate-of-return effects. Hydro is the most significant variable. The negative sign presumably reflects the importance of hydro's ability to come on load when required with a high reliability, thus enabling systems with large amounts of hydro to achieve the target reliability with a lower reserve margin. Nuclear has a positive (and significant) sign, as hypothesized, as do exports and average plant size. These variables are all highly significant.[19]

In interpreting the above results, we may note that, until recently anyway, system planners have tended to operate almost independently from the regulatory process and, to some extent, independently from the rest of the company. Thus, it may not be too surprising that the above empirical results relating rate of return and reliability are weak and the results on technological aspects strong.[20]

**Table 4-2
Ordinary-Least-Squares Stepwise Regression of Owned Reserve against Indicated Variables, Pooled Data for Thirty-Nine Electric-Only Utilities, 1971 to 1978**

	Return on Equity	Load Factor	Imports	Exports	Fossil Fuel	Nuclear	Gas	Hydro	Average Plant Size	Constant	F	Adj R²
				Regression Using Return on Equity (ROE)								
ROE lagged 5 years	−0.338 (0.73)	0.408 (2.29)	−3.904 (2.93)	2.326 (1.85)	X	0.647 (4.65)	−0.378 (2.93)	−0.737 (12.11)	0.485 (5.48)	−7.960	40.107	0.504
ROE lagged 6 years	−0.145 (0.34)	0.422 (2.34)	−3.336 (2.73)	2.632 (2.17)	X	0.667 (4.75)	−0.357 (2.76)	−0.725 (11.84)	0.483 (5.42)	−12.266	39.543	0.500
	Return on Assets	Load Factor	Imports	Exports	Fossil Fuel	Nuclear	Gas	Hydro	Average Plant Size	Constant	F	Adj R²
				Regression Using Return on Total Assets (RTA)								
RTA lagged 5 years	X	0.397 (2.24)	−4.002 (3.02)	2.399 (1.91)	X	0.660 (4.78)	0.373 (2.89)	−0.726 (12.31)	0.471 (5.46)	−11.539	45.833	0.505
RTA lagged 6 years	0.429 (0.49)	0.408 (2.26)	−3.332 (2.73)	2.630 (2.17)	X	0.677 (4.85)	−0.351 (2.70)	−0.712 (11.58)	0.465 (5.20)	−16.456	39.576	0.500

Note: Since the rates of return are lagged by 5 or 6 years, the data actually go back to 1965. Each cell gives the regression coefficient for the corresponding variables. The values in parenthesis denote corresponding values t values. The total number of cases was 309. "X" indicates not sufficiently significant to enter stepwise regression.

Concluding Remarks

We see some implications of these results for theory and public policy which we now summarize.

1. The AJ effects are much more complicated under uncertainty than has previously been indicated.
2. Reliability, while being a crucial dimension in the analysis, offers no straightforward way to test the AJ effect under uncertainty. The support for our own hypothesis in this regard is inconclusive at best.
3. Technological relationships are revealed to be dominant in the empirical analysis, in many respects consistent with the descriptions in the system planning literature.

In view of the fact that this chapter has raised as many questions as it has answered, reliability may well be a fruitful area for further study. Such issues as whether current methods of reliability planning are efficient, as questions by Telson (1973, 1975), the extent to which regulators should be concerned with reliability, and the possibility of incorporating consumer preferences in reliability planning are all possibilities for future research that come to mind as a result of our analysis and excursions into the real world of electric utilities and regulation. In addition, this chapter has suggested a general framework for studying regulation under uncertainty. This framework is an attempt to deal more explicitly with the nature of the regulatory process itself, and it points to the possible significance of parameters other than the allowed rate of return s, which has traditionally received all the attention. Further empirical, policy-oriented research on the operation and effects of the regulatory process present a promising direction for future research.

Notes

1. See Crew and Kleindorfer (1976) and Rees (1980) for a review of previous results on welfare-optimal reliability levels. These involve setting capacity (or reliability) so that expected losses in consumers' surplus due to excess demand rationing are just equal to the long run marginal cost of increasing capacity.

2. Peles and Stein (1976, p. 287, n7) assumes that price is set *ex post* after demand is known. This presumably means that their firm always meets demand, although their explanation leaves this open—"*Quantity sold* is assumed to equal *quantity produced*" (p. 279, emphasis added).

3. Littlechild's (1972) arguments that interruptible gas rates and airline standbys represent examples of prices being set *ex post* do not strike us as

very convincing. Indeed, in such cases, price is set *ex ante* for the bulk of the customers, those who pay the regular price for the right to get a particular flight or the right to maintained gas supplies. In addition, the rate charged to the standbys has to be fixed *ex ante*. What they pay *ex post* may exceed this, whether or not they get the flight. However, the *ex post* price need not be market-clearing, as apparently assumed by Littlechild and others, for capacity may often be underutilized with all standbys aboard. Thus the situation, while not straightforward, hardly seems to provide a strong case for *ex post* pricing. For an interesting discussion of interruptible pricing, see Tschirhart and Jen (1979).

4. We do not discuss Perrakis (1976a) because we consider it of limited interest since price is assumed set *ex post*.

5. Reliability is defined as the probability that demand will be less than capacity. Thus if regulation increases capacity, this may not be an AJ effect as long as reliability is increasing.

6. In Baron and Taggart (1978) the AJ effect is taken to mean that the expected value of $\{K(p)/\mathcal{L}(K(p), p, \tilde{u})\}$ is greater than the expected value of $\{\bar{K}(p)/\mathcal{L}(\bar{K}(p), p, \tilde{u})\}$, although they deal with only the case where demand is exactly met ($\alpha = 1$). This expected-value definition of the AJ effect would be an alternative to our stricter requirements.

7. The complexity of the tradeoff between additional capital and reliability at high levels of reliability has received some attention by the industry and the regulators in recent years, as surveyed by Robeson, Norland, and Gannon (1978). Robeson, Norland, and Gannon summarize the results of eleven studies undertaken from 1971 to 1977. Most of these studies attempt to quantify the output losses that would result from reduced reliability and, as they note, implicitly assume a linear relation between losses and unsupplied energy. This is unlikely to be the case since possibilities such as interruptible service were not considered. Presumably, where they are acceptable, the losses from interruption must be less than the benefit received by the customer, thus raising the question of the use of linearity assumptions and emphasizing the complexity of the problem and the scope for further research in this area.

8. We verify these comparative-statics properties for a simple case in the next section.

9. We show that T is specified by equation 4.18. Consider two cases:
Case 1: $D(p, u) > K$. In this case

$$\Pi = (p - w)\min\{D(p, u), K\} - rK \geq (s - r)K$$

since $D > K$ and $p - w \geq s$ are assumed.
Case 2: $D(p, u) \leq K$. Here we find that

$$\Pi = (p - w)D(p, u) - rK$$

so that $\Pi > (s - r)K$ if and only if $(p - w)D > sK$.

Taking cases 1 and 2 together, we see that the rate of return exceeds s whenever either $D(p, u) > K$ or $[D \leq K$ and $(p - w)D > sK]$. The set T is therefore the complement of these events, that is,

$$T = \{u \mid D(p, u) \leq K \text{ and } (p - w)D(p, u) \leq sK\}$$

which reduces to equation 4.18 since $p - w \geq s$ and $(p - w)D \leq sK$ already imply $D(p, u) \leq K$.

10. The cumulative distribution function G is defined as $G(u) = \Pr\{\tilde{u} < u\}$.

11. Note, however, that changing s also affects the objective function.

12. The results for the additive case are obtained in a straightforward manner from the analysis in Crew and Kleindorfer (1979a), with the only difference being that the reserve margin for the additive case is defined as $N_a = K - X(p)$ as opposed to $N_p = K/X(p)$ for the multiplicative case. Showing that N_a (or N_P) increases with decreasing s demonstrates that reliability increases with decreasing s. The parameter values for this special case are restricted to $\eta = 1$, $\alpha = 0$, and $0 < \gamma < 1$.

13. We used reported rates of return as a surrogate for allowed rate of return s used in the theory.

14. It is defined more precisely as

$$L = \frac{\text{actual output}}{8{,}760 \cdot \text{peak demand}} \, 100$$

15. The data distinguish between "owned reserve" as defined above and "total reserve." Clearly, owned reserve is the variable of interest here.

16. Indeed, the standard F-test described in Maddala (1977, pp. 194–201, 322–326) allows one to reject (at the .01 level) the hypothesis that coefficients for the regression model described below are stable across companies.

17. Although system planners such as Billinton (1970) and Endrenyi (1978) would argue for the use of probability methods in planning for reliability, they acknowledge the continued use of the simple rules of thumb for percentage reserve margins that had originally been the basis of reliability planning. This is confirmed by Telson (1973, pp. 117–21) who surveyed the criteria used by various systems through the United States.

18. We also ran a regression using a three-year moving average, lagged five years, of the rate of return on equity. Again, there was no significance on

rate of return. All the other terms continued to be significant, with effects similar to those in table 4–2.

19. We ran some additional tests on the individual firms which confirmed the significance of these results. Since we had only eight years of usable data on each firm, we confined attention to regressions of reserve margin against the four most important factors determined from the regression on the total sample, that is, hydro, nuclear, average plant size, and return on equity. Of the thirty-nine regressions run, sixteen had significant F values at the .05 level. Of these, sixteen had significant positive signs associated with average plant size. No other significant nonparametric patterns emerged from these individual firm regressions.

20. The results could be subjected to further analysis by performing a generalized-least-square analysis (GLS) instead of the ordinary-least-squares (OLS) used. Additional data could be added as they became available. However, we would be surprised if any such improvements would affect the above results in a major way.

Appendix 4A

Here we prove theorem 1 concerning the comparative statics of equations 4.22 to 4.24. First assume that both equations 4.23 and 4.24 are binding at optimum over a nonempty interval $[s, \bar{s}]$. Then we can solve equations 4.25 and 4.26 explicitly for N and K to yield $N = A(\alpha)$, a constant, and from equation 4.25.

$$\frac{K}{X(p)} = N = \frac{A(1-\gamma)(p-w)}{s} \qquad (4A.1)$$

From this $dN/ds = 0$ for $s \in [s, \bar{s}]$ and, from equation 4A.1,

$$\frac{d}{ds}\left(\frac{p-w}{s}\right) = \frac{d}{ds}\left(\frac{N}{A(1-\gamma)}\right) = 0 = \frac{s\, dp/ds - (p-w)}{s^2}.$$

From this, $dp/ds > 0$ for $s \in [s, \bar{s}]$. This implies $dX(p)/ds < 0$ and, with $dN/ds = 0$, we must have $dK/ds = d(NX)/ds < 0$. Thus, theorem 1 is valid if equations 4.23 and 4.24 are both binding.

Now assume that the reliability constraint 4.24 is not binding, but the rate-of-return constraint 4.23 (or 4.25) is binding in some interval $s \in [s, \bar{s}]$. In this case, equations 4.22 to 4.24 reduce to the problem

$$\max\{\bar{\Pi}(p, K) \mid K = A(1-\gamma)(p-w)X(p)/s\} \qquad (4A.3)$$

which, by substituting for K, is equivalent to

$$\max \hat{\Pi}(p, s) = \bar{\Pi}[p, A(1-\gamma)(p-w)X(p)/s] \qquad (4A.4)$$

which is a function of p and s. To determine the comparative statics of equations 4.22 to 4.24, it suffices to study the solution $\hat{p}(s)$ to equation 4A.4, from which the corresponding optimal $\hat{K}$ and $\hat{N}$ for equations 4.22 to 4.24 are given by

$$\hat{K} = \frac{A(1-\gamma)(\hat{p}-w)X(\hat{p})}{s} \qquad \hat{N} = \frac{\hat{K}}{X(\hat{p})} = \frac{A(1-\gamma)(\hat{p}-w)}{s} \qquad (4A.5)$$

From equation 4.22 we may write $\hat{\Pi}(p)$ in equation 4A.4 as follows:

$$\hat{\Pi}(p, s) = R(p)H(p, s) \qquad (4A.6)$$

where $R(p) = (p - w) X(p)$ and where

$$H(p, s) = \left\{ \int_0^{A(1-\gamma)} \left[u - \frac{rA(1-\gamma)}{s} \right] dG(u) \right.$$

$$+ \int_{A(1-\gamma)}^{A(1-\gamma)(p-w)/s} \left\{ \frac{s-r}{s} A(1-\gamma) + \eta[u - A(1-\gamma)] \right\} dG(u)$$

$$\left. + \int_{A(1-\gamma)(p-w)/s}^{\infty} [s - r + \eta(p - w - s)] \frac{A(1-\gamma)}{s} dG(u) \right\} \quad (4A.7)$$

Using subscripts to denote partial differentiation, we compute the following quantities of interest:

$$\hat{\Pi}_p = R_p H + R H_p = 0 \quad (4A.8)$$

by optimality;

$$H_p = \frac{\eta}{s} A(1-\gamma) [1 - G(N)] > 0 \quad (4A.9)$$

where $N = N(s) = A(1-\gamma)(p-w)/s$;

$$\hat{\Pi}_{ps} = R_p H_s + R H_{ps} \quad (4A.10)$$

$$R_p = (p - w) X_p + X < 0 \quad (4A.11)$$

since equation 4A.8 implies $R_p H = -R H_p$, with $H_p > 0$ by equation 4A.9 and $\hat{\Pi} = RH > 0$ by optimality;

$$R_{pp} = (p - w) X_{pp} + 2X_p < 0 \quad (4A.12)$$

by the assumed concavity of R;

$$H_s = \frac{A(1-\gamma)}{s^2} \left\{ r - \eta(p - w)[1 - G(N)] \right\} \quad (4A.13)$$

$$H_{ps} = \frac{\eta A(1-\gamma)}{s^2} \left\{ \frac{(p-w)g(N)}{s} A(1-\gamma) - [1 - G(N)] \right\} \quad (4A.14)$$

Applications to Electric Utilities

$$H_{pp} = -\eta \left[\frac{A(1-\gamma)}{s}\right]^2 \left[\frac{(p-w)g(N)}{s}\right] < 0 \qquad (4\text{A}.15)$$

$$\hat{\Pi}_{pp} = R_{pp}H + 2R_pH_p + RH_{pp} < 0 \qquad (4\text{A}.16)$$

since R_{pp}, R_p, $H_{pp} < 0$ and H, H_p, $R > 0$; and

$$sH_s + H = \int_0^{A(1-\gamma)} u\, dG(u)$$
$$+ \eta \int_{A(1-\gamma)}^{N} u\, dG(u) + \gamma(1-\eta)A(1-\gamma) > 0 \qquad (4\text{A}.17)$$

Now from the implicit function theorem and $\hat{\Pi}_p = 0$, we have

$$\frac{dp}{ds} = -\frac{\hat{\Pi}_{ps}}{\hat{\Pi}_{pp}} \qquad (4\text{A}.18)$$

Thus, since $N = A(1-\gamma)(p-w)/s$, we see that

$$\hat{\Pi}_{pp} \frac{s^2}{A(1-\gamma)} \frac{dN(s)}{ds} = -s\hat{\Pi}_{pp}\left(\frac{dp}{ds} - \frac{p-w}{s}\right)$$

$$= -s\hat{\Pi}_{ps} - (p-w)\hat{\Pi}_{pp}$$

$$= -sR_pH_s + \eta\frac{RA(1-\gamma)}{s}\left[1 - G(N)\right.$$

$$\left. - \frac{A(1-\gamma)(p-w)}{s}g(N)\right]$$

$$-(p-w)(R_{pp}H + 2P_pH_p + RH_{pp})$$

$$= -sR_pH_s + \frac{\eta RA(1-\gamma)}{s}[1 - G(N)]$$

$$-(p-w)(R_{pp}H + 2P_pH_p) \qquad (4\text{A}.19)$$

Now the second term in the last expression is positive since $p - w$, H, $H_p > 0$ and R_{pp}, $R_p < 0$. Also from equations 4A.8 and 4A.9 we see that

$$-sR_pH_s + \frac{\eta RA(1-\gamma)}{s}[1 - G(N)] = -R_p(sH_s + H) \qquad (4A.20)$$

which is positive by equations 4A.11 and 4A.17. Thus, we see from equation 4A.19 that $\hat{\Pi}_{pp}dN/ds > 0$. Since $\hat{\Pi}_{pp} < 0$, we finally have the asserted result, $dN(s)/ds < 0$.

To prove $dK/ds < 0$, we proceed exactly as above with N, noting from equation 4A.5 that

$$\frac{dK}{ds} = A(1-\gamma)\frac{sR_p\,dp/ds - R}{s^2}. \qquad (4A.21)$$

Appendix 4B
A Note on Data Sources

The data for the results of the third section were derived from published statistics. Data on peak demand, reserve margins, load factors, and quantities of the different types of generation were taken from the *Electric Light and Power* annual survey of the top 100 electric utilities, which commenced publication in 1971.[1] The data for the gas dummy were derived by examination of the *Electrical World Directory*. The data on numbers of plants owned by each company, rate of return, and exports and imports of power were derived from the annual *Statistics of Privately Owned Electric Utilities in the United States* published by the U.S. Department of Energy.

From the sample of 100 companies, several companies were eliminated, leaving the seventy-eight companies used. Two were eliminated because they were publicly owned. Four were eliminated because they were not present for each year of the period. Sixteen were eliminated because they were holding companies, which presented problems in reconciling data on exports and imports and rate of return with the data provided in *Electric Light and Power*.[2] Even with the elimination of these companies, some of the largest in the industry, enough large companies remained to get a wide size range.

Notes

1. The survey is a very useful and accessible source of data on electric utilities. In addition to the data used here, it contains data on heat rates (a measure of fuel efficiency), on total system reserves, and on the transmission network.

2. The *Electrical World Directory of Electric Utilities* was used for checking which companies were holding companies.

5 Fuel-Adjustment Clauses and Profit Risk

Frank A. Scott, Jr.

Regulatory commissions face the specific problem of deciding how often to regulate the firm's activities. On the one hand, commissions can prevent monopoly profits and ensure adequate earnings by conducting rate reviews frequently. On the other hand, by conducting rate reviews infrequently and allowing utilities to keep interim profits, regulators can provide an efficiency stimulus similar to that provided by competition. This interval of regulatory inaction, called regulatory lag, thus has recognized benefits. When prices are stable, a regulatory commission can permit extended periods between rate reviews without jeopardizing the goal of an adequate but not excessive rate of return.

When prices fluctuate, however, shortcomings of this use of regulatory lag appear. Rising input prices in the face of a fixed output price result in an inadequate rate of return being earned by the regulated firm. Falling input prices in the face of a fixed output price result in an excessive rate of return being earned. Fluctuating input prices thus transform regulatory lag from a benefit to a drawback. Regulatory commissions must find ways to speed up the rate-review process while still satisfying the goals of regulation. One method that negates some of the deficiencies of regulatory lag but retains some of the benefits is the automatic revenue-adjustment clause. When applied to fuel and used in regulating electric utilities, this tool is more commonly known as a fuel-adjustment clause.

The purpose of a fuel-adjustment clause is to compensate the regulated firm for changes in the cost of the fuel input without requiring a formal rate review. In principle, fuel clauses are designed to change the output price by an amount equal to the change in the average cost of production due to a change in fuel costs. Since the output price is adjusted automatically, the firm's profits theoretically remain invariant with respect to changes in the cost of fuel. Under such a system, presumably the regulatory commission can forgo frequent rate reviews even when fuel prices are fluctuating and still ensure an adequate but not excessive rate of return for the firm.

This chapter was developed from my doctoral dissertation, which was supported in part by a fellowship from the Institute of Public Utilities at Michigan State University. Roger Sherman, John Pettengill, Biff Bentley, and David Whitcomb provided useful comments on earlier drafts.

It is our intention to examine the effect of a fuel-adjustment clause on the variation in a regulated firm's profit. We also analyze the relation between profit variance and the attractiveness of the firm's securities to investors. In the first section, we outline a model of a public utility facing lagged regulation. In the second section, we demonstrate the effect of a fuel-adjustment clause on the variance of a firm's profit. In the third section, we show how reducing profit variance can increase the market value of the firm. We also demonstrate that under a fuel-adjustment clause the firm can further increase its market value by increasing the relative use of fuel in production. In the fourth section, we examine empirically the relation between fuel clauses and profit variance. Finally, we present conclusions in the last section.

Model of the Regulated Firm

Now we look more closely at the regulated public utility. We assume the firm produces a homogeneous output (electricity) using three inputs: capital, labor, and fuel. At discrete (but not necessarily equal-length) intervals, the regulatory commission conducts rate hearings during which it reviews the firm's costs and revenues. It then determines an output price that the utility is allowed to charge until the next rate review. This price ostensibly will permit the utility to earn a fair return on its investment. The utility thus faces a period between hearings in which its output price—not its rate of return—is fixed.

This assumption of lagged regulation impies some delay between cost changes and any output-price changes that are imposed by the regulator. The firm may earn more or less than the allowed return, depending on whether costs decrease or increase in the interim between rate reviews. The addition of a fuel adjustment clause implies a hybrid of continuous and lagged regulation. Under a fuel clause, the output price is revised continuously for changes in fuel costs and only at discrete intervals for changes in other operating costs. Again the actual rate of return earned by the firm will vary between rate reviews. The fuel-adjustment clause, however, removes that portion of the variation in earnings due to fuel-cost changes.

It is now appropriate to specify the profit of the firm. In any period t, the firm's actual profit is

$$\pi_t = P_t D(P_t) - w_t L_t - f_t F_t - r_t c_t K_t \qquad (5.1)$$

where π_t = profit in period t
P_t = output price in period t
$D(P_t)$ = quantity demanded at price P

Fuel-Adjustment Clauses and Profit Risk

L_t = labor input
F_t = fuel input
K_t = capital input
w_t = wage rate
f_t = unit price of fuel
c_t = unit price of capital goods
r_t = market interest rate[1]

Since public utilities are normally granted legal monopolies in their service areas, they are the sole suppliers in those areas and thus are able to see an interdependence between price and output level in the demand for their services. With each price the demand curve associates a unique quantity demanded. Being a public utility, the firm must satisfy all demand at the market price P. We assume that the firm produces exactly the quantity demanded, so $D(P_t)$ appears in the profit equation.

Regulation and Profit Variance

Regulation affects profit risk as well as profit level. Since it is normally assumed that investors dislike risk, regulatory conditions which reduce risk should increase the attractiveness of the firm's securities. In this section we analyze the impact of different regulatory conditions on profit risk. We first look at the covariance between the firm's profit and the profit of a market portfolio made up of the securities of all firms, and we show its relationship with the variance of the firm's profit. Then we see how regulatory lag and fuel-adjustment clauses affect the variance of the firm's profit.

An important determinant of the risk associated with a firm's securities is the covariance between the return on that security and the return on a market portfolio consisting of the securities of all firms. A positive covariance means that fluctuations in this firm's profit cannot be entirely diversified away by investors who hold portfolios. If investors dislike risk, then making profit more stable will increase the attractiveness of this firm's securities.

This relationship can easily be seen by looking at the definition of correlation in terms of covariance,

$$\rho_{im} = \frac{\sigma_{im}}{\sigma_i \sigma_m} \qquad (5.2)$$

where ρ_{im} = correlation between ith firm's profit and profit of market portfolio

σ_{im} = covariance between ith firm's profit and profit of market portfolio

σ_i = standard deviation of profit of ith firm
σ_m = standard deviation of profit of market portfolio

Rearranging equation 5.2 gives

$$\sigma_{im} = \rho_{im}\sigma_i\sigma_m \qquad (5.3)$$

The covariance of the firm's profit with the market depends directly on the standard deviation of the firm's profit σ_i. In a market consisting of many firms, we can safely consider σ_m to be exogenous to the individual firm. The correlation between the firm's profits and the market is not exogenous, since the firm's own actions influence ρ_{im}. In the following analysis, however, we assume that the introduction of a fuel-adjustment clause does not significantly alter ρ_{im}. The firm can thus increase its attractiveness to investors by reducing the variance of its profit. This is our starting point. We now look at the effect of different regulatory conditions on the variance of the firm's profit.

With lagged regulation, the output price is predetermined in the lag period between rate reviews. Profit during the lag period is

$$\pi_t = P_1 D(P_1) - w_t L_t - f_t F_t - r_t c_t K_t \qquad (5.4)$$

where P_1 is the output price set in the last rate review. Since $P_1 D(P_1)$ in equation 5.4 is constant and $w_t, f_t, r_t,$ and c_t are independent, the variance of profit is

$$\text{var } \pi_t = L_t^2 \sigma_w^2 + F_t^2 \sigma_f^2 + K_t^2 \text{ var } (r_t c_t) \qquad (5.5)$$

As the above equation indicates, under lagged regulation fluctuations not only in capital goods prices and the interest rate but also in wages and fuel prices can contribute to the variance of the firm's profit.

We now look at variance of profit when there is a fuel-adjustment clause. Under a fuel clause, the output price is updated continuously for changes in fuel costs and at discrete intervals for changes in other costs. Profit should remain relatively invariant with respect to changing fuel costs, thus reducing the variance of profit during the lag period.

Under a fuel-adjustment clause, the output price during the lag period is determined to be

$$P_t = P_0 + \frac{\alpha f_t F_t}{D(P_t)} \qquad (5.6)$$

where α is the percentage of a given cost change that the regulator permits to be passed through to output price and where

Fuel-Adjustment Clauses and Profit Risk

$$P_0 = \frac{sc_0K_0 + w_0L_0 + (1 - \alpha)f_0F_0}{Q_0} \quad (5.7)$$

Equations 5.6 and 5.7 are derived in appendix 5A.

Since the output price can now be adjusted, the profit during the lag period will be

$$\pi_t = P_t D(P_t) - w_t L_t - f_t F_t - r_t c_t K_t \quad (5.8)$$

By rewriting equation 5.8 and substituting from the fuel-adjustment clause, equation 5.6 for $P_t D(P_t)$ yields

$$\pi_t = P_0 D(P_t) + \alpha f_t F_t - w_t L_t - f_t F_t - r_t c_t K_t$$

or $$\pi_t = P_0 D(P_t) - w_t L_t - (1 - \alpha) f_t F_t - r_t c_t K_t \quad (5.9)$$

From equation 5.9 we can analyze the variance of profit under a fuel-adjustment clause. For simplicity we assume that the regulator allows all fuel costs to be passed through to output price, that is, $\alpha = 1$, and that the firm is unable to alter the heat rate F/Q of its plants in the observed time interval.[2] Substituting for P_0 in equation 5.9, we find that the profit during the lag period is

$$\pi_t = \left[\frac{(sc_0K_0 + w_0L_0)}{Q_0}\right] D(P_t) - w_t L_t - r_t c_t K_t \quad (5.10)$$

The variance of profit during the lag period will depend on variations in output $D(P_t)$ and on variations in input prices w_t and $r_t c_t$. Since we have already specified the probability distributions of w, r, and c, we need to analyze the distribution of output during the lag period. The variance of output depends on the elasticity of demand as well as on the variance of output price. From the definition of elasticity of demand, η,

$$dQ = \eta \frac{Q}{P} dp \quad (5.11)$$

Thus output will vary according to

$$\text{var } Q = \left(\eta \frac{\overline{Q}}{\overline{P}}\right)^2 \text{var } P \quad (5.12)$$

From the fuel-adjustment clause we know that

$$P = P_0 + \frac{\alpha f F}{Q} \qquad (5.13)$$

Thus, with a constant heat rate and $\alpha = 1$, the output price will vary according to

$$\text{var } P = \left(\frac{F}{Q}\right)^2 \sigma_f^2 \qquad (5.14)$$

The variance of output will be

$$\text{var } Q = \eta^2 \left(\frac{Q}{P}\right)^2 \left(\frac{F}{Q}\right)^2 \sigma_f^2$$

or

$$\text{var } Q = \left(\eta \frac{F}{P}\right)^2 \sigma_f^2 \qquad (5.15)$$

Using equation 5.9, we can now analyze the variance of profit during the lag period when a fuel-adjustment clause determines the output price:

$$\text{var } \pi_t = P_0^2 \left(\frac{\eta F}{P}\right)^2 \sigma_f^2 + L_t^2 \sigma_w^2 + K_t^2 \text{ var}(r_t c_t) \qquad (5.16)$$

If the regulator allows less than 100 percent of fuel costs to be passed through to the output price, then equation 5.16 will contain the additional term $(1 - \alpha)^2 F_t^2 \sigma_f^2$. A value of less than 1 thus will increase the variance of the firm's profit.

We are now ready to compare the variance of profit under each different regulatory scheme. To determine whether a fuel-adjustment clause in effect between rate reviews reduces the variance of profit, we compare equation 5.16 with equation 5.5. Profit will vary less under a fuel clause if the condition

$$P_0^2 \left(\frac{\eta F}{P}\right)^2 \sigma_f^2 < F_t^2 \sigma_f^2 \qquad (5.17)$$

is satisfied.

By performing the appropriate substitutions and transformations, this condition becomes

$$\left(\frac{scK + wL}{Q}\right)^2 \left(\frac{\eta F}{P}\right)^2 < F^2$$

$$\left(\frac{scK + wL}{PQ}\right)^2 \eta^2 < 1$$

$$\frac{scK + wL}{PQ} < \frac{1}{\eta} \qquad (5.18)$$

Fuel-Adjustment Clauses and Profit Risk

If the factor shares of capital and labor are less than the reciprocal of the elasticity of demand, then a fuel-adjustment clause reduces the variance of profit between rate reviews. Since the combined factor share of capital and labor is less than 1 and since the short-run demand for electricity is relatively inelastic, we can infer that a fuel clause does reduce the variance of profit.

Input Selection in Maximizing the Value of the Firm

As demonstrated in the previous section, a fuel-adjustment clause reduces the variance of profit and hence profit risk. In this section we extend the analysis and examine the effect of a fuel clause on the market value of the firm. We also look at the firm's choice of inputs and how a fuel clause alters the input-mix decision. We make use of the capital asset pricing model of financial markets developed by Sharpe (1964), Lintner (1965), and Mossin (1966). The specific form of the model used here is taken from Schramm and Sherman's "A Rationale for Administered Pricing" (1977, p. 128). Schramm and Sherman analyze a firm seeking to maximize its market value. The value of this firm when the capital market is in equilibrium is given by

$$V = \frac{E(\pi) - \rho \, \text{cov}(\pi, \pi_m)}{i} \qquad (5.19)$$

where V = value of firm
$E(\pi)$ = expected profit of firm
ρ = price of profit risk per unit of total capital-market value
$\text{cov}(\pi, \pi_m)$ = covariance between profit for firm and profit for portfolio of all firms in market
i = riskless rate of interest

Several points should be made about equation 5.19. The two components under the firm's control are the level of expected profit and the covariance of profit with the market portfolio. Although regulation restricts its options, a public utility still exerts some influence over both factors. The other two components determining market value, ρ and i, can be considered exogenous to the individual firm. The market price of risk ρ is not truly exogenous, but in a market with a significant number of firms, the impact on ρ of any individual firm is negligible. Finally, we emphasize the relation between expected profit and covariance with the market portfolio. If the firm's profit is positively correlated with profits of other firms, then the firm can trade off profit level for profit stability in order to increase its market value. Since a fuel-adjustment clause supposedly increases profit stability while keeping profit level constant, firms implementing fuel clauses should see an increase in their market values.

Now we are ready to analyze the maximization problem of the firm. The firm seeks to maximize its market value V

$$\max V = \frac{1}{i} E(\pi) - \frac{\rho}{i} \text{cov}(\pi, \pi_m) \tag{5.20}$$

subject to demand and production-function constraints and to any regulatory constraints imposed by regulatory authorities. In a market with many firms, the individual firm considers i, ρ, and π_m to be exogenously determined. Its own profit π is given by equation 5.1.

To solve this maximization problem, an unregulated monopolist would determine the value-maximizing price and then produce at minimum cost the corresponding quantity demanded. The regulated public utility lacks such freedom, for the regulator determines price in its industry. Instead, this firm can influence the output price only indirectly. If the regulator uses a method related to inputs, such as rate-of-return regulation or a fuel-adjustment clause, to set price, then the firm can affect the output price by varying the relative levels of input used in production. Rate-of-return regulation bases the output price on the quantity of fuel used as well as on the fuel prices.

Since the regulatory agency sets the output price, the decision variables of the regulated firm are capital, labor, and fuel. The levels of these inputs affect not only expected profit $E(\pi)$ but also covariance of profit with the rest of the market, $\text{cov}(\pi, \pi_m)$. By varying the levels of inputs, the firm can change its market value V. The relevant first-order conditions for maximum are

$$\frac{\partial V}{\partial K} = \frac{1}{i} \frac{\partial E(\pi)}{\partial K} - \frac{\rho}{i} \frac{\partial \text{cov}(\pi, \pi_m)}{\partial K} = 0 \tag{5.21}$$

$$\frac{\partial V}{\partial L} = \frac{1}{i} \frac{\partial E(\pi)}{\partial L} - \frac{\rho}{i} \frac{\partial \text{cov}(\pi, \pi_m)}{\partial L} = 0 \tag{5.22}$$

$$\frac{\partial V}{\partial F} = \frac{1}{i} \frac{\partial E(\pi)}{\partial F} - \frac{\rho}{i} \frac{\partial \text{cov}(\pi, \pi_m)}{\partial F} = 0 \tag{5.23}$$

Rewriting these three equations yields

$$\frac{\partial E(\pi)}{\partial K} = \rho \frac{\partial \text{cov}(\pi, \pi_m)}{\partial K} \tag{5.24}$$

$$\frac{\partial E(\pi)}{\partial L} = \rho \frac{\partial \text{cov}(\pi, \pi_m)}{\partial L} \tag{5.25}$$

Fuel-Adjustment Clauses and Profit Risk

$$\frac{\partial E(\pi)}{\partial F} = \rho \frac{\partial \operatorname{cov}(\pi, \pi_m)}{\partial F} \qquad (5.26)$$

The partial derivatives of expected profit with respect to capital, labor, and fuel will depend on whether the firm faces lagged regulation with or without a fuel-adjustment clause. The same can be said of the partial derivatives of the covariance between the firm's profit and the market. Since these derivatives reflect the effect of changing input levels on expected profit and on profit risk, the method used by the regulator to set output price will influence the value of the derivatives and hence the firm's selection of a production technique. Now we consider the effects of a fuel-adjustment clause on input selection.

An examination of equations 5.24 to 5.26 reveals that the firm will employ each input up to the point where the gain in market value via an increase in profit level will be exactly offset by the loss in market value via an increase in profit risk. Ignoring the effects of inputs on profit level and concentrating on profit risk, we find that lagged regulation with no fuel-adjustment clause creates no systematic bias in the firm's selection of inputs. Recalling equation 5.5, we see that all three inputs contribute similarly to profit variance. The firm has no incentive to substitute systematically toward or away from any input, since all three contribute directly to the variance of profit.[3]

The addition of a fuel-adjustment clause changes things considerably. A fuel clause alters the effect of inputs on the variance of profit. Looking back at equation 5.16, we see that capital and labor contribute to profit variance as before. Under a fuel-adjustment clause (FAC), however, the fuel contribution has been reduced. As a result, the effect on covariance is

$$\frac{\partial \operatorname{cov}(\pi, \pi_m)}{\partial F} < \frac{\partial \operatorname{cov}(\pi, \pi_m)}{\partial F}$$
(with FAC)   (without FAC)

Fuel contributes less to profit risk when a fuel clause is in effect. As a result, the firm can increase its market value by using relatively less capital and labor and more fuel than when no fuel clause is used. The addition of a fuel clause does introduce a systematic bias into the firm's selection of inputs.

Empirical Tests

In this section we examine empirically the relation between fuel-adjustment clauses and the variance of profit. We propose to test whether utilities with fuel-adjustment clauses actually experience a reduction in the variance of their profit. We approach the problem in two different ways. The first is a statistical test that involves the selection of a relatively homogeneous sample of firms that can be separated into FAC and non-FAC groups. We adjust for firm size and growth in demand for both groups and test whether the fuel-adjustment clause makes any difference in profit variance.

The second approach involves tracking the profits of a small group of firms over a period when each operated with a fuel clause. Given data on the amount of income derived from the fuel-adjustment clause, we can determine what profits would have been in the absence of a fuel clause. As a result, we can compare profits for the same firm operating with and without a fuel-adjustment clause. Although it requires several strong assumptions, this exercise provides another means of gauging the effect of automatic adjustments on the variance of a firm's profit. We now turn to the first approach, the statistical test.

Profit Variance of Firms with and without Fuel-Adjustment Clauses

The first test requires a homogeneous sample of firms that can be separated into FAC and non-FAC groups. We draw our sample from a group of firms surveyed in 1973 by the Stock Research Department of Salomon Brothers brokerage firm.[4] The survey contains information on fuel-mix data and fuel-adjustment clauses. Of the eighty firms responding, only eight firms both had no fuel-adjustment clause and generated a significant portion of their load from fossil-fueled plants. Twenty other firms were randomly selected that both generated a significant portion of their load from fossil-fueled plants and had a fuel-adjustment clause.

To determine the effect of fuel-adjustment clauses on the variance of profit, we must measure profit. We define profit to be net electric-utility operating income as contained in *Statistics of Privately Owned Electric Utilities in the United States*.[5] We examine the net revenue of the twenty-eight utilities over the period from 1970 to 1975, a period of widely fluctuating fuel prices.

In looking at the variance of profit for these twenty-eight firms, we find three potential effects at work. The variance of profit is affected by the existence of a fuel-adjustment clause, by growth in demand, and by the size of the firm. Firms in rapidly growing regions will probably experience greater profit variance about mean profit than firms in areas of no growth. And larger firms will probably see their profits fluctuate more in nominal terms than smaller firms simply because the values are larger. To remove these two influences so that we can concentrate on the effects of fuel-adjustment clause alone, we adjust for firm size and we detrend net revenue.

We adjust for firm size by dividing nominal net revenue in each year by net revenue in 1970 for each firm. We adjust for growth in demand by fitting a trend line through the adjusted (for firm size) net revenue over the six-year period. The residuals from this procedure should reflect the effect of fuel-adjustment clauses on variance of profit. By comparing the residuals of the two groups we can test whether fuel-adjustment clauses reduce the variance of profit.

We are now ready to formulate the first test. The null hypothesis states that fuel-adjustment clauses do not reduce fluctuations in profits; that is, the residuals from the above procedure are the same for both FAC and non-FAC firms. The alternative hypothesis is that fuel clauses reduce fluctuations in profits. To test the hypothesis, we compute the sum of the squared residuals around the fitted trend line for each firm. We add the sum of squared residuals (SSR) of each regression for the twenty FAC firms and for the eight non-FAC firms, and we use as a test statistic the ratio of the two sums:

$$F = \frac{\sum_{i=1}^{8} SSR_i/8}{\sum_{i=1}^{20} SSR_i/20}$$

If we assume that the two populations are normal and the two sums are independent, then under the null hypothesis this ratio follows the F distribution, with 8 and 20 degrees of freedom.

The results of this test are contained in table 5–1. As can be seen, the null hypothesis is rejected at the 95 percent confidence level. A significant difference exists between the fluctuations in profits of the two samples, and the group with fuel-adjustment clauses has the lower variance in profit. While admitting that other factors besides firm size, growth in demand, and fuel-adjustment clauses may influence variance of profit, we suggest that the existence of a fuel clause provides the best explanation of the difference in profit variance between the two groups.

Simulated Profits of Three Utilities Operating with and without a Fuel-Adjustment Clause

The second test of the effect of a fuel-adjustment clause on variance of profit is illustrative rather than statistical. We compute profits for three Virginia

Table 5–1
Test of Equality of Variances of Profit for FAC and Non-FAC Firms

FAC Firms, $n = 20$	Non-FAC Firms, $n = 8$
$\sum_{i=1}^{20} \dfrac{SSR_i}{20} = 0.061$	$\sum_{i=1}^{8} \dfrac{SSR_i}{8} = 0.166$

$$F = \frac{\sum_{i=1}^{8} \dfrac{SSR_i}{8}}{\sum_{i=1}^{20} \dfrac{SSR_i}{20}} = 2.713$$

$$F_{.05}(8, 20) = 2.45$$

utilities as they were with a fuel-adjustment clause and as they would have been without a fuel-adjustment clause for the period from 1971 to 1975. We perform this exercise for three firms operating in the state of Virginia: Virginia Electric and Power Company (Vepco), Appalachian Power Company (Apco), and Delmarva Power Company. By comparing the fluctuations in profits of these firms as they actually were and as they would have been without a fuel clause, we can gauge the effect of a fuel-adjustment clause on the variance of profit.

We calculate the actual profits of these three firms under a fuel-adjustment clause, using data on net electric-utility operating income from *Statistics of Privately Owned Electric Utilities in the United States*. We also calculate the simulated profits of these same firms had they not used fuel-adjustment clauses. The data on fuel-adjustment revenue needed for this step come from testimony by the Division of Public Utilities staff of the Virginia State Corporation Commission.[6]

Before proceeding, we must mention several assumptions that are implicit in this analysis. This exercise assumes that no additional rate requests would have been made if the firms had operated without fuel clauses. Since the data on fuel-adjustment revenue come from the Virginia State Corporation Commission, this exercise also assumes that no quantity adjustments would occur if electricity rates changed. State regulatory commissions usually assume zero elasticity of demand when projecting total revenue. With these heroic assumptions in mind, we continue with the illustration.

When inflation and growth in demand are taken into account, the profit stream of all three firms is noticeably smoother when a fuel-adjustment clause operates. Statistical verification of this effect comes from fitting a

Table 5-2
Fitting Trend Lines to Simulated Profits

Company	R^2	Sum of Squared Residuals
Vepco		
Profits with FAC	.8661	2.816×10^9
Profits without FAC	.0651	5.063×10^9
Apco		
Profits with FAC	.9821	5.728×10^7
Profits without FAC	.4735	9.503×10^8
Delmarva		
Profits with FAC	.7807	4.594×10^5
Profits without FAC	.0541	1.748×10^6

simple time trend line through profits for each firm with and without a fuel clause for the period from 1971 to 1975. The regression results are contained in Table 5-2. As indicated by the smaller sums of squared residuals, profits in each case vary less around the trend when a fuel clause is used. Especially in 1974 and 1975 when fuel prices increased dramatically, the fuel-adjustment clause shielded profits from wide fluctuations. Once again, a fuel-adjustment clause seems to have reduced the variance in firms' profits.

Conclusions

The market value of the firm depends on not only the level of expected profit but also the degree of profit risk. In the theory of capital-market equilibrium, risk is measured by the covariance between the firm's profit and the profits of other firms. We showed earlier that if the firm's profit is positively correlated with the market, the covariance term can be reduced by reducing the variance of the firm's own profit. Reducing the variance of its profit thus should increase the market value of the firm.

One regulatory mechanism which enables the regulated firm to reduce the variance of its profit is the fuel-adjustment clause. A fuel clause reduces the variance of profit regardless of the firm's input mix, since it removes that portion of the variance due to fluctuations in fuel costs. A fuel-adjustment clause also alters the firm's incentives to use fuel, however, because the firm can reduce the variance of its profit by increasing the relative use of fuel.

To test whether fuel-adjustment clauses reduce the variance of profit, we examined profit variance for samples of firms both with and without fuel-adjustment clauses. The results indicated that fuel-adjustment clauses significantly reduce variance in profit. To further illustrate the effect of a fuel clause on stability of earnings, we tracked the profits of three Virginia utilities for the period from 1971 to 1975 as they were with a fuel-adjustment clause and as they would have been without a fuel-adjustment clause. A fuel clause produced a noticeably smoother stream of profits than was evident without a fuel clause.

Notes

1. We assume that wages, fuel prices, capital-good prices, and the interest rate have expected future values of w, f, c, and r. In any period t, however, actual values of w_t, f_t, c_t, and r_t may differ from expected values by some random elements. Actual wages, fuel prices, capital-good prices, and the interest rate are distributed as follows:

$$w_t \sim (w, \sigma_w^2)$$

$$f_t \sim (f, \sigma_f^2)$$

$$c_t \sim (c, \sigma_c^2)$$

$$r_t \sim (r, \sigma_r^2)$$

We further assume that all four are distributed independently of one another.

2. The heat rate is the number of British thermal units required to produce one kilowatthour of electricity.

3. The firm, of course, will tend to use less of those inputs whose prices fluctuate wildly and more of those inputs whose prices are stable. Our use of the term *systematic substitution* does not refer to this phenomenon.

4. The results of the survey are contained in Salomon Brothers (1973).

5. U.S. Department of Energy (formerly FPC) annual.

6. Testimony of Virginia S.C.C. Staff in Case No. 19818, Investigation of the Fuel-Adjustment Clause of Virginia Electric and Power Company.

Appendix 5A

To derive the formula for a fuel-adjustment clause, we refer to a clause actually used. The fuel-adjustment clause used by the Virginia State Corporation Commission for Appalachian Power Company states that

> [w]hen the estimated cost of fossil fuel consumed by the Company at its electric generating stations during the billing month is above or below a base cost of 1.049 cents per kiloWatthour, the bill for service shall be adjusted by an amount equal to the product of (a) the kiloWatthours for the period for which the bill is rendered and (b) the factor "F" as defined below:
>
> F (in ¢/KWH) = (Cost of Fossil Fuel Consumed in ¢/KWH $\times$ 1.10282) $-$ 1.15686¢/KWH
>
> Any difference between the estimated cost of fossil fuel consumed during the billing month and the actual cost of such fuel consumed will be reflected in the calculation of the fuel adjustment factor in the second succeeding month.[1]

The constant 1.10282 in the definition of the fuel-adjustment factor is called the base-adjustment factor. It adjusts the fuel factor for system losses, franchise taxes, and hydroelectric generation. The constant 1.15686 cents per kilowatthour in the definition of the fuel-adjustment factor is the base fuel cost adjusted. This is simply the base fuel cost in March 1975 (1.049 cents per kilowatt hour) times the base-adjustment factor.

The fuel-adjustment factor (FAF) in any month t is thus

$$FAF_t = \alpha \frac{f_t F_t}{Q_t} - \beta$$

where α = base-adjustment factor (constant)
β = base fuel cost adjusted (constant)

and f_t, F_t, and Q_t are price per unit of fuel, units of fuel used in production, and output, respectively, in month t. The relationship between output price and the fuel-adjustment factor is

$$FAF_t = P_t - P_{3/75}$$

Here $P_{3/75}$ is the price set by the regulatory commission in March 1975. Presumably it was set so that the firm could cover its operating expenses and earn the allowed rate of return S:

$$P_{3/75} = [sc_0 K_0 + w_0 L_0 + f_0 F_0] / Q_0$$

Substituting the definitions of FAF_t and $P_{3/75}$ into the relationship between output price and the fuel-adjustment factor and then solving for P_t give

$$P_t = \frac{[sc_0 K_0 + w_0 L_0 + f_0 F_0]}{Q_0} + \frac{\alpha f_t F_t}{Q_t} - \frac{\alpha f_0 F_0}{Q_0}$$

$$P_t = \frac{[sc_0 K_0 + w_0 L_0 + (1-\alpha) f_0 F_0]}{Q_0} + \frac{\alpha f_t F_t}{Q_t}$$

Letting $P_0 = [sc_0 K_0 + w_0 L_0 + (1-\alpha) f_0 F_0]/Q_0$, a constant, we get

$$P_t = P_0 + \frac{\alpha f_t F_t}{Q_t}$$

This form corresponds to the general formula for fuel-adjustment clauses. The output price changes when fuel costs per unit of output change. Either a change in fuel price (f_t) or a change in the heat rate (F_t/Q_t) triggers the fuel-adjustment mechanism. We retain α in the general formula to allow for changes in the percentage of costs passed through to output price. Although α is normally set at 100 percent, it can be changed by the regulatory commission.

Note

1. Va. S.C.C. Tariff No. 7, issued May 12, 1975.

6 The Demand for Telecommunications: A Nontechnical Exposition

Lester D. Taylor

The telecommunications industry is in a period of sharp, rapid change. Technology is continuing to advance rapidly, the lines between the telecommunications computer industries are being severely blurred, and competition is now a fact of life in the private-line, toll, and terminal-equipment markets. Contributions from these markets, which in the past have been used to subsidize basic service to residential customers, are beginning to disappear, and pressures are mounting to raise basic-service rates and to begin pricing local calls on a measured basis. And in the midst of all this, Congress is rewriting the Communications Act of 1934. Thus, times in the telecommunications industry are both exciting and highly uncertain, and in ten to fifteen years the industry will almost certainly be quite different from what it is at present.

One cannot analyze the directions that the industry is likely to take in the years ahead without understanding the structure and determinants of telecommunications demand. A recent study by Meyer et al. (1979) of competition in the telecommunications industry, for example, has concluded that, contrary to what was just stated, competition in toll will not necessarily put upward pressure on basic-service rates. Part of the basis for this conclusion is an assumption, which is questionable in my opinion, that the price elasticity of demand for toll calls is elastic (that is, is greater than 1 in absolute value) so that a decrease in toll rates will lead to an actual increase in toll revenues. Suppose, however, that, as the existing empirical evidence suggests,[1] the Meyer et al. assumption of an elastic toll demand is wrong. What, then, will be the response of residential customers to the resulting higher basic-service charges? Answering this question will require knowledge of the price elasticity of demand for access to the telephone network and of the relationship between demand for access and demand for toll calls. Finally, with technology advancing at its present rapid pace, the reactions of consumers to this technological advance and the new products and services that it introduces, especially with regard to the use of time, will be of great

---

I am indebted to Michael Crew, Michael Murphy, John Panzar, and other participants at the Rutgers conference for comments and criticism and to Sonja Eskind and Brenda Vidal for secretarial assistance.

93

importance in defining the future dimensions of the industry. Thus, it is clear that knowledge of the basic determinants of telecommunications demand is central to an understanding of both the likely evolution of the industry in the years ahead and the development of a coherent set of public policies for guiding this evolution. The purpose of this chapter is to provide a nontechnical understanding of these basic determinants.

We begin with a discussion of the characteristics of telecommunications demand which set it apart from the demand for other goods and services.[2] These characteristics include:

1. A distinction between the demand for access to the telephone network (or system) and the demand for use of the network once access is acquired.
2. The dependence of the demand for access on the demand for use
3. The presence of access (or network) externalities which impart a public-good aspect to the telephone system and considerably complicate modeling the demand for its services
4. The importance of option demand in determining the demand for access
5. The importance of the opportunity cost of time

The distinction between the demand for access and the demand for use is fundamental to an understanding of telephone demand and follows from the fact that one must be connected to the telephone network before the network can be used. The purchase of access can thus be viewed as the purchase of the right to make and receive calls. Use, accordingly, is conditional on access; yet access, in turn, is dependent on the benefits that arise from use. If the net benefits from use are not at least as great as the purchase price of access to the network, then access will not be purchased. For most households, the net benefits from use exceed the purchase price of access, probably by a comfortable margin, and consequently we observe that about 95 percent of U.S. households subscribe to the telephone system.[3]

Determinants of the Demand for Access

As just noted, people will not purchase access to the telephone network unless they expect to use it to make and receive calls. Accordingly, the point of departure in determining the demand for access has to be the demand for use. Therefore, let us turn our attention to Figure 6–1b which shows the demand for telephone calls as a function of the price of a call. Assume that the price of a call is π_0. In this case, the number of calls demanded would be q^0 at a cost of $\pi_0 q^0$, represented by the rectangle $0\pi_0 dq^0$. Let us now ask ourselves how much the consumer would be willing to pay in order to be able to make q^0 calls. This will be given by the area between the demand function

Demand for Telecommunications

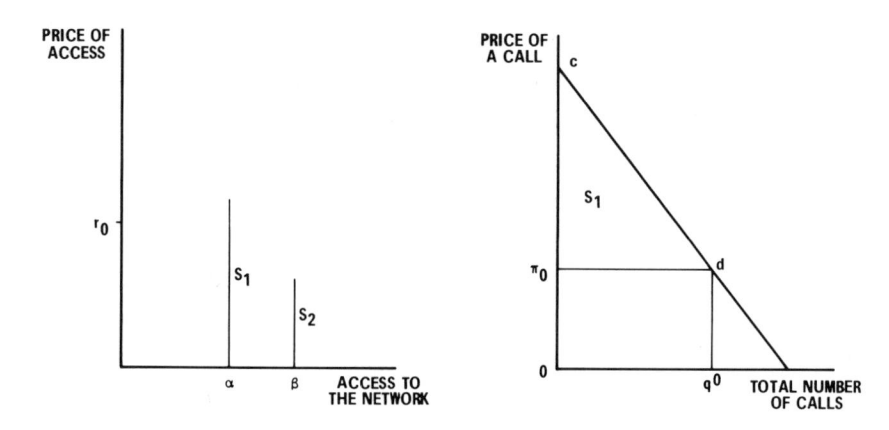

Figure 6–1 Demand for Access and Use

and the q axis from the origin and the point q^0, which is equal to the area $0cdq^0$. Let this quantity be denoted by A. The difference between what the consumer would be willing to pay in order to make q^0 calls, A, and what has to be paid, $\pi_0 q^0$, is equal to the consumer's surplus associated with the q^0 calls. The consumer's surplus S_1 is given by the triangle $\pi_0 cd$ and represents the net benefits to the consumer from use of the telephone network referred to earlier.

Let us now consider the demand for access. As stated above, the consumer will demand access to the network if the net benefits from use are greater than the purchase price of access. Assume that this price is r_0. Access will then be purchased if the consumer's surplus from use S_1 is greater than r_0. If S_1 is less than r_0, access will not be purchased. Refer now to figure 6–1a, which depicts the access–no access decision graphically. The purchase price of access is represented on the vertical axis, while the consumer's surplus from use, equal to the area $\pi_0 cd$ in figure 6–1b, is represented by the vertical spike at the point α on the horizontal axis with height equal to S_1. In this case, S_1 is assumed to be greater than r_0, so that access to the network is, in fact, demanded.

Let us now assume that there is a second consumer whose consumer's surplus from making and receiving calls is equal to S_2, as represented by the vertical spike at the point β in figure 6–1a. For this consumer, the net benefits from use are less than the purchase price of access ($S_2 < r_0$). Consequently, this consumer will not demand access to the network.

More generally, let us assume that we have a population consisting of M potential subscribers to the network. The question, then, is: How many of these potential subscribers will be actual subscribers? In other words, what determines the size of the telephone network? To this end, let us consider figure 6–2b, which refers to the aggregate demand for telephone calls in the population. This demand function is derived on the assumption that everyone belongs to the telephone network, and this function is obtained as the horizontal summation of the M individual demand functions. As before, let the price of a call be π_0. From the figure, we see that Q_0 calls will be made, where $Q_0 = \sum_{i=1}^{M} q_i^0$, with q_i^0 being the number of calls made by consumer i.

Let the net benefits (that is, the consumer's surplus) associated with q_i^0 for the ith consumer be given by S_i^0, and assume that the S_i are ordered by descending size, so that $S_1^0 > S_2^0 > \ldots > S_M^0$. These net benefits represent the willingness to pay for access by the M consumers in the population and are described by the step function in figure 6–2a. The number of consumers is measured along the horizontal axis in this figure, while the net benefits from use are measured along the vertical axis. As before, asume that the access purchase price is r_0. At this price (measured on the vertical axis), we see that to the left of point N_0 on the horizontal axis, the net benefits from subscribing to the network are greater than r_0, whereas to the right of N_0, the opposite is true. At point N_0, we have $S_i = r_0$, so that consumer N_0 is the marginal subscriber, and the telphone network consists of N_0 subscribers. The Q_0 calls in figure 6–2b, then, will be made by these N_0 subscribers. On the other hand, if the purchase price of access were r_1, which is greater than r_0, then the number of subscribers would be reduced to N_1. The Q_0 calls would now be made by these N_1 subscribers, and the marginal subscriber would be consumer N_1. The previously marginal subscriber N_0 would no longer belong to the network.

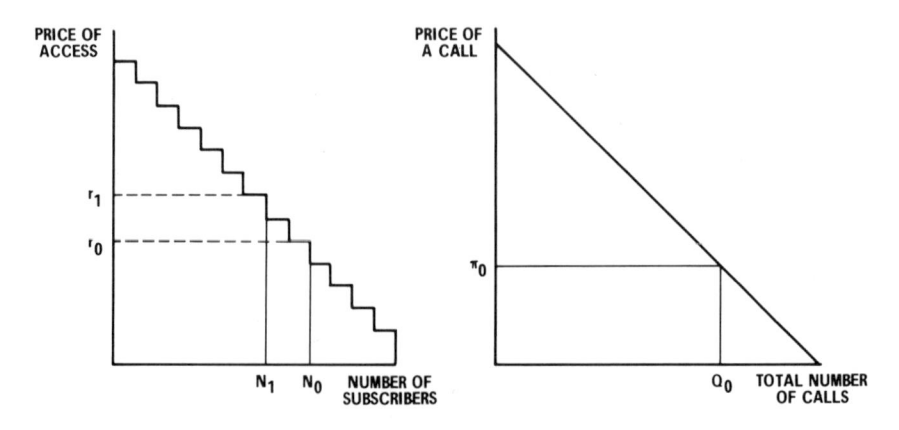

Figure 6–2 Access Price and Network Size

Demand for Telecommunications

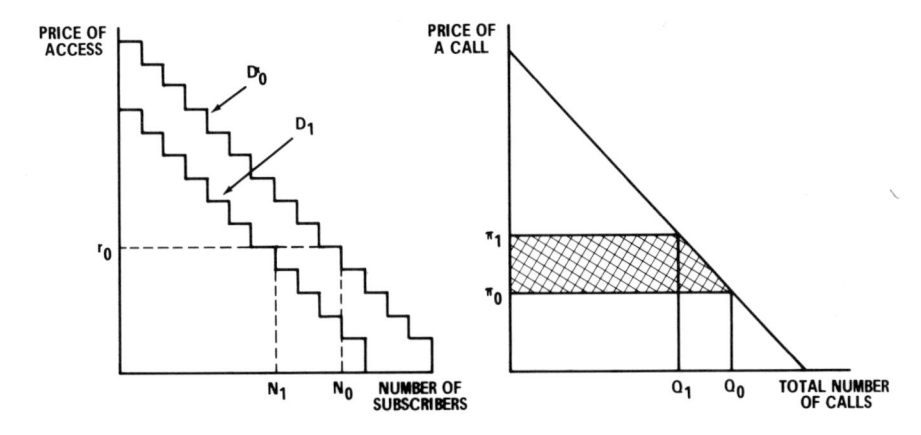

Figure 6-3 Call Price and Network Size

It must be emphasized that the aggregate demand for access depends on the price charged for calls. An increased charge for calls reduces the net benefits from use for all consumers, and since this decreases the willingness to pay for access, the aggregate demand for access is accordingly shifted to the left. This is illustrated in figures 6-3a and b. At a price of π_0 per call, we see from figure 6-3b that Q_0 calls will be made. The aggregate demand for access corresponding to π_0 is given by the curve labeled D_0 in figure 6-3a. In this case we see that N_0 consumers will demand access.

Let us now assume that the price per call is increased to π_1. In figure 6-3b, we see that Q_1 calls will be made at this price and that the aggregate consumer's surplus is reduced by the amount indicated by the hatched area. This decrease in willingness to pay shifts the aggregate demand for access to the left, as indicated by the curve labeled D_1 in figure 6-3b. With an unchanged purchase price of access of r_0, the number of consumers demanding access to the network is seen to be reduced to N_1 from N_0.

This exercise brings home the dependence of the demand for access to the telephone network on the demand for use of the network. Note that the word is *dependence* rather than *interdependence*: the demand for access depends on the demand for use, but the demand for use depends on the demand for access only in the rather trivial sense that there has to be access before there can be use.[4]

Network Externality and Benefits from Incoming Calls

In developing the dependence of the demand for access on the demand for use, we have ignored the complications caused by the existence of the network externality, the benefits from incoming calls, option demand, and the opportunity cost of time. The network externality and the benefits from incoming calls are discussed in this section. Option demand is discussed in the next section, while the opportunity cost of time is discussed in the fourth section, "Opportunity Cost of Time."

The network (or access) externality arises from the fact that when a new subscriber joins the telephone system, there is one more telephone that can be reached. This makes the network more valuable to existing subscribers and increases their willingness to pay to remain in the system. As a consequence, consumers will be willing to pay more to join a large system than to join a small system. Hence it follows that the aggregate demand curve for access in a large system will lie to the right of its location in a small system.

Let me now turn to the benefits from incoming calls. These have been ignored to this point because they, too, arise in the form of an externality. The externality in this case is the so-called call externality, and it refers to the benefit conferred on the party called by the party making the call. This benefit is treated as an externality because, except for collect calls and inward wide-area telecommunications service (WATS), the cost of a call is borne by the caller. Undoubtedly in many instances the called party does not feel benefited by a call, but on balance the externality is clearly positive, and summing over these externalities yields the benefits from incoming calls for the system as a whole.

What, then, is the importance of these two externalities for telephone demand? This question has found extensive analysis in the literature,[5] and our discussion here focuses on only the most basic of the points that have been advanced. The access externality, as already noted, makes a large system more valuable to a subscriber than does a small system, so that willingness to pay for access will vary directly with the number of subscribers already on the system. Since more telephones can be reached in a large system, more calls per telephone will be made, and individual demand curves will lie farther to the right. So, too, will the aggregate demand curve. Consumers' surpluses will be larger, and consequently the aggregate demand function for access will also lie farther to the right.

The access externality has two important implications. The first, which has been analyzed extensively by Artle and Averous (1973), Rohlfs (1974), and Von Rabenau and Stahl (1974), refers to the equilibrium size of the telephone network. Because of the externality, the equilibrium size of the system will be larger than what it would be in the absence of the externality. Less clear, however, is the fact that the equilibrium size of the system may not be unique. One particularly interesting possibility occurs when there are two equilibria, the first with only a few telephones and the second with a large number. Suppose that equilibrium is initially at the smaller value, and let there be a displacement from this equilibrium, triggered (say) by an increase

Demand for Telecommunications

in the income of a nonsubscriber of sufficient size to cause this nonsubscriber to become a subscriber. In this situation, the system may not remain at the lower equilibrium but, because of the network externality, may increase in size until it reaches the higher equilibrium. Such growth would be endogenous within the system because it could occur in the absence of any further changes in income.

The mechanism involved in the event is simple to understand: As the number of telephones increases, the network externality makes belonging to the system more valuable and causes some nonsubscribers who were previously on the margin of subscription to become subscribers. The size of the system would increase once more, thus becoming more valuable to belong to, and in turn this would cause a new group of nonsubscribers to join the system. This endogenous growth would continue to the point where the last round of new subscribers failed to make belonging to the system sufficiently valuable to cause the newest group of marginal nonsubscribers to subscribe.

The second important implication of the access externality involves a normative question and relates to the way that access to the telephone network ought to be priced from a social point of view.[6] The problem is as follows: An individual consumer makes the decision to join the telephone network on the basis of the private benefits to him or her. However, this consumer's joining the network confers a benefit on all existing subscribers, so that the social benefits of her or his joining the system are greater than the private benefits. If access is priced according to the principles of marginal cost, then the equilibrium size of the system would be too small. The reason is that the price charged would be equal to the marginal private benefit of belonging to the system, but the price would be below the marginal social benefit. Proper social pricing in this situation requires that access be subsidized. And the obvious—and important—question is: From where is this subsidy to come? We return to this question below.

The benefits from incoming calls, which arise from the call externality, are straightforward to deal with because they are well defined (at least in principle) and can simply be added onto the net benefits from outgoing calls. Since the benefits from incoming calls are on balance positive, it is clear that individual willingness to pay for access to the telephone system will be larger than it would be if incoming calls yielded no benefit. Hence, the equilibrium size of the system will be larger than what it would be otherwise.

Option Demand

A further complication in analyzing telephone demand arises from the fact that benefits are associated with not only completed calls but also calls that may not be made. When an individual subscribes to the telephone system, in effect she or he is purchasing options to make and receive calls. Some of these options will be exercised with certainty, while others will be made only randomly, because many calls will be made contingent on particular states of nature whose realizations are random and therefore not known at the time that access to the telephone system is purchased. Calls of an emergency nature, as for fire, police, or ambulance, are obvious cases in point, but compelling urgency is not the only determinant, for options may be purchased because preferences themselves are random.

Option demand was first discussed by Weisbrod (1964), and it has since figured prominently in the economics of irreplaceable natural resources and places of natural beauty. Thus *option demand* refers to the benefits arising from availability of a service whether or not there is any intention to use the service or facility. As Krutilla (1967, p. 780) argues, "... the option may never be exercised."

Although the telephone network may be viewed by only telephone engineers as something of great beauty, it is clear that option demand is an important factor in telephone demand and indeed is probably a major element of access demand. Accordingly, let us assume that during a given period (say a month), a consumer is willing to pay an amount for options to make R calls. These R calls are in addition to the calls that the consumer knows with certainty will be made. Let θ denote the proportion of these calls that will, in fact, be made. (The value of R may be very large, but for most consumers θ will be small.) Assume that both R and θ are known to the consumer. Assume, further, that the expected value of the options which will be exercised, θR, is included in q^0 (as defined in the first section), so that the net benefits from these calls are already included in the consumer's surplus associated with q^0.

On the other hand, the net benefits from the $(1 - \theta)R$ options not being exercised are not represented in the consumer's surplus associated with q^0, which means that this measure of the net benefits from using the telephone system understates the amount that the consumer is actually willing to pay in order to have access to the system.[7] Let ω denote the benefit yielded by an option that is not exercised. (Since the value of this benefit will probably vary with the called involved, ω should be viewed as a mean.) The benefits associated with the $(1 - \theta)R$ unexercised options will then be equal to $\omega(1 - \theta)R$, and this is the amount by which the consumer's surplus associated with the q^0 calls will understate the consumer's willingness to pay for access to the network.

Option demand springs from uncertainty, but uncertainty can take many different forms. As stated at the outset of this section, many calls are contingent on certain objective states of nature, while others are contingent on certain subjective states of mind. A call to the fire department illustrates

Demand for Telecommunications 101

the former, while a call to a friend in another city on an impulse or whim illustrates the latter. The distinction is of importance, at least in principle, because the consumer's preferences can be viewed as known and fixed in the first case, but random in the second.

Uncertain states of nature can be interpreted as risk (in the economist's traditional sense of the word), in which case having access to the telephone system can be viewed (assuming that the consumer is risk-averse) as the purchase of an insurance policy. However, uncertain preferences are another matter, and it seems best to treat this form of uncertainty as the uncertainty defined many years ago by Frank Knight. With Knightian uncertainty, the various states of mind cannot be described by a probability distribution. This form of uncertainty is no less important than risk in giving rise to an option demand for telephone calls, but it is obviously much more difficult to deal with analytically. However, this problem need not concern us for now, for (at present) there is little prospect of being able to distinguish empirically between the option demand arising from contingent states of nature and the option demand arising from uncertain preferences.[8]

It remains to take up the option demand associated with incoming calls. However, since incoming calls are, for the most part, beyond the control of the party receiving the call, it makes most sense to identify the option demand for incoming calls with the benefits yielded by these calls. If this is done, then there are no additional benefits to be allocated since the willingness to pay for access associated with the option demand for incoming calls is reflected in the benefits already attributed to these calls.

Opportunity Cost of Time

To this point, it has been assumed that the only constraint on a consumer's behavior is the amount of income available to be spent. The assumption is that the consumer allocates the income that is available among telephone calls and other goods and services so as to maximize the amount of satisfaction (or utility) that can be obtained. However, income is not the only constraint on a consumer's behavior, for consumption does not occur instantaneously, but requires time as well as income. A consumer not only must have the income to purchase a good, but must also have the time to consume it. Thus, proper analysis of consumer behavior must treat both time and income as constraints.

However, there is an important difference between time and income.[9] The amount of time available is fixed, but this is not the case for income. There are only twenty-four hours in a day, and nothing can be done to change this. A consumer has to decide how to allocate these twenty-four hours between the time spent in the workplace earning income and the time spent in the home "consuming" this income and keeping the body and mind in order. Income, in contrast, while fixed in the short run, can be increased in the long run because of enhanced productivity and the fact that time can be reallocated between time spent on the job and time spent in the home.

In general, the consumer will allocate his or her time in such a way that benefits in each use are equated on the margin. Doing this will maximize the amount of satisfaction from the time available. As a consumer's market wage increases, the value of time spent in earning money income increases, and if this consumer is to continue maximizing satisfaction, some adjustments will have to be made in order to bring the value of time spent in all activities into equality on the margin. These adjustments can take a variety of forms. Since with an increased money wage the same amount of income can be earned with less labor time, the consumer could take the increased labor productivity in the form of not only increased money income, but also increased leisure (including time spent in home production). Alternatively, the consumer could continue spending the same number of hours in the workplace (or even increase these hours) and reallocate her or his consumption expenditures in such a way as to increase the productivity of the time spent in home consumption and production. In this case, goods, which are now relatively less expensive in terms of time, will be substituted for time in home consumption and production.

Time and the telephone are so closely related because the telephone has been (and continues to be) a major vehicle for increasing the efficiency of time. As the market wage rate increases, the opportunity cost of time increases, and there is accordingly an increased incentive to economize on the use of time. The telephone provides a means for doing so. As the Bell System says, "Let your fingers do the walking." However, in delving into the relationship between time and the telephone, one has to look at the substitutes for the telephone, which at present essentially consist of the mail and travel. The mail involves relatively little out-of-pocket cost, while travel is expensive. But both are highly time-intensive relative to the telephone. As a consequence, whenever the opportunity cost of time increases, consumers have an incentive to substitute the use of the telephone for mail and travel.

However, while the telephone is highly efficient in the use of time, a telephone call also requires time as an input. Indeed, an unescapable feature of a telephone call is that it requires the undivided attention of (at least) two parties. Consequently, the full cost of a call includes not only the out-of-pocket cost of the call, but also the opportunity cost of the time that goes into it. In the case of a local call under flat-rate pricing of basic service, for example, the out-of-pocket cost of the call is zero, but the actual price of the call is the opportunity cost of the time required for the call to be completed. The opportunity cost of time has been virtually ignored in the empirical literature on telephone demand. I am aware of only one study, by Beauvais

(1977), that attempts to include the cost of time in a meaningful way in the price of a call.[10]

Some indirect evidence of the importance of the opportunity cost of time is offered in several econometric models of intrastate toll demand in which both the number of toll calls and the average duration of a call are explained as a function of income, price, and other variables.[11] Calls are a positive function of income, but duration is a negative function. In other words, as income increases, the number of toll calls increases, but the average duration of a call decreases. The former reflects the positive income elasticity of the demand for calls, while the latter reflects an increased opportunity cost of time. Finally, it should be noted that one of the reasons why telephone use in the United States is considerably higher than in other countries is that the opportunity cost of time is higher in the United States than in most other countries.

Some Final Observations

The purpose of this chapter has been to present a nontechnical exposition of the basic determinants of telephone demand. We have seen that the demand for access to the telephone network depends in a specific way on the demand for use of the network. We have also seen how the access and call externalities affect both the demand for access and the demand for use. In addition, we have noted how option demand is an important determinant of the demand for access when uncertainty, both of future states of nature and of preferences, is present. Finally, we noted briefly how telephone demand is dependent on the opportunity cost of time.

In closing, I would like to return to the access externality discussed in the second section. Near the end of that section, it was noted that, because of this externality, the benefits to society of an additional subscriber to the telephone system are greater than the private benefits to the subscriber, so that if access to the system is priced at marginal cost, the size of the system will be smaller than what is socially optimal.[12] Since an access price less than marginal cost is required for social welfare to be maximized, a subsidy is required.

In the past, this subsidy has been provided primarily by contributions from the toll market, where long-distance calls have been priced in excess of marginal cost.[13] However, with the advent of competition in the intercity toll market, price appears to be driven toward marginal cost, and the revenues which in the past provided the subsidy to access would seem to be disappearing. In response to this, the telephone companies see the lost revenues being made up from increased charges for access and local use, and this, in turn, is the motivation of usage-sensitive pricing of local calls.[14]

Unquestionably, local-service charges can be increased sufficiently to recover the revenues that are lost to competition. But the social problem would still exist, namely, the need, because of the access externality, for access to be priced below marginal cost. However, all this assumes that the access externality not only exists, but also is quantitatively significant. But this is an empirical question, and it may not be the case. Clearly, therefore, one of the first orders of business is to isolate the access externality empirically. If the externality turns out to be quantitatively important, then the larger question will have to be faced of who is to subsidize the price of access.[15]

Notes

1. See chapters 4 and 5 of Taylor (1980).

2. Telecommunications and telephone demand are used interchangeably throughout this chapter. Those desiring a more technical discussion of the telephone demand together with a survey and critique of the empirical literature are referred to Taylor (1980). It should be noted that not all the characteristics in the list that follows reflect purely demand-side phenomena. Some arise because of the way that telephone services are supplied.

3. See *Statistics of Communications Common Carriers*, Federal Communications Commission, Washington, D.C. This percentage is higher than for any other country and considerably higher than for most. There are undoubtedly many reasons for this, but one of the most important clearly has to be the historically high levels of income in the United States. In addition, historically access has been subsidized by contributions from the toll and terminal-equipment markets and probably has resulted in lower prices for access in the United States than in other countries. Moreover, installation charges are generally lower in the United States. For comparisons with Europe, see Mitchell (1979c). For a highly readable history of the U.S. telephone industry, see Brooks (1976).

4. I am ignoring the fact that, since use depends on income, the income available for making calls is reduced by the amount of the access purchase price. The demand for use thus depends on this price through an income effect. For a formal discussion of this, see chapter 2 of Taylor (1980). In normal circumstances, this income effect will be inconsequential because the access price is small relative to income. Also, as was pointed out by John Panzar in discussion at the conference, the dependence of access on use establishes a symmetry between the price of access and the price of use. For any change in the price of access, an equivalent offsetting change in the price of use can be found that leaves the demand for access unchanged, and vice versa. Finally, it should be noted that an access-plus-use charge is formally equivalent to a two-part tariff, and so the graphical analysis that has been

Demand for Telecommunications

presented here, except for the ignoring of the dependence of the demand for use on the access price noted at the beginning of this note, is really the economics of a good or service supplied on a two-part tariff. See Buchanan (1952–1953), Gabor (1966), and Oi (1971). See also Taylor (1975), Blattenberger (1977), and Taylor, Blattenberger, and Rennhack (1980).

5. See Artle and Averous (1973), Squire (1973), Rohlfs (1974), Von Rabenau and Stahl (1974), and Littlechild (1975). See also chapter 2 of Taylor (1980).

6. Willig (1980) provides an illuminating discussion of this and related issues.

7. I am ignoring the complications introduced by the access externality and the benefits associated with incoming calls.

8. I do not wish to make too much of the randomness of preferences in this context. What I feel is really the case is that calling behavior is random in the small rather than in the large. I do believe that preferences are stable in the sense that at the time that the purchase of access is being considered, consumers recognize that some calls will be subject to whim and fancy and plan accordingly. All of us have made calls that were prompted by an ephemeral mood, without subsequent regret. That such occasions are likely to occur gives rise to an additional willingness to pay in order to have access to the telephone system.

9. For a highly readable and insightful analysis of the economics of time, see Linder (1970). See also Becker (1965) and Gronau (1976).

10. For a discussion of Beauvais' analysis, see chapter 3 of Taylor (1980).

11. The studies in question have not yet been published.

12. Socially optimal in this context refers to a pricing policy that seeks to maximize the sum of consumers' and producers' surpluses.

13. For a discussion of the historical pricing policies in the telephone industry, see De Muth (1979).

14. For discussions of the issues involved in moving toward and implementing measured local service, see Garfinkel and Linhart (1979) and Cosgrove and Linhart (1979).

15. For a detailed discussion of the many issues involved in optimally pricing telephone services, see Rohlfs (1978).

7 Alternative Measured-Service Structures for Local Telephone Service

Bridger M. Mitchell

Introduction

Local telephone calls are undoubtedly the most frequently used utility service that is sold at a zero price in the United States. For residential telephone users, the cost of this service traditionally has been supported by a flat monthly subscription fee and by revenue transfers from business subscribers and the sale of long-distance calls.

A priori, one might expect such a system to cause a significant loss of economic welfare in a market of 1 billion residential local calls a month costing perhaps $350 million annually. But demand has generally been thought to be very price-inelastic, and prior to the advent of electronic switching, the transaction costs of measuring and billing each call were substantial. Thus the lack of a per-unit charge for a local residential call could be welfare-optimal, as suggested by a model based on limited empirical data (Mitchell 1978).[1]

As electronic technology—stored program control and digital switching—replaces electromechanical central-office equipment in the local telephone network, call-measurement costs are expected to decline substantially. The major telephone companies have begun to embrace a new pricing approach, termed *usage-sensitive pricing* or *local measured service*, that would charge customers for each outgoing call placed, and, in its more elaborate forms, for the duration and distance of the call and the time of day at which it is made.

This chapter examines several types of measured-service rate structures that could eventually supplant the ubiquitous flat-rate and analyzes in detail the effects of offering consumers a choice between a flat rate and a measured rate. New rate structures could cause large changes in some subscribers' bills, and a transition to measured rates might be designed to spread this impact over several years. Ignoring these redistributive issues, the analysis here concentrates on the long-term welfare effects, implicitly measured by

---

Ed Park has stimulated me to think more deeply about the issues raised here and saved me from several errors. I also thank Michael Crew and John Panzar for helpful comments. This research was supported by National Science Foundation Grant DAR 77-16286 to The Rand Corporation.

consumers' plus producers' surplus, of alternative rates. To highlight these effects, simple assumptions are made: Costs vary only with the number of subscribers and calls, and the detailed effects of consumer demand elasticities ("repression") are omitted. Although a more elaborate model would provide increased realism, it would not qualitatively change the basic results.

Cost Structures

The total costs of suplying local telephone calls are assumed to depend linearly on the number of subscribers n and the total number of calls x:

$$C = C(n, x) = F + C_A n + C_U x \qquad (7.1)$$

These costs are long run in nature, reflecting the local plant required to supply access lines and the trunking and switching capacity needed to meet busy-hour demands. If measured rates are charged, total costs are increased by the costs of measuring and billing usage.

$$C_M = C_{MA} n_M + C_{MU} x_M \qquad (7.2)$$

which are also assumed to vary linearly with the number of customers billed under measured rates n_M and their total number of calls x_M.

This basic cost function abstracts from the effects of variations in call duration and distance and varying utilization of capacity at different times of day. It also assumes that the joint supply of local calls and other services—principally long-distance calls—does not create an important difficulty in estimating the marginal costs of access C_A and usage C_U. A recent Bell System study indicates that these long-run marginal costs, in 1975 dollars, were approximately $11 per month per additional subscriber and 3 cents per call (Rohlfs 1979; Mitchell 1979a).

The fixed costs incurred to provide local service may well depend on what other telephone services are supplied. For this chapter, the amount F can be considered a revenue or contribution requirement. In practice, its value will depend importantly on cost allocation procedures used to "separate" costs between local and long-distance services.[2]

Alternative Rate Structures

The rate structure for local calls is summarized by the subscriber's outlay function $R(x)$, which gives the total expenditure required to purchase x calls per month.[3] Several basic types of rate structures are shown in figure 7–1.

Local Telephone Service

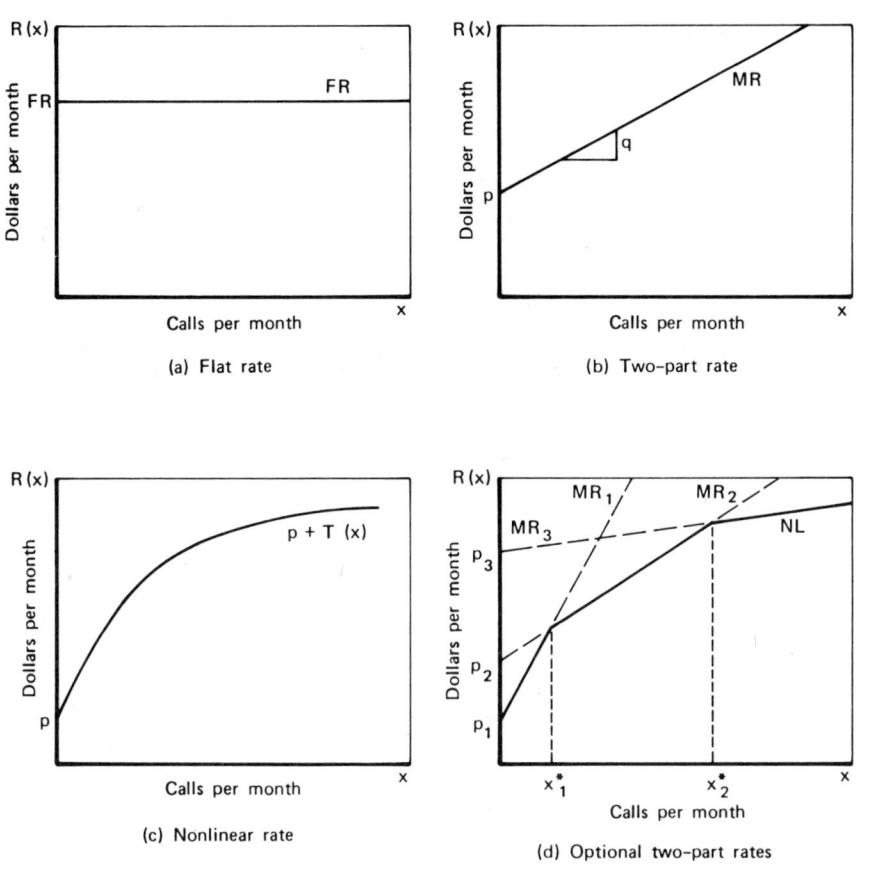

Figure 7-1 Alternative Rate Structures

(a) Flat rate
(b) Two-part rate
(c) Nonlinear rate
(d) Optional two-part rates

A *flat rate*

$$R(x) = FR = \text{constant} \qquad (7.3)$$

has been the predominant rate structure for U.S. residential customers.
  A *two-part rate*, or measured rate (MR),

$$R(x) = p + qx \qquad (7.4)$$

charges a monthly price p for access to the telphone network (to both place and receive calls) and a price q per outgoing call.

A *nonlinear rate*

$$R(x) = p + T(x) \tag{7.5}$$

also charges an access price p plus an amount $T(x)$ that varies, but not in direct proportion to the volume of calling. Usually, as shown in figure 7–1c, nonlinear rates are concave functions which provide volume discounts for larger consumption.

Optional two-part rates permit the subscriber to minimize his or her monthly bill by choosing from several rates with different access prices p_i and usage prices q_i. For example, suppose three rate plans are offered with $p_1 < p_2 < p_3$ and $q_1 > q_2 > q_3$. Then the bill-minimizing rates correspond to the solid curve in figure 7–1d. The *breakpoints* x_i^* are the quantities at which two rate plans have the same monthly bill.

Demand for Calls

An individual consumer, with tastes indexed by the parameter θ, may be assumed to possess a utility function $U_\theta(x_\theta, y_\theta - R(x_\theta), n)$ where x_θ is the number of telephone calls, y_θ is income, $y_\theta - R(x_\theta)$ is expenditure on other goods, and n is the number of telephone subscribers. The consumer's demand for telephone calls can be derived from two interrelated decisions—deciding whether to subscribe to telephone service and determining the number of calls to make if she or he subscribes (Littlechild 1975; Mitchell 1978). These relationships, aggregated over the joint distribution of consumers' preferences and incomes, permit the interdependent market demand curves for access n and volume of calls x to be derived. For a particular rate structure, these demands determine revenue, cost, and profit. In a regulated setting, profit π may be constrained to be zero or alternatively to be a specified negative value $-\pi_0$ if only a portion of the assigned fixed and overhead costs F is to be recovered by local rates.

Second-Best Pricing

In the context of the assumed cost function 7.1, marginal-cost pricing amounts to charging the two-part measured-service rate

$$MR = C_A + C_U x \tag{7.6}$$

In the case of telephone service, achievement of the ideal efficiency effects of marginal-cost pricing is limited by several factors.

Local Telephone Service

First, as noted above, measuring equipment requires added investments, and monthly billing operations increase expenses. The appropriate marginal-cost rate will include these costs

$$MR = C_A' + C_U'x \tag{7.7}$$

where $C_A' = C_A + C_{MA}$ and $C_U' = C_U + C_{MU}$. Unless these extra resources return significant economies in the use of the telephone system, a simpler flat-rate price structure is preferable.

Second, membership in the telephone network usually creates a positive economic externality. The value to an individual consumer of being connected to the telephone network is increased when other consumers are also connected. As a result, the total value to society of an additional subscriber is greater than just the private value that he or she places on telephone service. Economic welfare may be increased by pricing access to the telephone network at something less than its marginal cost and by increasing other rates to subsidize the access service.

Finally, marginal-cost pricing would cause a deficit for a telephone company with economies of scale and scope; a zero-profit constraint requires that some prices exceed marginal cost.

"Second-best" prices maximize social welfare subject to one or more constraints. The prototype problem is maximization of consumers' plus producer's surplus subject to a minimum-profit constraint. When the market for the firm's services can be segmented into separate and independent demands, the optimal prices are given by the Ramsey principle: Increase the price of each service over its marginal cost in inverse proportion to its elasticity of demand (Ramsey 1927; Baumol and Bradford 1970).

Second-best rates may be considered in terms of each of the rate structures of figure 7–1. Under a flat rate (figure 7–1a) there is only one price.[4] To satisfy the budget constraint, it must be equal to average cost; equivalently, the flat rate equals a pro rata share of fixed costs plus the marginal cost of access and the average cost of usage:

$$FR = \frac{(F + nC_A + C_U \Sigma x)}{n}$$

$$= \frac{F}{n} + C_A C_U \bar{x} \tag{7.8}$$

The two-part rate structure (figure 7–1b) and permits each call to be priced at marginal cost $q = C_U'$, and would therefore seem to provide the best pricing solution (if measuring costs are sufficiently small)

$$MR = p + qx = \left(\frac{F}{n} + C_A'\right) + C_U'x \tag{7.9}$$

But if demand for access to the local network is at all price-elastic, this access price will exclude some potential subscriber i who is willing to pay her or his marginal costs $C'_A + C'_U x_i$. In general, it will increase welfare to set $q > C'_U$ in order to lower p somewhat. The second-best two-part rate structure most likely will require setting both the access price p and the usage price q above marginal costs (Ng and Weisser 1974).[5] If customers can be segmented by differences in their demand elasticities, these markups above marginal costs will vary inversely with demand elasticities according to a generalization of the Ramsey formula that accounts for interdependence between the demand for access and the demand for calls (see Mitchell 1978). However, if network externalities are sufficiently large, it may even be optimal to price access below marginal cost.

A nonlinear rate structure (figure 7–1c) allows the firm to discriminate among customers according to volume of consumption ("size") and thus to achieve greater welfare gains than are possible under a two-part rate. As long as local telephone calls are not readily resold, the firm can collect more revenues from some groups of consumers and use them to set a lower access price than under a two-part rate. In general, in the optimal nonlinear rate structure, the marginal price of an additional call $R'(x) = dR(x)/dx$ will exceed marginal cost for all but the largest quantity $x_{\max}$, at which point $R'(x)$ should just equal marginal cost (Willig 1978).

Optional two-part rates (figure 7–1d) allow the customer to choose from several measured-rate plans. In advance of consumption the consumer selects the plan under which she or he will be billed. If the consumer knows his or her demand *with certainty*, optional rates will provide a piecewise linear approximation to a nonlinear rate structure (Faulhaber and Panzar 1977). Thus, in figure 7–1d the three optional rates MR_1, MR_2, and MR_3 are equivalent to the nonlinear rate structure NL shown by the solid line. In this case, a sufficient variety of suitably designed options can provide almost all the welfare gains of a nonlinear rate schedule.

Typically, however, a consumer's calling rate is somewhat uncertain. Furthermore, the number of calls made may also vary systematically from month to month. These factors mean that the consumer who must choose one rate plan in advance and be billed under it for several months will tend to have higher payments than would result under the "equivalent" nonlinear or piecewise-linear rate schedule. For example, consider the consumer who makes x_1 calls in the first month and x_2 the next month, for an average calling rate of $\bar{x}$. If he or she must choose one of the two optional rate schedules shown in figure 7–2, the lowest overall bill is obtained under MR_2. The consumer pays monthly charges of R_1 and R_2 for an average of $\bar{R}$. If the consumer could instead select a separate rate schedule for each month, she or he would pay only R'_1 and R_2, reducing average charges to $\tilde{R}$.

Will second-best measured-service rate structures necessarily improve

Local Telephone Service

welfare? If consumer demand curves are linear and there are no network externalities, a two-part measured-service rate increases net welfare as long as the cost savings from reduced usage are more than twice the measuring costs (Mitchell 1979a). By lowering the price of access to the network and increasing the number of subscribers, nonlinear and optional rate structures will provide somewhat larger net welfare gains.

However, measuring costs per call may be large enough to make mandatory measured-service rates undesirable. In these instances, is it possible to achieve net welfare gains by metering only some subscribers?

Optional Flat and Measured Rates

If measured service is offered as an alternative to a flat rate, this reduces the resources devoted to measuring, but it also limits any welfare gains from positive per-unit pricing to a subgroup of the market. If measuring costs must be incurred for all subscribers, then any of the second-best measured-service rate structures discussed above, with positive per-unit prices for *all* calls, will be welfare-superior to an optional flat-rate structure. However, if measuring and billing costs can be limited to only those customers who select the

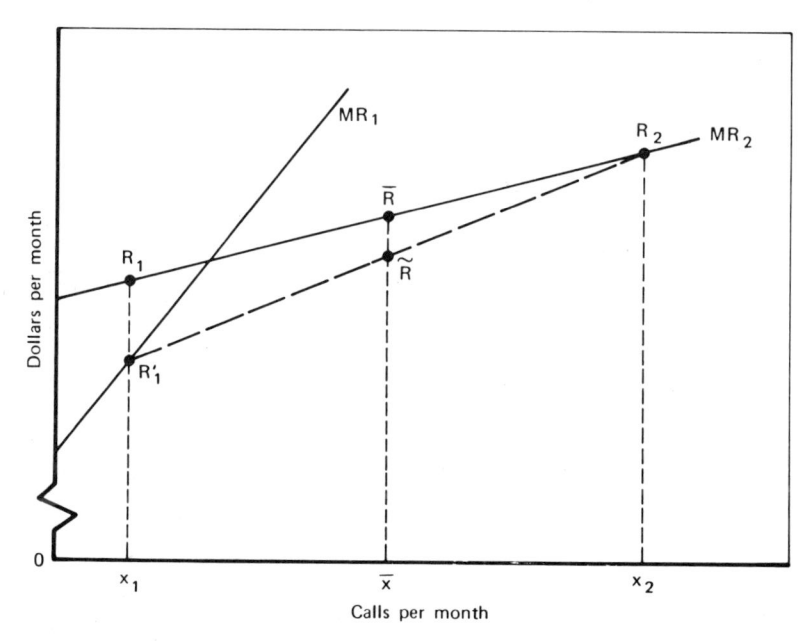

Figure 7-2 Average Bills under Optional and Nonlinear Rates

measured rate, it is possible for the option of measured or flat rates to increase net welfare over a single flat rate even when a mandatory measured rate would not.

In the U.S. telephone industry, different policies are being developed to measured service. The Bell System has announced its plan to offer measured service on an optional basis, giving the subscriber a choice between a flat rate and one or more measured rates. As shown in figure 7–3, AT&T's prototypical rate structure would offer the consumer a choice of three rate plans (Garfinkel and Linhart 1979). Rate MR_1 would have a low access price p_1 and a substantial per-call price q_1; it would be the least costly plan at very low levels of usage. Rate MR_2 would have a higher minimum price p_2 and would provide an allowance of, for example, $A = 30$ calls per month, with additional calls billed at q_2 per call. High-usage consumers, making more than, for example, $x_2^* = 150$ calls per month, would minimize bills by selecting the flat rate FR.[6] In contrast to the AT&T approach, General Telephone has announced that it will convert local areas to measured service on a nonoptional basis, so that all customers will be billed under a single measured rate with no allowance (Schmidt 1979).

When flat rates and measured rates are offered as options, it is necessary to determine which consumers will select which rates in order to calculate market demands. To satisfy the budget constraint, the rates must jointly recover the contribution requirement F plus all the variable costs.

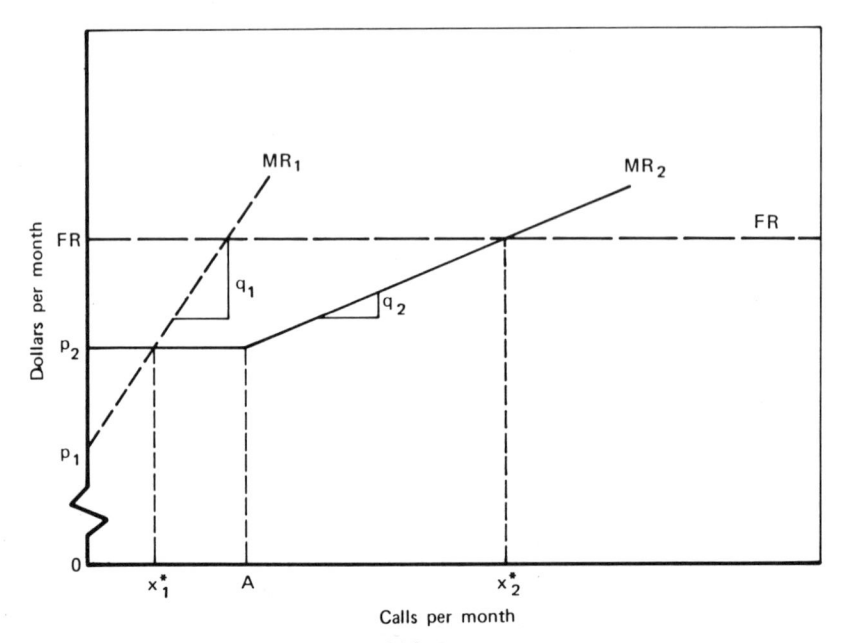

Figure 7–3 Optional Rates Planned by the Bell System

Local Telephone Service

To examine the effects of optional flat and measured rates, I consider a flat rate and a single measured rate with no call allowance and assume that the new rates must satisfy the same budget constraint which applied when all customers had flat-rate service, the rate given in equation 7.8. Because consumers' choices of rate plans interact with the rates that can be set, the first problem is to determine what, if any, pairs of *MR* and *FR* rates are consistent with consumer choice. One can then analyze the welfare effects of optional flat and measured rates.

Equilibrium Optional Rates

It is illuminating to view the determination of equilibrium *MR* and *FR* rates as the outcome of a dynamic process. Assume, first, that there are no fixed costs or contributions to be earned by local service ($F = 0$) and that the average usage is $\bar{x}_0$ calls per month. Figure 7–4 shows the initial flat rate (FR_0) that recovers the marginal costs of access (C_A) and usage (C_U).

For a measured rate that covers only marginal costs (inclusive of measuring costs)

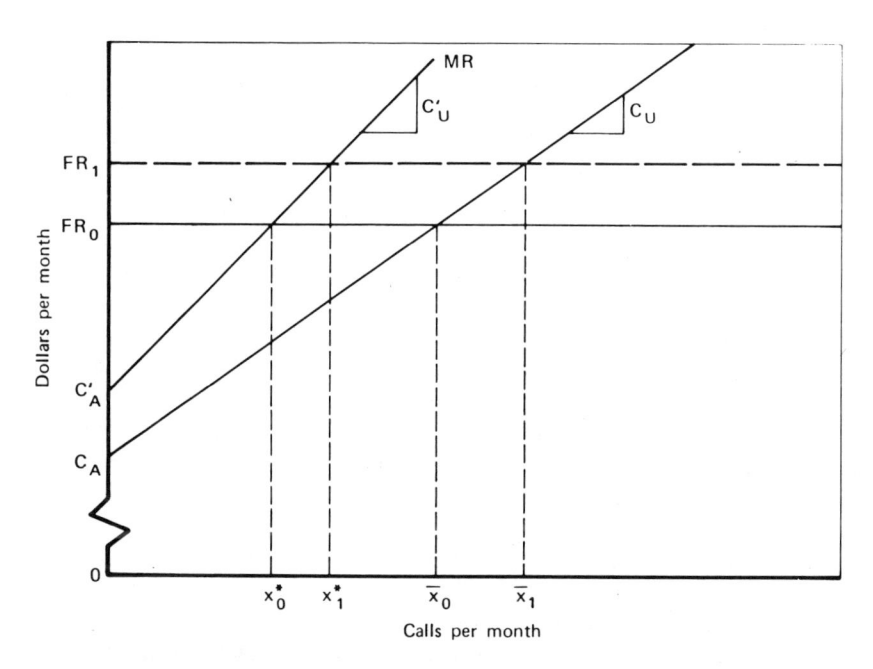

Figure 7–4 Unstable Flat Rate: No Fixed Costs and Measured Rate Equal to Marginal Costs

$$MR = C'_A + C'_U x \qquad (7.10)$$

the breakeven point—where flat and measured rates result in the same bill—occurs at x_0^*. If each consumer knows how many local calls he or she makes each month and selects the rate plan to minimize the telephone bill, then the consumer will choose a rate plan by comparing his or her monthly usage to the breakeven value. A subscriber with usage $x < x_0^*$ will select the measured rate, and users with $x \geq x_0^*$ will choose the flat rate.[7]

The result of this self-selection process is that the average usage of flat-rate subscribers will not be $\bar{x}_0$, but a higher value such as $\bar{x}_1$. To meet the budget constraint, the initial flat rate must be raised, perhaps at the next rate hearing, to FR_1.[8] But now consumers with usage between x_0^* and x_1^* will select the measured rate, further increasing the average usage of the flat-rate group.

In the limiting case of zero measuring costs ($C'_A = C_A$, $C'_U = C_U$), this process continues indefinitely, and there is no equilibrium flat rate (Mitchell 1979a). However, positive measuring costs are sufficient to ensure that a (very high) equilibrium flat rate does exist.[9]

Suppose, however, that local telephone rates are required to generate a positive monthly contribution ($F > 0$). If the measured rate covers only the marginal access, usage, and measuring costs, then all the contribution F must be raised from the subscribers choosing the flat rate. When low-usage customers ($x < x_0^*$) switch to measured service, the flat rate must now be raised by a greater amount than shown in figure 7–4, in order to make up for the contributions lost from measured-rate subscribers. In this case, despite the presence of measuring costs, a sizable contribution requirement will mean that there is no stable flat rate.

However, if each measured-rate customer pays more than her or his marginal cost, it will be possible to achieve a stable flat rate. Figure 7–5 shows such a case, assuming for ease of illustration that consumers' usage is uniformly distributed between 0 and $x_{\max}$. The initial flat rate is again FR_0. When the measured rate $MR = p + qx$ is offered with $p > C'_A$, $q > C'_U$, the breakeven quantity is x_0^* and consumers of this size switch to the measured rate. This shift reduces the ith consumer's contribution by $FR_0 - R(x_i)$. The total reduction in revenue is (proportional to) area D, although measured-rate subscribers still provide reduced contributions shown by area E. By increasing the flat rate to FR_1, the forgone contributions (area D) can be recouped from flat-rate subscribers (area G).[10]

This analysis demonstrates that when consumers minimize bills and local service must earn a positive contribution, the optional measured rate must generally be priced above marginal costs if the flat rate is to remain viable.

Clearly there are many possible measured-rate–flat-rate combinations that could satisfy the budget constraint. Setting the measured-rate parameters

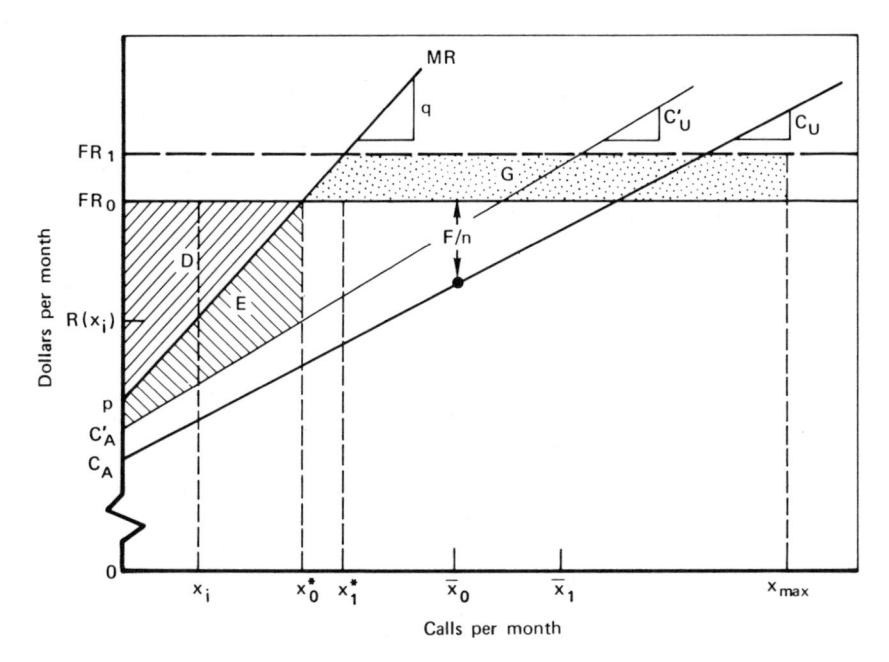

Figure 7-5 Stable Flat Rate: Fixed Costs and Measured Rate Greater than Marginal Costs

close to marginal costs will result in attracting the greatest number of customers to the measured rate; this policy will require large increases in the initial flat rate. Conversely, a measured rate well above marginal costs will be attractive to only a few small users, leaving the flat rate almost unchanged.

To narrow the choice among possible pairs of measured and flat rates, one may wish to prohibit cross subsidization between the rates. The measured rates will be *subsidy-free* when it covers marginal costs at each level of usage:

$$MR_i \geq C'_A + C'_U x_i \qquad (7.11)$$

For customers selecting the flat rate, the corresponding requirement is that these customers *as a group* cover their marginal costs (Mitchell 1979a; Kahn and Zielinski 1976). Therefore, the subsidy-free condition

$$FR \geq C_A + C_U \bar{x}_{FR} \qquad (7.12)$$

applies to the flat-rate subscriber with average flat-rate usage $\bar{x}_{FR}$.[11]

Welfare Analysis

When measuring costs are so high that mandatory measured rates are undesirable, optional flat and measured rates may, nevertheless, increase welfare. This possibility arises because the measured-rate option can potentially induce new subscribers to join the network.

Suppose that the measured rate could be offered to only those consumers who were not subscribers under the initial flat rate. Because the measured rate reduces the minimum price of access it would attract some consumers unwilling to pay the flat rate to have telephone service. Any such subsidy-free measured rate would unambiguously increase welfare, because each consumer who becomes a new subscriber is better off by purchasing telephone service and is paying all her or his marginal costs. Let the total welfare gain for this new group be ΔW_1.

However, existing subscribers cannot be excluded from choosing the measured rate, so that the welfare effects on this group must also be accounted for. Existing subscribers who shift to measured service will cause new costs of measuring and billing. Facing positive per-unit prices, they will also make fewer calls and thus reduce the costs of usage. If these cost savings less the value of the forgone calls were to exceed the added measuring costs, there would be a net welfare gain for this group. Let the net amount be ΔW_2. But, by hypothesis, this quantity will be negative for subscribers as a whole. A fortiori, it will be negative for the smaller users who choose the measured rate, because a portion of the costs of measuring each subscriber is invariant with usage (C_{MA}) and because low-usage customers are probably less price-elastic (Park, Mitchell, and Wetzel 1980).

Finally, the addition of new subscribers to the network may increase the value of telephone service to existing subscribers. Let the total value of this externality be ΔE.[12] Then the overall net welfare effect of the optional flat and measured rates will be the sum of these three terms:

$$\Delta W = \Delta W_1 + \Delta E + \Delta W_2 \qquad (7.13)$$

In summary, introducing a measured rate as an option to a flat rate may achieve a net gain in welfare, and this gain could be achieved even if, because of the costs of measuring all subscribers, a mandatory measured rate would create a net loss. If measuring costs were less substantial, both optional and mandatory measured rates would increase welfare; which rate structure is welfare-optimal will depend on the magnitudes of measuring costs and demand elasticities and the distributions of customer preferences. At sufficiently low measuring costs, a mandatory rate, by imposing a positive per-unit price on all calls, would achieve the greater improvement.

At present rate levels, some 98 percent of U.S. households have access to a telephone. The potential welfare gains from adding new subscribers are, therefore, quite limited. However, elimination of the current support that local service receives from interstate toll rates could cause local flat rates to rise substantially. In these circumstances, local measured rates might prevent the welfare loss that would accompany a reduction in the number of subscribers.

Implementing a Measured Rate

The previous analysis is based on the assumption that each consumer chooses the rate that minimizes the monthly bill. But the available empirical evidence on consumer choices casts some doubt on the validity of that assumption.

Market Experience

A study of consumer choices in several states in which optional measured-service plans are available finds that a substantial fraction of telephone subscribers are on a rate plan that results in a higher monthly bill than the minimum for their level of usage (Infosino, forthcoming). Significant numbers of subscribers take the flat rate at usage levels well below the monthly breakeven point, and some rather high-usage users elect measured service when the flat rate would be cheaper.[13] Overall, the number of customers who buy measured service is substantially smaller than the number who could reduce their telephone bills by doing so.[14]

The major causes of this behavior are not well understood, but several possible reasons can be advanced. Consumers lack accurate information about their telephone usage; most interview data show that they systematically overestimate the number of calls they make each month. Moreover, some consumers may be unaware that alternatives to the customary flat rate are available or may continue with a flat rate simply out of habit.

Furthermore, variation in a subscriber's calling pattern occurs because of both regular (for example, seasonal) factors and random events. Because of this variability, the rate plan that minimizes the bill for a given month's usage may not be the least costly in the longer term. And consumers may prefer the assurance of a certain monthly sum to an uncertain, fluctuating one.[15] A final possibility is that for this commodity—local telephone conversations—consumers have a particular dislike of paying for each item consumed. To avoid feeling "cost-conscious" when picking up the telephone to call somebody nearby, such consumers are willing to pay a premium and choose the flat rate.

Ex Post Pricing

Instead of requiring each customer to choose between a flat rate and a measured rate in advance, with the attendant uncertainty about which rate will be least costly, the telephone company could calculate the customer's bill under each plan and charge the minimum rate for her or his actual usage. Such an *ex post pricing* scheme would be equivalent to a single, nonlinear rate structure that is the lower envelope of the pair of optional rates.[16]

The disadvantage of ex post pricing is that it requires every customer's usage to be measured. And if the expense of metering every call is to be incurred, a positive marginal price per call for all customers will be welfare-superior to charging nothing for some calls.

However, it is possible to avoid the costs of metering the customers who prefer a flat rate by offering ex post pricing *as a third option* to the flat rate and the measured rate.[17] For example, the optional ex post (EP) rate could be equal to MR for usage up to the breakeven point x_1^* and thereafter equal to FR plus the costs of measuring and billing calls in excess of x_1^*. As drawn in figure 7–6, beyond x_1^*, the EP rate is flat at a slightly higher level than FR. The EP rate will be subsidy-free provided that

$$EP \geq \begin{cases} C'_A + C'_U x & 0 \leq x < x_1^* \\ C'_A + C'_U \bar{x}_{EP}^* & x_1^* < x \end{cases} \quad (7.14)$$

where $\bar{x}_{EP}^*$ is the mean usage of those EP subscribers who make more than x_1^* calls per month. In fact if the metering process can be turned off when usage reaches x_1^*, the measuring costs of an optional EP plan might be no greater than those for the MR plan.

Consumers with high average usage and little uncertainty or monthly variability can choose FR to minimize their bills. Other consumers can select EP with the assurance that they will pay only the flat rate plus extra measuring costs if their usage lies above the breakeven level x_1^*. As drawn, the EP option dominates the MR rate, and no rational consumer would choose it. Alternatively, the telephone company might charge a premium to subscribers who select ex post pricing. This would raise the EP schedule somewhat and make the MR rate attractive to consumers with consistently low usage.

The concept of an optional ex post rate is readily extended to include added rate elements for the length of conversation, distance, and time of day. Indeed, if consumers have difficulty in choosing the minimum-cost option when rates depend on only the number of calls, they will find optional measured-rate plans with multidimensional rate elements even more complex.

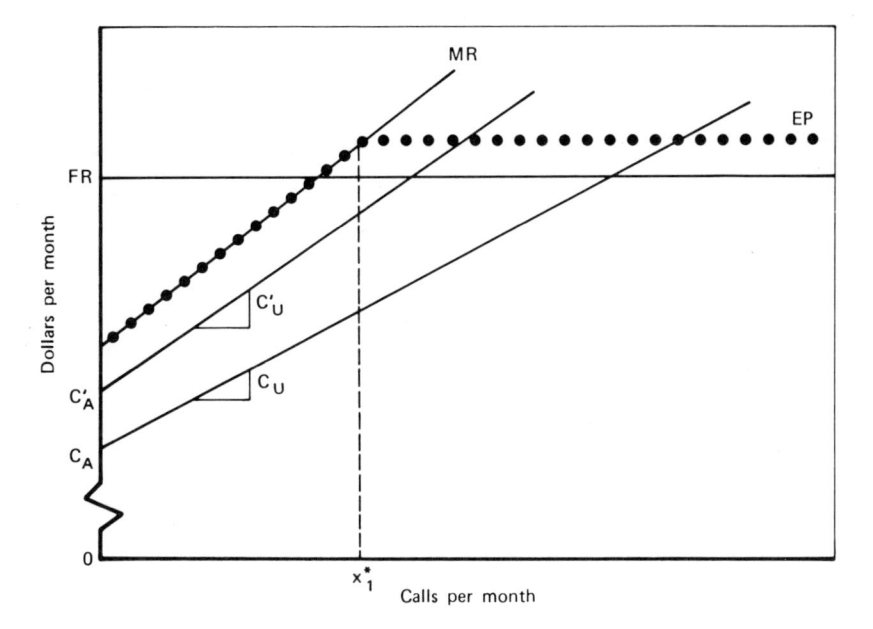

Figure 7–6 Ex Post Rate as an Option to Flat and Measured Rates

Evaluation

The ex post option would constitute a market test that could discriminate between alternative explanations of consumers' observed preferences for flat-rate service. By choosing the ex post option, consumers could obtain information about their own local telephone usage at low cost. If they presently select flat-rate service primarily because of uncertainty about what their bills would be under measured rates, then an optional ex post rate should be popular.

However, if consumers' choices to date reflect the behavior of informed subscribers who derive utility simply from being able to place local calls at a zero price, then providing an ex post option will not significantly increase the total number of consumers on a measured rate. In this case, the market data would provide a method of measuring the "utility premium" that subscribers attach to flat rates (Mitchell 1979c). The finding of a large premium would support the offering of optional flat-rate service on a subsidy-free basis. This approach would then be desirable because when measuring costs are small, mandatory measured service would otherwise be judged a welfare-superior rate structure.

Notes

1. Measuring costs depend strongly on the technology of the telephone network. Many European telephone administrations use a low-cost method of charging for local as well as long-distance calls, measuring usage with periodic pulses whose frequency varies inversely with the price per minute of calling. Every subscriber's monthly usage, in pulse units, is accumulated by a separate meter and billed as a summary amount (see Mitchell 1979*b*), 1979*c*).

2. Currently, the residential contribution F may be negative in some jurisdictions where high long-distance and business subscription rates have provided large revenue transfers to reduce local residential rates. But in the longer term, the supply of long-distance services by competing common carriers using microwave and earth-satellite transmission facilities is expected to reduce sharply the revenues available to support local services. In accord with the long-run perspective of this chapter, I assume that F is nonnegative.

3. In addition, there is a one-time service-connection fee.

4. However, if the market can be segmented, there is room for welfare-increasing price discrimination. The traditionally lower flat rates charged to residential subscribers are consistent with their higher elasticity of demand, although the levels of the rates do not necessarily correspond to those of the Ramsey formula (see Mitchell 1976).

Some of the differences between business and residential flat rates is also attributable to higher average levels of calling (and therefore higher costs) for business subscribers. It would, of course, be possible to discriminate between business and residential customers under measured-service rate structures as well. But because measured service rates will automatically vary with usage costs, there is less need to have separate rates by class of customer. I assume that a single rate structure applies for both business and residential service.

5. However, this relationship need not hold if consumers with differing tastes have intersecting demand curves. Compare Oi (1971).

6. Full-scale implementation of the AT&T rate structure would include separate charges for the initiation and duration of the call, differentiated by the distance it travels and the time of day at which it is placed.

7. Assuming that consumers select rate plans to minimize expenditure ignores the effects of price elasticity of demand ("repression") and the resulting shift in the frequency distribution of usage when a measured rate is introduced.

In a more exact analysis, each consumer would choose the plan that yields maximum surplus; this would not alter the qualitative results reached here. If the many separate decisions to place calls during the month also contain a random component, the surplus analysis becomes quite complex. A formally similar problem in the context of insurance reimbursement subject to a deductible is explored by Keeler, Newhouse, and Phelps (1977).

8. Panzar (1979) shows that when demand elasticity is taken into account and consumers have strictly positive minimum usage, a measured rate with an access price exceeding marginal cost can achieve (small) welfare gains without raising the flat rate.

9. Suppose that FR_1 is provisionally set equal to $C_A + C_U x_{max}$. Users between the breakeven point for this flat rate, x_1^*, and x_{max} will select the flat rate, but because their costs are each less than FR_1, a net contribution will result. Thus a slightly lower FR will both attract customers and satisfy the budget constraint.

10. The higher FR_1 causes a small increase in the breakeven quantity to x_1^*. Measured-rate consumers between x_0^* and x_1^* pay somewhat higher rates than under the original flat rate, but they also add measuring costs. The net amount has been included in the shaded area G.

11. By estimating the mean usage of flat-rate subscribers from data samples collected in periodic traffic studies, most of the costs of measuring this group's usage can be avoided.

12. The other effects of repricing from the initial FR_0 to the final MR and FR_1 only redistribute payments from one subgroup of existing subscribers to another.

13. The same type of "error" is observed when three rate plans are offered.

14. Somewhat paradoxically, in the one situation in which optional flat and measured-service rates are welfare optimal—relatively large measuring costs and small demand elasticities—the tendency of existing subscribers to choose the flat rate will increase welfare by reducing the measuring costs and the absolute size of ΔW_2 in equation 7.13.

15. However, it is unlikely that risk aversion in the consumer's utility function can explain the observed pattern, because the amounts of expenditure at risk in most cases are very small fractions of total income.

16. In fact, this rate structure has exactly the same form as the declining-block rate plans that have been widely used for electricity sales, except that the marginal price will be zero at high levels of usage.

17. This proposal is due to John Panzar.

8 Spatial Considerations in Public-Utility Pricing

Robert E. Dansby

Introduction

The theory of spatial economics has found little application in public-utility pricing.[1] Yet, many problems in this area seem to beckon use of the techniques from spatial economics. In this chapter, we apply spatial-economics concepts in analyzing two public-utility pricing problems of current interest.

The first problem concerns the pricing of electricity, with both production and transmission costs taken into account. Although there have been many recent papers on electricity pricing, few have taken explicit account of transmission costs.[2] The results below show, however, that a more general treatment of the spatial distribution of electricity demand leads to interesting new insights. Schmalensee (1978) showed that a uniform spatial distribution of demand and constant-returns production and transmission cost functions imply that welfare-optimal prices would exactly cover costs; also Schmalensee derives a similar result in nonspatial theory. In the next section, it is shown that for more general spatial demand distributions, welfare-optimal forms of practical electricity-pricing policies do not ensure the firm's viability when production and transmission cost functions exhibit constant returns.

The second problem concerns delineating the conditions under which the expansion of local-exchange calling areas is justified on cost/benefit grounds. The theory of nonspatial local-exchange pricing, for example, two-part tariffs and Ramsey pricing, is well established in the economics literature.[3] However, the evaluation of the merits of extended-area telephone service requires explicit consideration of the spatial characteristics of the relevant local exchanges. In the third section, "Extended-Area Local Service," social-welfare criteria for judging local calling-area expansion are derived; circumstances which imply that implementation of extended-area service (EAS) would decrease welfare are discussed. If, for example, traffic-measurement costs are relatively small, then a transition from toll pricing to EAS, between

---

The author is associated with Bell Laboratories and AT&T and is adjunct associate professor of economics at Rutgers University. The views expressed in this chapter should not be interpreted as reflecting official policy of the Bell System.

given exchanges, will decrease welfare. Some limitations on the application of the welfare criteria are also discussed. The fourth section, "Conclusions," contains a summary and suggestions for further research.

Spatial Consideration in Electricity Pricing

In this section, it is shown that spatial considerations can have an important influence on pricing decisions of an electric utility. In the case of electric utilities, the spatial distribution of customers becomes an important factor for two reasons: (1) Customers' locations influence the utility's investment in transmission facilities, and (2) the customer usage density affects the amount of transmission loss, that is, the cost of distribution on given lines. Both factors can be important in planning decisions of an electric utility, since they affect pricing and capital-investment decisions.

However, not much attention is given to these matters in the economics literature on public-utility pricing. Marginal-cost pricing principles are now common fare in discussions of electric-utility pricing policy, in the form of the immense literature on peak-load pricing.[4] The purpose of this section is to extend welfare-optimal electricity-pricing rules to account for transmission costs and the distribution of spatial demand; the result is interesting new insights concerning the influences of these factors on welfare-optimal prices.

The model used is reasonably general. The utility is assumed to face the problems of (1) selecting the appropriate size (design) of a production unit (generating plant) and transmission facilities to serve a particular geographic region and setting prices for service to the different regions. It is assumed that capacity investment (both production and transmission) and pricing decisions are made to maximize the sum of consumers' and producers' surplus.

The relevant social-welfare objective is derived by first considering the spatial distribution of demand. Customers are indexed by the taste parameter α. Each customer of a given type will have the same level of usage when faced with identical prices; however, the population density of particular α types may vary by geographic region. The demand of an individual type-α customer is denoted by $q(\hat{p}, \alpha)$, where $\hat{p}$ is the effective price and the domain of α is the unit interval. The number of customers of type α who are located a distance r from the plant site, in the direction θ, is denoted by $h(r, \theta, \alpha)$. The individual demand function q has the usual properties—nonnegative, continuous, differentiable, and downward-sloping with respect to $\hat{p}$. The population density h is also assumed to be continuous, but beyond that it is rather arbitrary.

The total demand of all customer types located at (r, θ) is then

$$Q(r, \theta) = \int_0^1 q(\hat{p}, \alpha) h(r, \theta, \alpha) \, d\alpha \qquad (8.1)$$

Spatial Considerations

and they generate revenue equal to $\hat{p}Q(r, \theta)$. The consumer surplus generated by customers located at (r, θ) is then

$$S(r, \theta) = \int_0^1 h(r, \theta, \alpha) \int_{\hat{p}}^\infty q(y, \alpha)\, dy\, d\alpha \qquad (8.2)$$

where an individual's consumer surplus is characterized by the usual Marshallian triangle.

The total cost of providing electricity to the various customers depends on the level of both production and transmission activities. Because of the technology used to produce electricity, there are joint cost elements in production and transmission. The common belief is that because of electricity-storage costs, the total cost of production and transmission is lower when both activities are carried on together. The total cost of producing electricity services will also depend on the layout of the distribution network and the site of the generating plant. Because power companies do not have complete freedom in selection of power sites, we assume the site to be arbitrary.[5] Moreover, the positions of transmission routes are determined by the relative positions of the power plants and major population centers. Thus, in this analysis, locations of the power plant and of transmission lines are taken as givens in decisions regarding capacity investment and pricing.[6] Hence we assume the power-generating plant is located at the origin in a polar-coordinate system. There are N major population centers served by the power plant, and the ith center is located in the direction θ_i relative to the location of the plant. The main transmission lines are laid out in the directions $\{\theta_1, \ldots, \theta_N\}$ (see figure 8–1).[7]

The cost of producing enough electricity to meet the demands Q and supplying it to the various population centers is given by the neoclassical cost function C. The first term is the cost of transmission due to line loss, and the second term characterizes all other costs of production and transmission:[8]

$$C = \sum_i^N \int_0^R c(r, \hat{Q}(r, \theta_i))\, dr + C(\hat{Q}(0, \theta_1), \ldots, \hat{Q}(0, \theta_N), \hat{Q}(0)) \qquad (8.3)$$

The second term includes all capital and operating costs of production, which depend on $Q(0)$, and transmission; these costs depend on the demand along each transmission line $Q(0, \theta_1)$. Here $\hat{Q}(r, \theta_i)$ is defined as the total demand in the region served by the ith transmission line which must be transmitted at least a distance r. The distance to the most remote customer is denoted by R. The ith main transmission line is assumed to provide service to all customers in the region bounded by $\bar{\theta}_i = (\theta_i + \theta_{i+1})/2$ and $\underline{\theta}_i = (\theta_i + \theta_{i-1})/2$. Thus, $\hat{Q}(r, \theta_i)$ is the total demand in the pie slice bounded by $\bar{\theta}_i$ and $\underline{\theta}_i$ which must be transmitted at least a distance r (see figure 8–2) and is given formally by

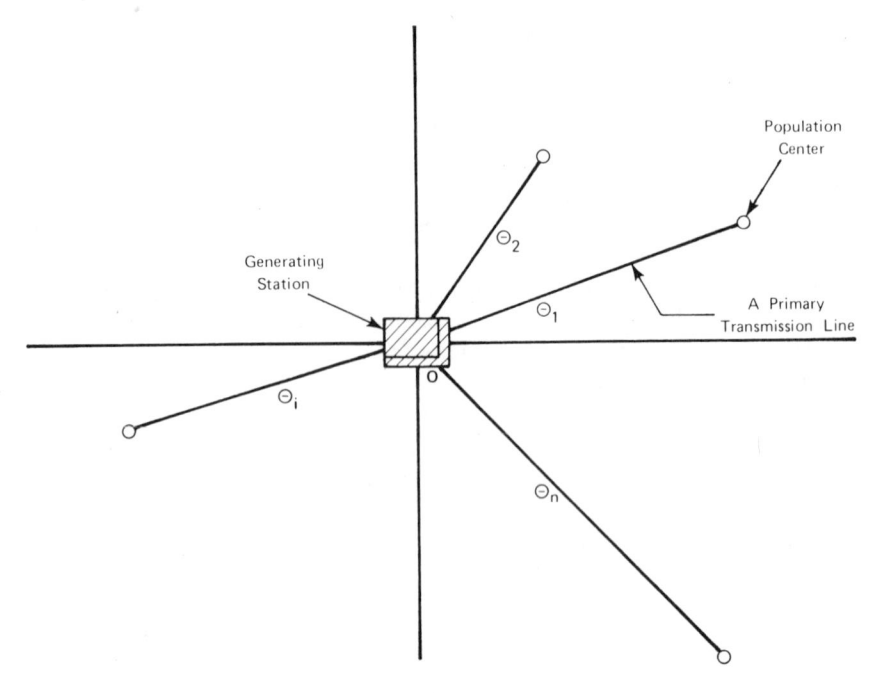

128 Issues in Public-Utility Pricing and Regulation

Figure 8-1 Relative Locations of Generating Station, Transmission Lines, and Population Centers

$$\hat{Q}(r, \theta_i) = \int_r^R \int_{\theta_i}^{\bar{\theta}_i} Q(x, \theta) \, d\theta \, dx \qquad (8.4)$$

The total demand, at r or beyond, in all market areas is given by

$$\hat{Q}(r) = \sum_i^N Q(r, \theta_i) \qquad (8.5)$$

Hence, $Q(0)$ is the *total demand* to be served by the utility, and $Q(0, \theta_i)$ is the total demand originating in region i.

The total cost includes costs of variable and fixed factors associated with production and transmission. The capacity of production and transmission facilities is subsumed by this formulation, as are the costs of fuel and of line maintenance and production and transmission operating cost.[9] The function in equation 8.3 reflects the fact that transmission costs depend on the number of main transmission lines, the amount of electricity carried over each line,

Spatial Considerations

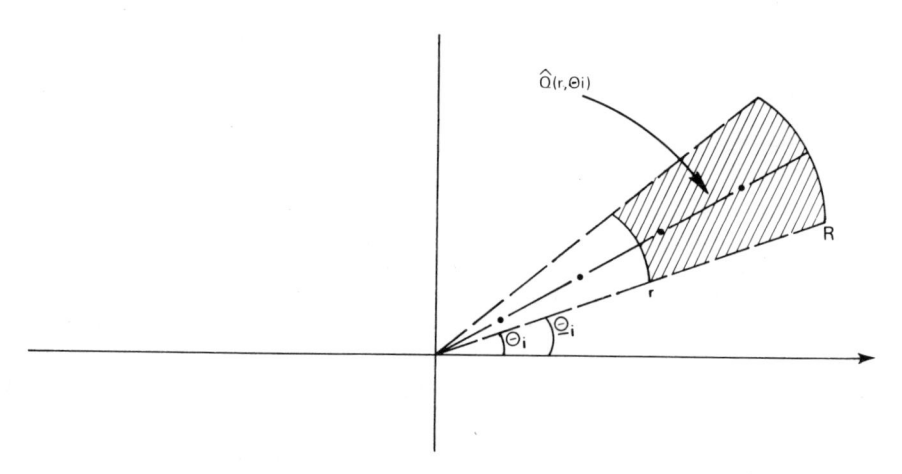

Figure 8-2 Regional Spatial Demand

and the spatial distribution of usage on each line. Moreover, the specification in equation 8.3 permits cost complementaries in production and distribution. Possible activity-specific economies of scale in production and transmission may also be manifested. For a given total usage on a line, transmission loss is usually higher when all usage is distant from the generating plant than when usage is evenly distributed along the transmission route. Where there are transmission losses, these are valued at the implicit cost of factors used to produce the "lost" kilowatts.

The objective of the utility is assumed to be maximization of aggregate net welfare, which is given by

$$W = \int_0^{2\pi} \int_0^R [S(r, \theta) + PQ(r, \theta)] \, dr \, d\theta - C \qquad (8.6)$$

where $Q(r, \theta)$, $S(r, \theta)$, and C are defined in equations 8.1, 8.2 and 8.3, respectively. Electric-utility rate schedules do not usually tie prices to the customers' distance from the generating facility. Moreover, rates are not usually permitted to differ across various intrajurisdictional regional markets. Hence the price P is a scalar and is the same in every transmission region. Revenue at (r, θ) is given by $PQ(r, \theta)$. In this formulation, production and transmission capacity enters implicitly into the cost function in equation 8.3. Thus there is no need to impose explicit capacity constraints. The public utility need only determine the optimal price; the optimal capacity of production and transmission facilities will then be determined implicitly by $\hat{Q}(0)$ and $Q(r, \theta_i)$, $i = 1, \ldots, N$, when evaluated at the optimal price.[10]

The welfare-optimal price of electricity must satisfy[11]

$$P^* = \sum_{i=1}^{N} \left[C_i + \int_0^R \frac{\partial c}{\partial \hat{Q}} \frac{\hat{Q}_P(r, \theta_i) \, dr}{\hat{Q}_P(0, \theta_i)} \right] \frac{\hat{Q}_P(0, \theta_i)}{\hat{Q}_P(0)} + C_{N+1} \quad (8.7)$$

The marginal cost of increasing total output is denoted by C_{N+1}. The term in the summation is the marginal total cost of transmission to all service regions. In nonspatial models, the welfare-optimal price would equal marginal production cost; the same is true in the spatial model if there are no transmission costs. However, in the realistic case where there are transmission costs in the spatial model, price is greater than marginal cost of total output, and the difference is the marginal total cost of transmission. The marginal total transmission cost in equation 8.7 is a weighted average of the marginal transmission costs specified to the various regions. Thus, with a pricing policy that ignores interregional differences in population density and transmission costs, there is implicit interlocation cross subsidy.[12] Moreover, if the public utility were permitted to charge a different price P_i in each of the $i = 1, \ldots, N$ transmission regions, then in some regions $P_i < P$, that is, under the uniform-price policy, region i is paying more than under region-specific pricing. On the other hand, those regions for which $P_i > P$ are paying less under the uniform-price policy. The magnitude of this interregional price differentiation depends on the extent of scale economies in production and distribution, as well as the spatial distribution of demand in the various regions.

The welfare-optimal, region-specific prices are given by [13]

$$P_i^{**} = C_i + \int_0^R \left[\frac{\partial c}{\partial \hat{Q}} \frac{\partial \hat{Q}(r, \theta_i)}{\partial P_i} \bigg/ \frac{\partial \hat{Q}(0, \theta_i)}{\partial P_i} \right] dr + C_{N+1} \quad (8.8)$$

where $C_i + C_{N+1}$ is the marginal cost of production and transmission to serve the ith regional market. The second term, involving the integral, is the marginal cost of transmission loss in the ith regional market. The extent of interregional price differentiation per unit demand is simply

$$P_i^{**} - P^* = C_i^{**} - \sum_{i=1}^{N} C_i^* F_{0i} + C_{N+1}^{**} - C_{N+1}^*$$

$$+ \int_0^R \left(\frac{\partial c^{**}}{\partial \hat{Q}} \frac{\hat{F}_{ri}}{\hat{F}_{0i}} - \sum_{i=1}^{N} \frac{\partial c}{\partial \hat{Q}} \hat{F}_{ri} \right) dr \quad (8.9)$$

Spatial Considerations

where $F_{ri} = Q_p(r, \theta_i)/Q_p(0)$ and $F_{0i} = F_{ri}$ evaluated at $r = 0$. The following proposition establishes an important feature of these price differentials.

Proposition 1:[14] If the production and transmission cost functions C and c exhibit constant returns to scale with C which are the same for all regions, then the regionally averaged price P^* equals the region-specific price P_i^{**} only if

$$\int_0^R \frac{\partial c}{\partial \hat{Q}} \left[\frac{\hat{Q}_p(r, \theta_i)}{\hat{Q}_p(0, \theta_i)} - \frac{\sum_i \hat{Q}_p(r, \theta_i)}{\sum_1 \hat{Q}_p(0, \theta_i)} \right] dr = 0$$

This result shows that the relationship between the optimal uniform regional price and optimal region-specific prices is largely determined by the spatial distribution of demand.[15] If the spatial distribution of demand is such that, in market region i, the ratio $\hat{Q}_p(r, \theta_i)/\sum_i \hat{Q}_p(r, \theta_i)$ is equal to $\hat{Q}_p(0, \theta_i)/\sum_{i=1}^N \hat{Q}_p(0, \theta_i)$ for all r, then $P^* = P_i^{**}$. The ratio $\hat{Q}_p(r, \theta_i)/\sum_i \hat{Q}_p(r, \theta_i)$ measures the relative value of the charge in aggregate spatial demand in the outer reaches of the region i, (that is, the change in the shaded section of figure 8–2) to the change in the aggregate spatial demand in the outer ring, between r and R, of the entire market. Similarly, $\hat{Q}_P(0, \theta_i)/\sum_{i=1}^N \hat{Q}_P(0, \theta_i)$ is the ratio of the change in aggregate spatial demand in region i to the change in total spatial demand in all market areas.

Thus, the uniform price P^* may, depending on the demand distribution, be different from each of the optimal region-specific prices. The uniform price P^* is interpreted as a regionally averaged price because it is the weighted average—the weights are $\hat{Q}_P(0, \theta_i)/\hat{Q}_P(0)$—of the region-specific marginal cost of production and transmission, that is, the term in brackets in equation 8.7. Because P^* is regionally averaged, the uniform-price policy necessarily induces some interregional cross subsidies. The importance of proposition 1 is that it shows that such subsidies can occur even with constant-returns-to-scale cost functions. Elimination of these cross subsidies among different classes of customers would require pricing-structure and usage-measurement methods that are not feasible. Here, then, is a case where the elimination of cross subsidies would likely be more expensive than permitting their continued existence.

Another implication of the spatial model is that constant returns to scale do not necessarily guarantee financial viability of the firm as it does in a nonspatial environment.

Proposition 2:[16] If the production and transmission cost functions exhibit constant returns to scale, then the optimal uniform price yields profit.

$$\Pi^* = \sum_{i=1}^{N} \left\{ C_i(\cdot)' \left[\frac{\hat{E}(0, \theta_i)}{E(0)} - 1 \right] + \int_0^R c(\cdot)' \left[\frac{\hat{E}(r, \theta_i)}{\hat{E}(0)} - 1 \right] dr \right\}$$

and the optimal region-specific prices yield profit

$$\Pi^{**} = \sum_{i=1}^{N} \int_0^R c(\cdot) \left[\frac{\hat{E}(r, \theta_i)}{\hat{E}(0, \theta_i)} - 1 \right] dr$$

This result establishes that the use of uniform rates or region-specific rates is sufficient to ensure that the firm will break even at the welfare optimum. The logic of this result is rather clear. The different regional markets are differentiated by cost and demand conditions. Moreover, within a given regional market, the elasticity of demand depends on the distance from the generating plant. Thus, a uniform-price policy is not flexible enough to account for interregional and interlocational differences in the markets. The region-specific price policy is not flexible enough to account for interlocational differences. If the price policy were permitted to reflect these different market characteristics, that is, if the prices could differ across regional markets and depend on distance, then profit would, as shown by Schmalensee, equal zero. However, practical considerations suggest that this pricing policy is not feasible for electricity supply. The uniform-price policy is reminiscent of those currently in use. The region-specific price policy may be a reasonable alternative for reducing the inefficiencies associated with strictly uniform price policies.

The optimal region-specific prices yield zero profit if the elasticity of demand in each region is independent of distance from the generating plant, that is, $\partial \hat{E}(r, \theta_i)/\partial r = 0$ for all r and i. On the other hand, the region-specific prices yield positive (negative) profit if the elasticity of demand increases (decreases) with distance from the generating plant. If the elasticity of total demand in each regional market is identical, that is, if $\hat{E}(0, \theta_i) = \hat{E}(0, \theta_{i+1})$ for all i, then the rules cited above also determine the level of profit under the optimal uniform-price policy. However, since $\hat{E}(0, \theta_i)/\hat{E}(0) - 1$ enters the optimal profit function corresponding to a uniform-price policy, there is a wider range of conditions under which constant returns fail to imply zero profit.

There is no paradox in these results, even though the result differs from the usual nonspatial zero-profit implication of constant returns. The catch here is that the pricing policy, because of practical considerations, is not permitted to be flexible enough to reflect the effect of spatial location on

Spatial Considerations

marginal cost. If price were permitted to vary with distance, then the optimal region-specific price $P_i(r)$ would yield zero economic profit, the result obtained by Schmalensee. However, even if the uniform-price policy is location-dependent, as in $P(r)$, profits may be nonzero in the constant-returns case because of interregional averaging.

Extended-Area Local Service

In this section we address a problem which arises in the management and pricing of local telephone service. Traditionally, the telephone company has designated certain geographical areas as local-exchange areas. Within these local-exchange areas, usually contiguous areas of a city whose people have a strong community of interest, telephone service is often provided under flat-rate tariffs; customers pay a fixed monthly charge for calls within the local exchange. The fixed charge does not depend on the number of calls or on the duration of calls made by the individual subscriber. Calls made to individuals outside the local-exchange area—toll calls—are billed at a rate which depends on distance and duration. As populations have migrated from city to suburbs and as cities have grown in geographic area, there have been pleas for an expansion of some local-exchange calling areas. In this section we examine the economic factors which influence the social-welfare impact of extended-area service (EAS) implementation.

The analysis of this problem requires a slightly different spatial model than was used in the last section, because account must be taken of not only where demand originates but also its "destination." The demand for calls to a location x by a customer located at any point r is denoted by $q(\hat{P}, r, x)$, where the $\hat{P}$ is the price per unit of calls. The value of $\hat{P}$ is dictated by whether the call from r to x is local or toll. For a local call, the price $\hat{P}$ equals zero; for a toll call, we assume the price $\hat{P}$ equals P. Suppose $\mathcal{A}$ is the set of points located in exchange A and $\mathcal{B}$ is the set of points located in exchange B. The total demand[17] for intraexchange calls $q_A(P)$ and interexchange calls $Q_A(P)$ by subscribers located in exchange A is then

$$q_A(\hat{P}) = \int_{\mathcal{A}} \int_{\mathcal{A}} q(\hat{P}, r, x) \, dr \, dx$$

and

$$Q_A(\hat{P}) = \int_{\mathcal{B}} \int_{\mathcal{A}} q(\hat{P}, r, x) \, dr \, dx$$

Similarly, for subscribers in exchange B, the demands for intraexchange calls $q_B(\hat{P})$ and for interexchange calls $Q_B(\hat{P})$ are defined by

$$q_B(\hat{P}) = \int_B \int_B q(P, r, x)\, dr\, dx$$

and

$$Q_B(\hat{P}) = \int_A \int_B q(\hat{P}, r, x)\, dr\, dx$$

The question of interest is whether an enlargement of a local exchange is economically justified on the basis of cost/benefit criteria. Here the cost/benefit criterion is taken to be social welfare, the sum of consumers' surplus and profit. Thus we compare the social welfare yielded by serving intraexchange calls on a flat-rate basis and interexchange calls on a toll basis to the social welfare yielded when both exchanges constitute a single flat-rate calling area. The social welfare produced when interexchange calls are priced on a toll basis and intraexchange calls are on a flat-rate basis is

$$W^0 = \int_0^\infty [q_A(y) + q_B(y)]\, dy + \int_P^\infty [Q_A(y) + Q_B(y)]\, dy - \rho_A^0 N_A$$
$$- P_B^0 N_B + P_0[Q_A(P_0) + Q_B(P_0)] + \rho_A^0 N_A + \rho_B^0 N_B$$
$$- c_1[q_A(0) + q_B(0)] - c_2[Q_A(P_0) + Q_B(P_0)] - F^0 \qquad (8.10)$$

The first two terms measure the consumer surplus derived from local and toll usage. We asume that there are N_A and N_B subscribers, respectively, in exchanges A and B; thus consumers' surplus is reduced by the access charges $\rho_A^0 N_A + \rho_B^0 N_B$ incurred by the subscribers, where the access charges ρ_A and ρ_B may differ in the two exchanges. The firm's profits are determined by the toll revenue $P_0 Q(P_0)$, the revenue from access charges ρN, the total cost of serving local calls $c_1[q_A(0) + q_B(0)]$, the total cost of serving toll demand $c_2[Q_A(P_0) + Q_B(P_0)]$, and the level of fixed costs F^0. The marginal cost of a toll call c_2 includes the marginal cost of measurement and the marginal cost of transmitting the toll messages. The marginal cost of serving a local call is c_1. The cost of serving local and toll calls is assumed to exhibit constant returns to scale.

Several simplifying assumptions are implicit in this definition of social welfare derived from telephone usage. First, the number of subscribers is assumed to be fixed and independent of any prices. The price changes being contemplated here might result in an increase in the number of subscribers; however, this effect is likely to be small. Moreover, we do not incorporate the fact that the consumer surplus derived by a subscriber may depend on the

Spatial Considerations

total number of subscribers in the two exchanges. This network externality is expected to be small relative to the surplus effects of a transition from toll pricing to EAS; thus its exclusion is not likely to adversely bias the conclusions. The frequency and duration components of toll demand are aggregated into a single usage measure Q. Finally, the practive of basing toll charges on the distance called is not explicitly taken into account.

There are two alternative methods for implementation of extended-area service between exchanges A and B. The first method, called one-way EAS, permits the customers in local exchange A to make calls to exchange B on a flat-rate basis, while exchange B must continue to make calls to exchange A on a toll basis. The second method, called two-way EAS, is to enlarge local exchange A as above, but to also permit customers in the extended area (exchange B) to make calls to local exchange A on a flat-rate basis. Under both one-way EAS and two-way EAS, calls originating in exchange A which terminate in exchange B are local calls. Calls that originate in exchange B are all defined to be local calls under two-way EAS; but under one-way EAS, calls that terminate in exchange B are local while calls that terminate in exchange A are toll. Thus, the calls $Q_A(\hat{P})$ become local calls under both one-way and two-way EAS. The calls $Q_B(\hat{P})$ are toll calls under one-way EAS and are local calls under two-way EAS.

The social welfare which results from an expansin of the local calling area of exchange A via one-way EAS is then

$$W^1 = \int_0^\infty [q_A(y) + q_B(y) + Q_A(y)]\,dy + \int_{P_1}^\infty Q_B(y)\,dy - \rho_A^1 N_A$$
$$- P_B^1 N_B + P_1 Q_B(P_1) + \rho_A^1 N_A + P_B^1 N_B - c_1[q_A(0) + q_B(0)$$
$$+ Q_A(0)] - c_2 Q_B(P_1) - F_1 \tag{8.11}$$

Similarly, the social welfare which results from an expansion of the local calling area of exchange A via two-way EAS is

$$W^2 = \int_0^\infty [q_A(y) + q_B(y) + Q_A(y) + Q_B(y)]\,dy - \rho_A^2 N_A - \rho_B^2 N_B$$
$$+ \rho_A^2 N_A + \rho_B^2 N_B - c_1[q_A(0) + q_B(0) + Q_A(0) + Q_B(0)]\,F_2 \tag{8.12}$$

These calculations simply reflect the reclassification of interexchange calls from toll calls to local calls. Here, both the access prices and the toll price may be adjusted when EAS is implemented. As a practical matter, the toll price is not usually changed when a local calling area is expanded. The fixed costs may also change when EAS is implemented and may depend on the type of EAS being considered.

The social-welfare differentials associated with a transition from toll pricing to one-way and two-way EAS, respectively, are then

$$W^1 - W^0 = \int_0^{P_1} Q_A(y)\,dy + \int_{P_1}^{P_0} Q_B(y)\,dy + P_1 Q_B(P_1)$$
$$- P_0[Q_A(P_0) + Q_B(P_0)] + c_2[Q_A(P_0) + Q_B(P_0)$$
$$- Q_B(P_1)] - c_1 Q_A(0) - (F_1 - F_0) \tag{8.13}$$

and

$$W^2 - W^0 = \int_0^{P_0} [Q_A(y) + Q_B(y)]\,dy - P_0[Q_A(P_0) + Q_B(P_0)]$$
$$+ c_2[Q_A(P_0) + Q_B(P_0)] - c_1[Q_A(0) + Q_B(0)] - (F_2 - F_0) \tag{8.14}$$

The welfare differential resulting from implementation of two-way EAS equals (1) the consumer-surplus gain from the reduction of toll prices to zero minus (2) the lost toll revenue plus (3) the savings in measurement and traffic-related costs minus (4) any increase in fixed costs. The consumer-surplus gain from EAS implementation is given by the first term in equation 8.14. The second, third, and fourth terms in equation 8.14 are described by the correspondingly numbered items above; these terms measure the change in profit that results for EAS implementation.[18] This interpretation of the factors affecting the change in welfare also applies to one-way EAS if toll prices remain fixed, that is, if $P_0 = P_1$, in equation 8.13. The additional terms in equation 8.13 measure the impact of toll-price adjustments that may accompany one-way EAS implementation. In most practical applications, toll prices will not be adjusted when one-way EAS is implemented; thus we focus the subsequent discussion on the two-way EAS case.

Note that the welfare differential $W^2 - W^0$ measures the net welfare benefit of a transition from the current toll price to two-way EAS. If current toll prices are not welfare-optimal, this calculation may be viewed as gauging the combined effects of (1) adjustment of current toll price toward the welfare-optimal toll price and (2) transition from optimal toll prices to two-way EAS. Clearly, if the current toll price is above marginal cost, that is, if $P^0 > c_2$, then the first adjustment will increase welfare.[19] Indeed, the welfare differential $W^2 - W^0$ is smallest when the toll price is welfare-optimal. On the other hand, the transition from optimal toll prices to two-way EAS may either increase or decrease welfare.

The net benefit of EAS implementation is also decreased if measurement costs are relatively small. In particular, the welfare differential $W^2 - W^0$

Spatial Considerations

decreases as the gap between the marginal cost of toll calls and the marginal cost of local calls decreases; the difference between c_2 and c_1 is, by definition, equal to the marginal measurement cost.[20] Moreover, if a transition to EAS significantly increases fixed costs, then net welfare will be diminished.

These points are made more explicit by considering the magnitude of $W^2 - W^0$ in the special case of linear demand. If the demand for interexchange calls is described by a linear-demand curve, then

$$\int_0^{P_0} Q(y)\, dy = P_0 Q(P_0) + \frac{P_0}{2}[Q(0) - Q(P_0)] \qquad (8.15)$$

and

$$Q(0) = Q(P_0)[1 - E(P_0)] \qquad (8.16)$$

where $E(P_0) = [P_0/Q(P_0)][\partial Q(P_0)/\partial P_0]$. Consequently, the welfare differential in equation 8.14 is given by

$$W^2 - W^0 = Q(P_0)[c_2 - c_1 + (c_1 - P_0/2)E(P_0)] - (F_2 - F_0)$$

where $Q(P_0) = Q_A(P_0) + Q_B(P_0)$.

It is clear from this formula that whether the transition from welfare-optimal toll pricing, where $P_0 = c_2$, to EAS decreases welfare depends on the relative magnitude of c_1, c_2, and elasticity of toll demand $E(P_0)$. An interesting insight is that even if there are no measurement costs, that is, if $c_2 = c_1$, then a transition to EAS will increase welfare if the toll price is significantly above the marginal cost of toll calling. Implementation of EAS would decrease welfare if there were no measurement costs and if the toll price were welfare-optimal.[21] As a general principle, we can then say that EAS should not be a favored policy alternative if measurement costs are relatively small and if toll prices are near the welfare optimum.

In the simple linear-demand case, toll pricing is preferable to EAS if

$$(c_2 - c_1) + (c_1 - P_0/2)E(P_0) < (F_2 - F_0)/Q(P_0)$$

that is, if the savings in measurement cost $c_2 - c_1$ plus the net change in usage costs $(c_1 - P_0/2)E(P_0)$ is less than the increase in fixed cost per unit demand. If there is no change in fixed cost, that is, if $F_2 = F_1$, then this rule states that toll pricing is preferable if the saving in usage costs is at least *twice* the costs of measurement.[22] However, this rule is only approximate when subject to the caveats mentioned in the next section.

Although the linear-demand case is useful for illustrative purposes, it has serious limitations in applications. From the existing studies on toll demand

and the demand effects of conversion from flat rate to measured service, it appears that linear-demand curves are inadequate for characterizing the behavior of toll demand over the range of prices considered here. It is reasonable to expect that the marginal utility value of an additional call decreases significantly as the toll price approaches zero. This suggests that the true demand curve is likely to be convex. Moreover, a linear-demand curve is not consistent with the observed data on toll demand and usage under EAS.[23] In particular, the elasticity of short-haul toll is on the order of $-.10$ to -1.7 [see Taylor (1979). However, the estimates of usage under EAS range as high as 10 times the usage under toll. Clearly, a linear-demand specification cannot be made consistent with these data. Moreover, from the observed data on toll demand, that is, current toll usage $Q(P_0)$, usage under EAS $Q(0)$, and the elasticity of toll demand at the current price $E(P_0)$, it is not possible to infer exactly the shape of the demand curve, especially since there has been no experience with toll prices that are in the range $(c_2, 0)$.

Consequently, it is difficult to use the cost/benefit methodology to obtain empirical estimates of the welfare impact of EAS. The data exist, however, to produce rather precise estimates of the profits differential $\Delta\pi$ that would result from EAS implementation. The primary data needed to calculate $\Delta\pi$ include current toll usage, usage under EAS, marginal cost of toll calls, marginal cost of local calls, and the current toll price. As we have indicated, the impact of EAS conversions on consumer surplus depends crucially on the shape of the demand curve, which is assumed to be convex. It is therefore useful to employ the known demand data, that is, P_0, $\hat{Q}(P_0)$, $\hat{Q}(0)$, and $\hat{E}(P_0)$, to construct bounds on the change in consumer surplus. First we construct a linear-demand curve which goes through the observed toll-usage level under EAS; this linear demand is denoted by the dashed line labeled M_1 in figure 8-3. Clearly, the line M_1 represents a usage under EAS equal to $\hat{Q}(0)$; however, the slope of M_1 at the current toll price may be higher than the observed slope given M_2. Thus, calculation using M_1 will give an upper bound on the change in consumer surplus, because the actual demand curve must be between the dashed line M_1 and the solid line M_2. Thus it is determined by this method that

$$\Delta cs \leq \frac{P_0}{2} [\hat{Q}(P_0) + \hat{Q}(0)] \qquad (8.17)$$

which is derived from equation 8.15. The second method involves using the solid line M_2 to calculate the change in consumer surplus. Note that line M_2 has an elasticity of demand which is consistent with the observed toll elasticity, but this curve implies a demand under EAS which is less than the observed or forecasted level. The actual demand curve is therefore tangent to M_2 at the current toll price P_0, and nowhere does it lie below M_2. Consequently, use of M_2 in calculating the change in consumer surplus will

Spatial Considerations

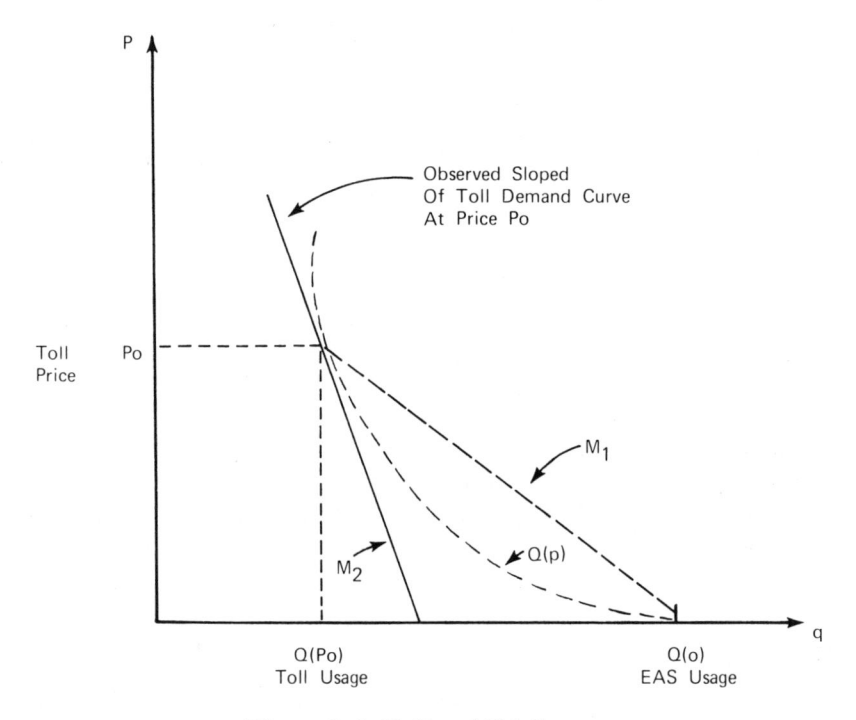

Figure 8-3 Toll and EAS usage

give an underestimate of the actual change. The change in consumer surplus is given by equation 8.15. Equation 8.16 then implies that

$$\Delta cs \geq P_0 \hat{Q}(P_0) \, [1 - \hat{E}(P_0)/2] \qquad (8.18)$$

Hence, the impact of EAS on consumer surplus is partially characterized by proposition 3:

Proposition 3:[24] If the aggregate demand curve is convex, implementation of two-way EAS between two exchanges will result in a change in consumer surplus which is no greater than $P_0/2[\hat{Q}(P_0) + \hat{Q}(0)]$ and is no less than $P_0 \hat{Q}(P_0)[1 - \hat{E}(P_0)/2]$. The difference between the upper and lower bounds on Δcs approaches zero as $[1 - \hat{Q}(P_0)]$ approaches $Q(0)/Q(P_0)$.

Therefore, these bounds on Δcs give a range within which the actual change in consumer surplus must fall. As $1 - E(P_0)$ more closely approximates $\hat{Q}(0)/\hat{Q}(P_0)$, these bounds give an increasingly precise gauge of the actual change in consumer surplus. The corresponding bounds on the change in welfare are

$$W^2 - W^0 < \left(c_2 - \frac{P_0}{2}\right)\hat{Q}(P_0) - \left(c_1 - \frac{P_0}{2}\right)\hat{Q}(0) - (F_2 - F_0)$$

and

$$W^2 - W^0 > \left[c_2 - c_1 + \left(c_1 - \frac{P_0}{2}\right)\hat{E}(P_0)\right]\hat{Q}(P_0) - (F_2 - F_0)$$

A final point is that these computations presume that conversion from toll pricing to EAS would be mandatory for all customers. It is therefore conceivable that this mandatory EAS could increase aggregate welfare, while the net benefit derived by specific groups of customers could be negative. These difficulties may be avoided if EAS and toll tariffs are offered as optional tariffs for calling between the two exchanges.[25] Moreover, if such a set of optional tariffs were offered, all consumers could be better off. However, it is not clear what the cost of implementing such a set of optional tariffs would be.

Conclusions

In this chapter, principles from spatial-economic theory have been used to gain insight regarding two public-utility pricing questions. The results show that in the case of electricity pricing, new insight is gained by taking explicit account of the spatial distribution of demand. The traditional nonspatial results that link profitability to the returns-to-scale properties of the cost function need not hold in a spatial model. For example, we have shown that welfare-optimal profits will be positive, even with constant returns to scale, if the elasticity of demand increases with distance from the generating site. Moreover, we have shown that a pricing policy which requires implicit averaging of cost leads to cross subsidies. Hence some customers end up paying more, and others less, than would be dictated by the marginal-cost pricing principle.

The section dealing with extended-area telephone service shows that EAS is not generally justified by cost/benefit criteria. However, two-way EAS can improve welfare in some limited circumstances. The cost/benefit test derived for making such judgments depends crucially on the shape of the toll demand curve. Since the demand curve is not known over the range of prices associated with an EAS conversion, we derived bounds on the change in consumer surplus and social welfare. These bounds can be evaluated by using observable data on toll and EAS usage. Moreover, the bounds are quite accurate gauges on the change in social welfare if the ratio of usage under

Spatial Considerations

EAS to current toll usage is approximately equal to 1 minus the current elasticity of toll demand.

These results are based on an analysis of mandatory EAS, between given exchanges, and it is therefore a partial-equilibrium-type analysis. A subject for future research is the extension of these basic welfare comparisons to include optional local and toll tariffs and both local and interstate services. Finally, this future research should explicitly take account of the dependence of toll tariffs on the distance called.

Notes

1. A comprehensive review of this literature is contained in Greenhut and Ohta (1975).

2. The extensive literature on peak-load pricing is surveyed in Crew and Kleindorfer (1979c).

3. See, for example, Panzar and Faulhaber (1977) and Baumol and Bradford (1970).

4. See Crew and Kleindorfer (1979c) for a discussion of peak-load pricing. A paper by Berkowitz (1977) examines the impact of transmission costs on power-grid structure; however, his formulation assumes that transmission costs depend linearly on the level of the load. Schmalensee (1978) is the first to take account of the dependence of transmission costs on demand density.

5. Zoning restrictions and consumer protests are among the factors which limit site selection.

6. The sensitivity of optimal capacity investment and prices to plant and transmission-line location could be investigated to determine the effects of these assumptions.

7. Note that the distribution of the population $h(r, \theta, \alpha)$ is defined relative to the location of the generating plant.

8. Because of transmission losses, the total amount of electricity produced by the utility must exceed the aggregate demands if these demands are all to be satisfied. Thus, since the cost of function C is defined as the cost of satisfying the demands $Q(r, \theta_i)$, it implicitly takes account of the "additional" production due to line losses.

9. See Panzar (1976) for a similar characterization of production-capacity cost.

10. Hence there is no need to make the assumption that total supply is limited to production capacity rather than transmission capacity.

11. This is derived by taking the partial derivative of W, in equation 8.6, with respect to the uniform price P and setting it equal to zero.

12. To the extent that interlocation cross subsidies exist, they are analogous to the price effects of nationwide average pricing in telecommunications. A similar interlocational subsidy may result from the averaging across distance bands, implicit in equation 8.7.

13. The optimal region-specific prices are derived from equation 8.6 after consumer surplus and revenue are written in their region-specific forms.

14. Proof of proposition 1: Suppose the marginal cost C_i is constant and identical for all i (for example, $C_i = C_0 V_i$) and the marginal cost C_{N+1} is constant. Then by the definition of F_{0i}

$$C_i^{**} - \sum_{i=1}^{N} C_i^* \hat{F}_{0i} = C_0 \left(1 - \sum_{i=1}^{N} \hat{F}_{0i}\right) = 0$$

Moreover, with constant returns $C_{N+1}^{**} = C_N^*$. If in addition $\partial^2 c / \partial \hat{Q}^2 = 0$, that is, there is constant marginal transmission cost, then the price differential equation 8.9 becomes

$$P_i^{**} - P^* = \int_0^R \frac{\partial C}{\partial \hat{Q}} \left[(\hat{F}_{ri}/\hat{F}_{01})^{**} - \sum_i^N \hat{F}_{ri}^* \right] dr$$

By noting $\hat{Q}_P(0) = \Sigma_i \hat{Q}_P(0, \theta_i)$ and recalling the definition of $\hat{F}_{ri}$, the result in proposition I follows.

15. The demand distribution $h(r, \theta, \alpha) = e^{\delta r} h(\alpha)$, for example, implies that $P^* = P_i^{**}$. In this example, the demand distribution is the same along each ray from the plant site.

16. The proof of proposition 2 derives directly from equations 8.7 and 8.8 by noting that constant returns imply that $\Sigma_i C_i \hat{Q}(0, \theta_i) + C_{N+1} Q(0) = C(\hat{Q}(0, \theta_i), \ldots, \hat{Q}(0, \theta_n), \hat{Q}(0))$ and $(\partial c / \partial \hat{Q}) \hat{Q}(r, \theta_i) = c(r, \hat{Q}(r, \theta_i))$. By definition, $\hat{Q}(0, \theta_i)(\hat{F}_{ri}/\hat{F}_{0i}) = [\tilde{\xi}(r, \theta_i)/\tilde{\xi}(0, \theta_i)] \hat{Q} \cdot (r, \theta_i)$. Thus, the calculation revenue minus total cost yields the cited result.

17. Thus we do not take explicit account of the distance component of toll charges, nor do we include explicit charges for duration or number of calls.

18. Note the symmetry between this rule for judging the net benefits of EAS and the benefits associated with measured-service implementation discussed in Mitchell (1976).

19. Note that $\partial(W^2 - W^0)/\partial P_0 = (P_0 - c_2)[\partial Q(P_0)/\partial P_0]$ which is positive if $P_0 > c_2$.

20. Since $\partial(W^2 - W^0)/\partial c_2 = Q_A(P_0) + Q_B(P_0) > 0$, the cited result follows.

21. If $c_2 = c_1$, then $c_1 > c_2/2$ and hence $W^2 - W^0$ is negative.

22. See Mitchell (1979) for a similar simple rule concerning the benefits of measured service.

Spatial Considerations

23. For a discussion of toll demand studies, see Taylor (1978). The demand effects associated with conversions from flat rate to measured service are discussed in Pavarini (1978).

24. The upper and lower bounds are established in equations 8.17 and 8.18. From these bounds it follows that

$$1 - E(P_0) \leq \frac{2 \Delta cs}{P_0 \hat{Q}(P_0)} - 1 \leq \frac{\hat{Q}(0)}{\hat{Q}(P_0)}$$

25. It is shown in Panzar and Faulhaber (1977) that the aggregate welfare produced by provision of a service increases monotonically as the number of optional tariffs for the service increases. The optional EAS and toll tariffs would offer the customer a choice among both rate schedules *and* the geographic region to which the schedules apply. Thus, optional EAS and toll pricing would present greater opportunity for self-selection than the options discussed in Panzar and Faulhaber (1977) and consequently should further increase welfare.

9

Implementing Time-of-Day Pricing of Electricity: Some Current Challenges and Activities

J. Robert Malko and
Ahmad Faruqui

Introduction

During the 1970s, the costs of providing electricity and customers' bills rose significantly because of general inflation, the energy dilemma, increases in system peak demand, rising fuel costs, and difficulties in obtaining financial capital.[1] In response to the problem of rising costs of providing electricity service, there have been increased efforts in the United States to change traditional electricity-pricing structures and to modify electricity-usage patterns.[2]

Since the conclusion of an important and forward-looking Madison Gas and Electric Company case in August 1974, several state regulatory commissions, utilities, and intervenors have been analyzing the desirability and feasibility of implementing time-of-day (TOD) pricing of electricity, and some state regulatory commissions have directed electric utilities to implement TOD tariffs.[3] In addition, each state rgulatory commission must consider and make a determination by November 1981 concerning the electricity rate-making standard of TOD rates in order to comply with the Public Utility Regulatory Policies Act (PURPA) of 1978.[4]

This chapter is organized into the following three major sections with associated objectives. First, a brief review of PURPA, which is part of the National Energy Act (NEA) of November 1978, is presented, and pro-

---

Dr. Faruqui is a project manager in the demand and conservation program of the Electric Power Research Institute. The views expressed here are those of the authors and do not necessarily represent the views of the Electric Power Research Institute. The authors wish to express their appreciation to the following who contributed to the preparation of this chapter: Robert E. Ashburn, of Long Island Lighting Company; John Asmus, of San Diego Gas and Electric Company; Haso C. Bhatia, of the Michigan Public Service Commission; Jennifer Fagan, of the Wisconsin Public Service Commission; Leo E. Gargin and Warren Farguson, of the Southern California Edison Company; Ronald J. Liberty and Maureen Frechette, of the New York Public Service Commission; Stephen P. Reynolds, of the Pacific Gas and Electric Company; Jackalyne P. Pfannanstiel of the California Public Utilities Commission; John L. Walker, of the Wisconsin Power and Light Company; Alfred J. Roberts and Dennis Whitney, of the Los Angeles Department of Water and Power. The authors, of course, assume responsibility for the contents of this chapter.

visions concerning time-of-day pricing are emphasized. Second, a framework for considering and implementing cost-based TOD rates is proposed and examined. Issues concerning price elasticity and load-shape modifications are emphasized in this section. Third, some actual TOD-pricing implementation activities for industrial, commercial, and residential customers in California, Michigan, New York, Virginia, and Wisconsin are discussed.

Public Utility Regulatory Policies Act of 1978

This section review the major features and provisions of NEA and discusses the electricity rate-making standards specified by PURPA.

Basic Features

After approximately eighteen months of debate and deliberation, NEA was passed by the U.S. Congress in October 1978 and became law on November 9, 1978.[5] At the signing of this energy legislation, President Carter stated: "Today we can rightfully claim that we have a conscious national policy for dealing with the energy problems of the present and also to help us deal with them in the future."[6]

The NEA has five major parts: (1) the National Energy Conservation Policy Act of 1978, (2) the Powerplant and Industrial Fuel Use Act of 1978, (3) the Public Utility Regulatory Policies Act of 1978, (4) the Natural Gas Policy Act of 1978, and (5) the Energy Tax Act of 1978.

Major PURPA provisions pertain to (1) rate-making standards for electric-utility rate structures, (2) cogeneration, (3) wholesale rates, (4) aid to the states and consumer representation, (5) gas utilities, (6) small hydroelectric facilities, and (7) crude-oil transportation systems. In addition, PURPA contains significant miscellaneous provisions relating to the authorization of funding for the National Regulatory Research Institute and clarification of natural-gas transportation policies.

Electricity Rate-Making Standards

In order to attempt to partially solve the problem of rising costs of providing electricity during the 1970s, Congress decided that retail electricity rates should be structured to encourage the following objectives: (1) conservation of energy supplied, (2) efficient use of facilities and resources, and (3) equitable rates to consumers.[7]

Now, PURPA specifies that each state regulatory commission should

Time-of-Day Pricing of Electricity 147

consider and make a *determination* concerning the appropriateness, relative to the above three purposes and applicable state law, of implementing the following *six rate-making standards*: (1) cost of service, (2) declining block rates, (3) TOD rates, (4) seasonal rates, (5) interruptible rates, and (6) load-management techniques.[8] Also PURPA defines special or additional rules for considering and making a determination concerning the following rate-making standards: cost of service, TOD rates, and load-management techniques.[9]

This chapter concentrates on the rate-making standard of TOD pricing of electricity in order to provide assistance to regulatory agencies, electric utilities, and other groups that are analyzing the desirability and feasibility of implementing TOD rate structures. With respect to the PURPA provisions relating to TOD pricing of electricity, the features of reflecting costs of providing service and cost-effectiveness considerations are emphasized in the legislation for each customer class.

By November 1980 (two years after enactment of PURPA), each state regulatory commission must start the *consideration* process or establish a hearing date for the consideration of TOD rates and the other rate-making standards with respect to each electric utility for which it has rate-making authority *and* to which PURPA applies.[10] By November 1981 (three years after enactment of PURPA), each state regulatory commission must finish the consideration process and make a determination concerning the appropriateness of implementing time-of-day rate structures and the other rate-making standards.[11] Large nonregulated utilities must follow a similar procedure. In summary, the decision concerning the appropriateness of implementing TOD tariffs is the responsibility of each state regulatory body based on state law, as supplemented by specific provisions of PURPA.

Framework for Considering and Implementing Cost-Based TOD Rate Structures

Load management of electricity usage, including direct (mechanical) controls on end-use equipment and time-differentiated tariffs, represents a partial solution to the problem of rising electricity costs. Load management has the dual objectives of reducing growth in peak demand, thereby reducing the requirement for capacity expansion, and shifting a portion of the load from inefficient peaking units to more efficient base-load plants, thereby obtaining some savings in gas and oil peaking fuels. By moward toward achieving these objectives, electric utilities can decrease operating and capacity costs, reduce the rate of increase of consumer bills, and provide a partial solution to the national energy dilemma.

Time-differentiated pricing of electricity is an indirect form of load management that prices electricity to reflect differences in the cost of providing service by time of day and season of year. Time-of-day pricing reflects or tracks costs in a more accurate manner than do traditional block-rate structures; TOD pricing logically follows from marginal- or incremental-cost pricing theory, but is compatible with embedded (historical average accounting) cost of service.

Time-of-day pricing offers more potential for improving system-load factors than do traditional block rates. By providing a cost-based price signal that will motivate customers to modify usage patterns, the implementation of TOD rates can reduce growth in system-peak demand and shift load from peak to off-peak periods. A cost/benefit analysis is required to determine how effective and efficient TOD pricing will be.

This section of the chapter proposes a general framework for considering and implementing cost-based TOD rates and analyzes the roles that estimation of price elasticities and load-shape modifications play in that framework.

General Framework

The experience of regulatory commissions and utilities which have already implemented time-differentiated tariffs for electricity provides useful information for formulating a general framework to consider and implement cost-based time-of-use prices. The proposed framework consists of the following activities and steps: load research, rate design, cost/benefit analysis, information flow with customers, actual application, and reporting and analysis of results (actual experience).[12] Figures 9–1 and 9–2 illustrate these activities and steps and their interrelationships. Figure 9–3 presents the following: a definition of the problem—increasing electricity costs; a proposal for a partial solution—load-management alternatives (TOD rates and direct load controls); and a description of various consideration or implementation activities with emphasis on rate-design and cost-benefits issues. And PURPA explicitly addresses some of these consideration and implementation activities, specifically load research, rate design, and cost/benefit analysis.

Elasticities and Load-Shape Modifications

Elasticity measures provide an important input into the cost/benefit analysis of TOD rates. They help quantify the load-shape modifications introduced by the time-differentiated rates. As such, they are helpful in assessing the financial benefits of TOD rates: reduced capacity needs, improvements in system-reliability levels, and, possibly, energy conservation. Elasticity

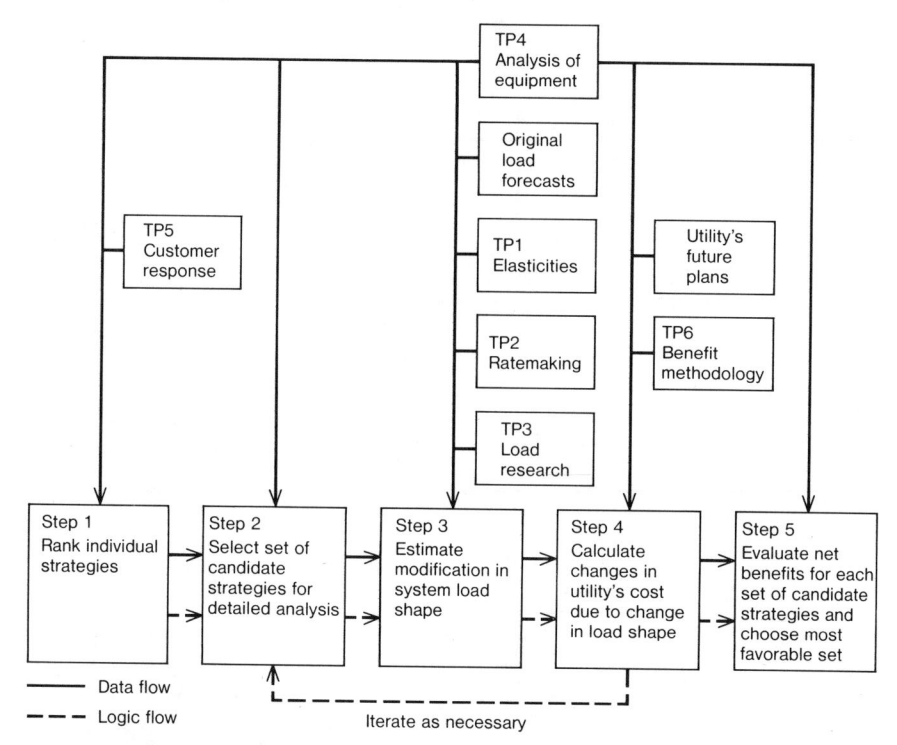

Figure 9-1 Five-Step Procedure for Evaluation of Load-Management Strategies

Source: Electric Utility Rate Design Study *Equipment for Load Management: Communication, Metering, and Equipment for Using Off-Peak Energy.* Topic Paper 4, October 1979. Electric Power Research Institute, Palo Alto, California.

Note: TP indicates topic papers of the Electric Utility Rate Design Study.

measures have other uses; among them are allocation of system revenues by customer class and assessment of the aggregate-revenue impact of TOD rates.

In spite of these obvious benefits, the potential usefulness of elasticity measures continues to be surrounded by controversy. The extent of this controversy can be well gauged from the following contrasting and conflicting viewpoints:

> Through the influence of Alfred Marshall economists have developed a fondness for certain dimensionless expressions called elasticity coefficients. On the whole, it appears that their importance is not very great except possibly as mental exercises for beginning students.... Not only are elasticity expressions more or less useless, but in more complicated systems they become an actual nuisance.[13]

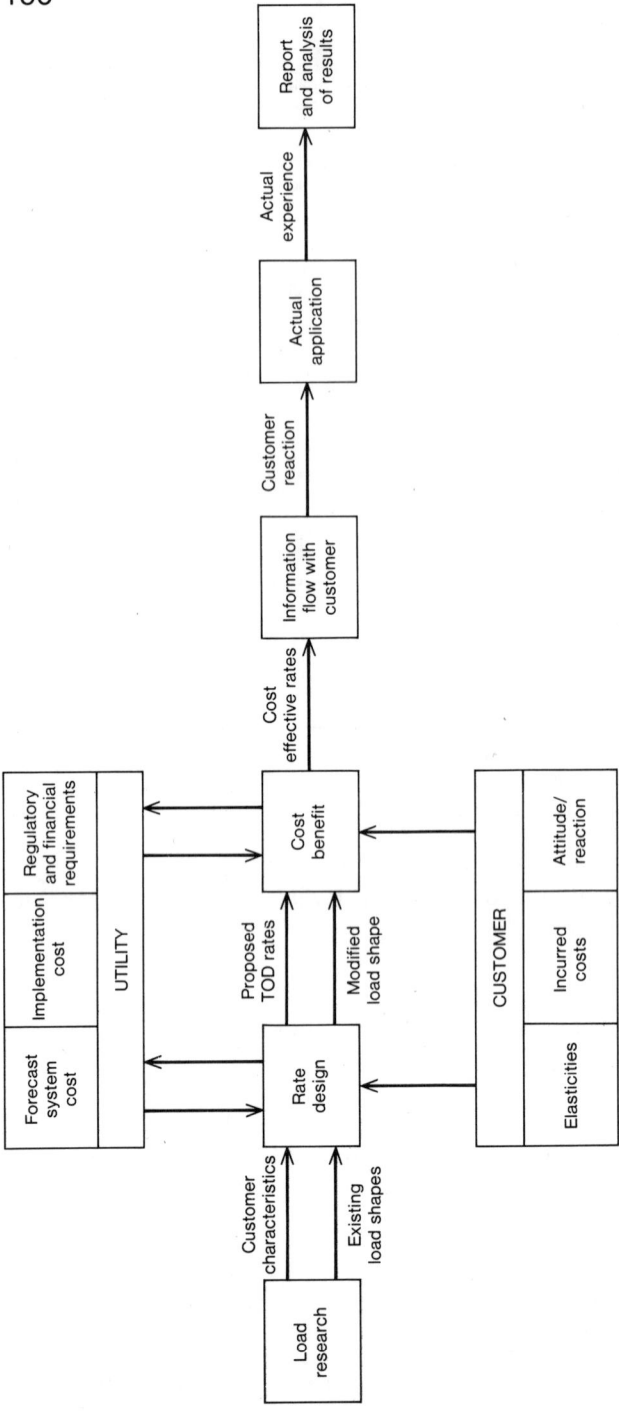

Source: J. Robert Malko, Dennis J. Ray, and Nancy L. Hassig, "Time-of-Day Pricing of Electricity in Some Midwestern States," presented at the Midwest Economic Association Annual Meeting, Chicago, Illinois, April 1979.

Figure 9-2 Activities for Consideration and Implementation of Time-of-Day Pricing

Time-of-Day Pricing of Electricity 151

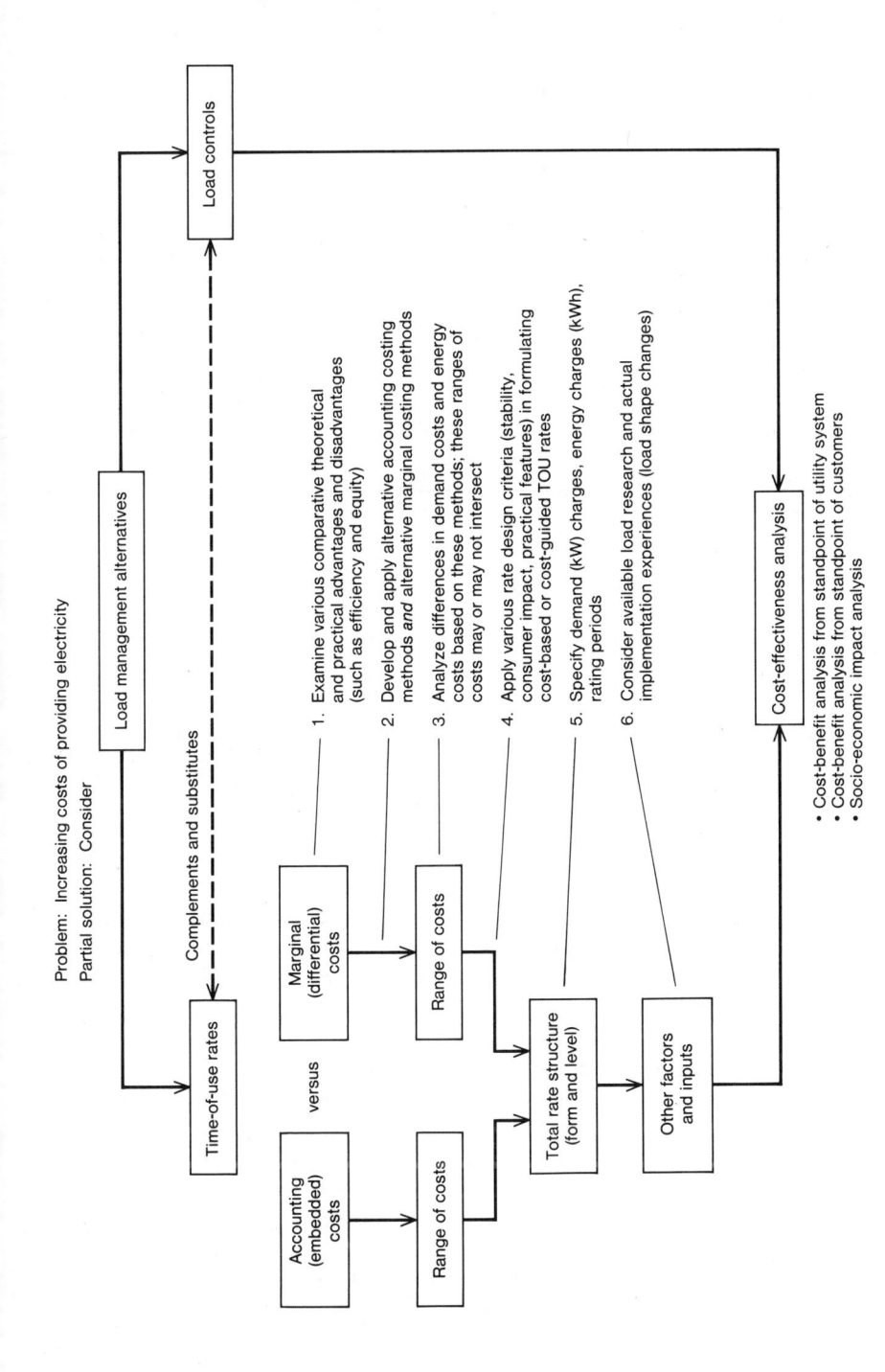

Problem: Increasing costs of providing electricity
Partial solution: Consider

1. Examine various comparative theoretical and practical advantages and disadvantages (such as efficiency and equity)
2. Develop and apply alternative accounting costing methods *and* alternative marginal costing methods
3. Analyze differences in demand costs and energy costs based on these methods; these ranges of costs may or may not intersect
4. Apply various rate design criteria (stability, consumer impact, practical features) in formulating cost-based or cost-guided TOU rates
5. Specify demand (kW) charges, energy charges (kWh), rating periods
6. Consider available load research and actual implementation experiences (load shape changes)

- Cost-benefit analysis from standpoint of utility system
- Cost-benefit analysis from standpoint of customers
- Socio-economic impact analysis

Figure 9–3 Some Activities for Considering Load-Management Alternatives

...elasticities are *the* most important quantities in modern microeconomic analysis.... Price (own- and cross-price) elasticities, income elasticities, *compensated* elasticities and *uncompensated* elasticities are all phrases that now form part of the jargon used by analysts of the TOD experiments.[14]

This section discusses the usefulness of elasticity measures in predicting load-shape modifications. First, an outline of an economic model of the load shape is developed. Second, the extent to which elasticities can be used to approximate results obtainable from this model is examined. Third, some of the recent evidence on elasticity magnitudes is presented. Finally, concluding comments are made concerning the proper role of elasticities in assessing the cost-effectiveness of TOD rates.

System planners at an individual utility decide on the optimal mix of base load, intermediate-load, and peak-load capacities for generating electricity based on the customer demand conditions in their service area. A convenient tool for summarizing these demand conditions is the annual load-duration curve. This curve plots minimum capacity levels against the duration periods for which they are needed throughout the year.

Figure 9–4 illustrates the impact of TOD rates on the annual load-duration curve for a hypothetical system. Here TOD rates are predicted to reduce the need for peak-load capacity (by $kW_1 - kW'_1$) and increase the needs for intermediate-load (by $kW_2 - kW'_2$) and base-load (by $kW_3 - kW'_3$) capacities.

The question naturally arises as to how the impact of TOD rates on the annual load-duration curve is to be quantified. One way of handling this question is to analyze the impact of TOD rates on daily-load curves and to then "build up" the modified *annual* load-duration curve from the modified *daily*-load curves.

System load is plotted against hour of occurrence in a daily-load curve. Since the system load at any hour is an aggregate of the individual loads of a diverse group of customers, it is analytically advantageous to decompose the system-load curve into a set of customer-class load curves. The impact of TOD rates on these customer-class load curves can then be analyzed with reference to, for example, three pricing periods.

Figure 9–5 illustrates the impact of TOD rates on the daily residential-load curves for a hypothetical system. For simplicity, the curves are represented as step functions. Time-of-day rates shift load away from the peak period to the intermediate and base periods. These shifts in load can be characterized in terms of a simple demand model in which individual residential customers regard the electricity consumed in the three pricing periods as three different, but substitutable, commodities. Each period's electricity demand can be expressed in terms of electricity prices in the three periods, customer's income level, energy composition of the appliance stock, lifestyle of the customer's household, and so on.

Time-of-Day Pricing of Electricity

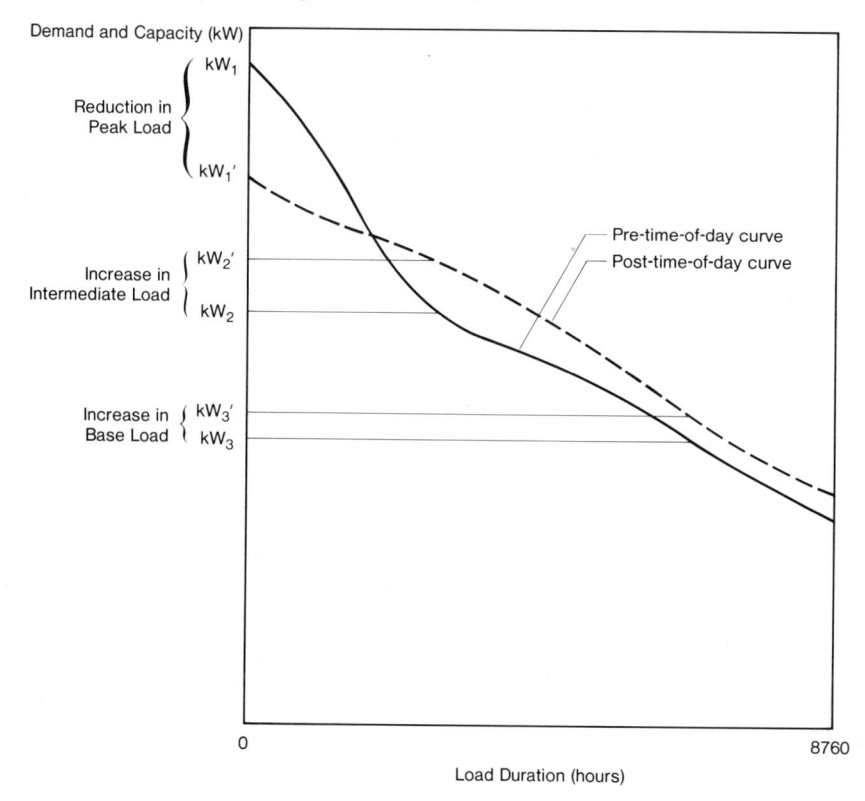

[Figure: Load-duration curve with y-axis "Demand and Capacity (kW)" showing labels kW₁, kW₁' (Reduction in Peak Load), kW₂', kW₂ (Increase in Intermediate Load), kW₃', kW₃ (Increase in Base Load); x-axis "Load Duration (hours)" from 0 to 8760; two curves labeled "Pre-time-of-day curve" (solid) and "Post-time-of-day curve" (dashed)]

Figure 9–4 Impact of Time-of-Day Pricing on a Hypothetical Annual Load-Duration Curve

The impact of TOD rates on electricity consumed in the three pricing periods can be analyzed in terms of point estimates of the own-price elasticity of demand in the three periods. However, except under highly restrictive assumptions on the type of TOD rates and the nature of customer preferences, such an analysis can be quite misleading. A transition from non-TOD rates to TOD rates involves, in general, a variation in electricity prices in all three pricing periods. The impact on base-period demand cannot be inferred accurately from a knowledge of the own-price elasticity of base demand alone, because this is a *ceteris paribus* parameter. Also required is a knowledge of the relevant cross-price elasticities. However, knowledge of price-elasticity measures, both own and cross, is still insufficient for generating demand predictions, since the impact of TOD rates on base demand will generally be conditioned by the levels of nonprice variables. A high income level will reduce the need to respond to price variations, and a low income level will augment that need. An all-electric household will exhibit a

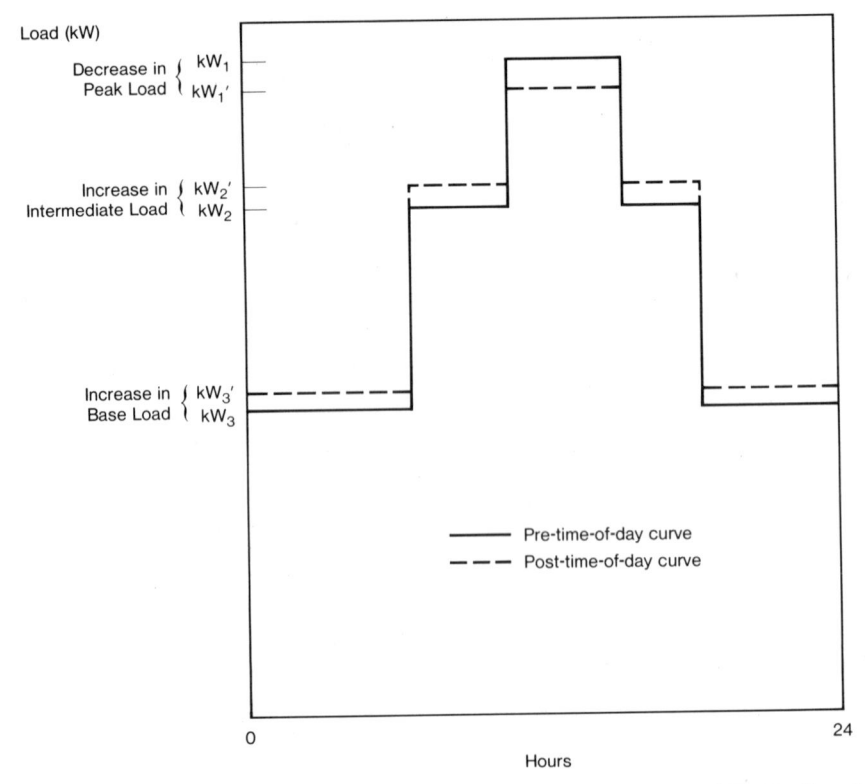

Figure 9-5 Impact of Time-of-Day Pricing on a Hypothetical Daily-Load Curve

greater response than a household which runs mostly on oil, gas, and coal. Finally, a household where all members are present at home during peak hours will be less able to respond than one in which most members are absent.

It follows that a summary statistic such as the own-price elasticity of demand will generate misleading predictions of the impact of TOD rates on daily-load shapes, unless it is supplemented by data on cross elasticities with respect to electricity prices in other periods, income, appliance composition, and demographic variables. In addition, data will be needed on "initial conditions" such as the benchmark shares of peak, intermediate, and base loads in daily consumption before a set of point-elasticity estimates can be applied to a given utility system.

It should be noted that even a complete set of point-elasticity estimates will not generate accurate predictions of load-shape modifications except in cases where the underlying customers' preferences are characterized by constant-elasticity demand functions. In general, it will be preferable to utilize the full system of three electricity demand equations to predict the impact of TOD rates on utility loads rather than a set of point-elasticity estimates.

Before we review some of the available elasticity estimates, it is pertinent to briefly recall the stochastic nature of econometric estimates. Uncertainties can be introduced in such estimates by factors such as economic model specification, statistical technique of estimation, sample design, and choice of data. Uncertainties can be caused by other factors as well.

It is possible that households in the observed sample have failed to respond fully to a given set of TOD rates, because the rates were not differentiated enough to circumvent the "discreteness" frequently present in household decision making. This factor will introduce a downward bias in estimated elasticity measures. On the other hand, it is possible that households have responded fully to the TOD rates, so that the substitution potential has been completely exhausted. Any further differentiation in the rates will not further alter the load shape. In such cases, elasticity estimates will be upward-biased. Finally, it should be recognized that substitution possibilities will, in general, differ between the short run, when only appliance-usage levels are variable, and the long run, when appliance-efficiency levels are additionally variable. Thus, elasticity estimates will be sensitive to particular assumptions made about the dynamics of consumer adjustment. All these factors will impinge on the usefulness of elasticities as predictors of load-shape modifications. They will impede the ready transferability of elasticity estimates between utility systems and may, in certain cases, also impede transferability within a given utility system.

Table 9-1 presents some of the available elasticity estimates for residential customers. The most striking characteristic of these estimates is their lack of consensus. The Arizona and Wisconsin numbers indicate that, even from a qualitative viewpoint, the peak elasticity does not relate in a unique manner to the off-peak elasticity—across the different analyses, with their different model specifications, estimation techniques, and data bases. Evidence on industrial and commercial elasticities is very limited, primarily because no experimental data are available for these customer classes. Nonexperimental evidence goes back to January 1977 for some utility systems; however, these TOD rates employ only a single-rate structure, making estimation of elasticities extremely difficult.

In conclusion, it seems fair to say that elasticity measures have a role to play in quantifying the impact of TOD rates on key variables such as system-capacity loads, but that point estimates of own-price elasticities alone cannot generate reliable predictions. The available evidence on such measures points to a lack of consensus. A considerable portion of this variation may be due to the use of a summary, *ceteris paribus* measure that is more akin to a

Table 9-1
Ranges of Uncompensated "Partial" Own-Price Elasticities of Residential Electricity Demand by Time-of-Day

	Connecticut[a]	Arizona[b]		Wisconsin[c]	
	Narrow Peak (4 hr)	Narrow Peak (3 hr)	Broad Peak (5 to 8 hr)	Narrow Peak (6 hr)	Broad Peak (9 to 12 hr)
Peak Period		−1.454	(−1.362, −1.428) RTI		
		−0.412 LL			
Summer		−0.679	(−0.169, −0.483) AH	(−0.412, −0.655)	(−0.475, −0.844) CC
			(−0.723, −0.780) AT	−0.806	(−0.812, −0.826) AT
Winter	(−0.455, −0.657)				
Midpeak Period		−1.547	(−1.479, −1.723) RTI		
		−0.261 LL			
Summer		−0.479	(−0.378, −0.474) AH		
			(−0.309, −0.527) AT		
Winter	(−0.240, −0.497)				
Offpeak Period		−1.640	(−1.516, −2.034) RTI		
		−0.461 LL			
Summer		−0.409	(−1.88, −0.362) AH	(−0.514, −0.769)	(−0.300, −0.636) CC
			(−0.570, −0.643) AT	−0.094	(−0.210, −0.239) AT
Winter	(−0.294, −0.360)				

Source: D.J. Aigner and D.J. Poirier, *Electricity Demand and Consumption by Time-of-Use: A Survey* (Palo Alto, Calif.: Electric Power Research Institute, 1980), table 4-2, p. 4-4.

[a]From Lawrence and Braithwait (1977), table 6, pp. 1–167. Ranges for Connecticut are constructed over results of the months of November 1975 and January 1976 and over subperiods of the day (two of which were designated peak; three, midpeak; one, offpeak.

[b]The entry noted "AT" is from Atkinson (1977), tables 8 and 9, pp. 33 and 34, respectively. Since he pools the data over months, the ranges are constructed for the broad-peak period only.
Aigner and Hausman (AH) attempt to correct for truncation bias in their results. They use the one summer month of August. Moreover, since length of the peak period is an independent variable in their model, a single elasticity is reported, although separate elasticities for individual pricing periods could have been calculated. The ranges are constructed by contrasting with their results without truncation accounted for. See table 2, p. 16; table 4, p. 21.
Lau and Lillard (1978) (LL) work only with households that faced the narrow-peak period, over the period from May to October 1976. They pool the data over months. Results reported appear in table 3, p. 27.
The Research Triangle Institute 1978 (RTI) uses data aggregated over the period from July to September 1976.

[c]The first entries are from Caves-Christensen (1978), tables 6 and 7, pp. 25 and 26, respectively, and are marked "CC." Ranges were constructed over the results for the months of July and August 1977, over alternative definitions of the peak period (in the case of "broad peak"), and over alternative TOD rate differentials from 2:1 to 8:1.
The second entries, marked "AT," are from Atkinson, table 11, p. 39. since he pools the data over the two available months and over prices, the ranges constructed are for the broad-peak period only.

function than to a constant in most practical applications. Future work in this area may appropriately abandon reliance on volatile point-elasticity measures and turn to full economic models of the load shape as predictors of load-shape modifications.[15]

Time-of-Day Pricing in Practice

This section presents a brief survey of recent experience in the United States with TOD rates. Experience in certain key states is emphasized in order to present a concise, yet representative, picture. The experience of large industrial and commercial customers is examined, followed by a discussion of the experience of residential customers.

Industrial–Commercial Customers

This section presents the following information for each of the major California, Wisconsin, Michigan, and New York electric utilities which have instituted TOD rates:

Implementation date

Coverage (number of customers involved; minimum demand levels; share in system electric sales, revenues, and peak load; whether mandatory or optional)

Rate-structure features (costing methodology; number of pricing periods; ratios of peak to off-peak energy charges; peak-demand charge; seasonal differentials)

Analysis of impacts (shift in noncoincident maximum load)

California. A resolution adopted by the California legislature during the summer of 1974 directed the California Public Utilities Commission (PUC) to investigate the feasibility of TOD rates.[16] Three investor-owned utilities—Pacific Gas & Electric (PG&E), Southern California Edison (SCE), and San Diego Gas & Electric (SDG&E)—responded to the subsequent California PUC request by implementing TOD rates on a mandatory basis for large commercial and industrial customers in 1977, starting with PG&E in February followed by SCE and SDG&E in the fall. Both fully allocated costs and marginal costs were considered in designing these TOD rates. In addition, a major study, partially funded by U.S. Department of Energy, is being conducted to examine the applicability of marginal-costing methodologies for rate design in California. A fourth utility, the Los Angeles Department of Water and Power (LADWP), adopted TOD rates in January 1979.

In the PG&E service area, 830 customers, each with a maximum demand exceeding 1,000 kilowatts (kW), are on TOD rates. Collectively they account for approximately one-quarter of system electricity sales and one-seventh of system peak load. The TOD rate structure has three pricing periods. The peak–off-peak energy–price ratio varies from 1.62:1 (1.045 ¢/killowat hours (kWh) to 0.645 ¢/ kilowatt hours (kWh)) to 2.20:1, depending on customer demand levels. A demand charge of $4.20/kW is assessed during the peak period for customers with maximum demands exceeding 4,000 kW; the other customers pay a lower rate of $2.50/kW. some of the energy and demand charges vary seasonally.[17]

Approximately 3.3 percent of the summer noncoincident maximum demand of 150 large power customers, each with maximum demands exceeding 4,000 kW, has been reduced in response to TOD rates. The winter reduction is estimated at 2.3 percent. Industries with large responses have been cement, paper, and steel. In all cases, most of the load shifting has occurred in periods of excess plant capacity. A considerable portion of the reduction in peak-period loads has been due to rescheduling of maintenance operations to off-peak hours. None of the customers have yet made technological alterations in their capital stock to accommodate the TOD rates, but a few have indicated that future decisions may be influenced by the revised rates.

Now, PG&E has found the industrial-commercial TOD rates to be cost-effective, given that load shifting was achieved at negligible additional metering and billing costs.[18] Also SCE and SDG&E have reported similar findings.[19]

In the SCE service area, 861 customers, each with individual maximum demands exceeding 1,000 kW, are on TOD rates. Collectively they account for approximately one-third of system electricity sales and one-quarter of the peak load. The TOD rate structure has three pricing periods. The ratio between the energy charges for the peak and off-peak periods is 1.27:1 (1.408 ¢/kWh to 1.108 ¢/kWh). The demand charge for peak-period use is $2.10/kW. The rates do not vary seasonally.[20]

As a consequence of the implementation of TOD rates, approximately 3.6 percent of the maximum noncoincident load has been reduced for 111 large power customers, each with maximum demands exceeding 5,000 kW. The most responsive industries include cement, steel, rubber, and chemicals. As in the case of PG&E, load shifting varies directly with the degree of excess plant capacity.[21]

In the SD&E service area, approximately 131 customers, each with individual maximum demands in excess of 1,000 kW, are on TOD rates.

Time-of-Day Pricing of Electricity 159

Collectively they account for approximately one-fifth of system energy sales. Customers with maximum demands over 4,500 kW contributed 9 percent to the summer peak load in 1978. The rate structure features three pricing periods. The peak–off-peak energy-price ratio is 2.19:1 (1.38 ¢/kWh to 0.63 ¢/kWh). The peak-period demand charge is assessed at $5.84/kW for customers with maximum demands less than 4,500 kW; for larger customers, the demand charge is based on coincident monthly demand and is set at $6.41/kW.[22]

In the LAWDP service area, 180 large commercial and industrial customers, each with maximum demands exceeding 2,000 kW, were placed on TOD rates in January 1979. Collectively they account for one-fifth of the system electricity sales. The rate structure features two pricing periods. Only the energy charge is time-differentiated, with a ratio of 2.5:1.[23]

Wisconsin. On a number of occasions, including the previously cited Madison Gas and Electric Company case, the Public Service Commission of Wisconsin has stated that it has a strong commitment to implementing TOD rates for customer classes that already have the necessary metering.[24]

Time-of-day rates in Wisconsin have been implemented by Wisconsin Power and Light (WP&L), Madison Gas and Electric (MG&E), and Wisconsin Power Company (WEPCO), starting with WP&L in January 1977. All three utilities have instituted mandatory TOD rates based primarily on marginal-costing methodologies.

In the WP&L service area, 419 customers, each with individual demands exceeding 200 kW, are on TOD rates. Collectively they represent 36 percent of system electricity sales, 28 percent of revenues, and 24 percent of peak load. The rate structure has two pricing periods. The peak–off-peak energy-price ratio is 2.06:1 (2.53 ¢/kWh to 1.23 ¢/kWh). The peak-period demand charge is $4.75/kW. A report surveying the first-year impact of the rates is available.[25]

In the MG&E service area, 111 customers, with individual demands exceeding 300 kW, are on TOD rates. Collectively they account for one-third of the system electricity sales and approximately one-quarter of both system revenues and peak load. There are two pricing periods in the rate structure. The peak–off-peak energy–price ratio varies from 2.53:1 to 3.40:1, depending on customer definition (2.53 ¢/kWh to 1 ¢/kWh and 3.4 ¢/kWh to 1 ¢/kWh). The demand charges vary from $5.96/kW to $6.45/kW.[26]

In the WEPCO service area, 491 customers, with individual demands exceeding 300 kW, were placed on TOD rates in January 1978. Collectively they account for 37 percent of system sales and approximately one-quarter of both system revenues and peak load. The rate structure has two pricing periods, and the peak–off-peak energy-price ratio is 2.00:1 (2.8 ¢/kWh to 1.4 ¢/kWh). The demand charge is assessed at $3.96/kWh.[27]

Michigan. Two Michigan utilities have been authorized by the Michigan Public Service Commission (PSC) to bill their large power customers on TOD rates. Collectively, these customers account for approximately 45 percent of system electricity sales and peak load for both utilities. Detroit Edison has 2,259 customers on such rates, and Consumers Power has 1,725. During the spring of 1976 TOD rates were implemented for both companies. The rates are optional from the legal standpoint, but have proved to be effectively mandatory from the economic viewpoint.

Embedded-costing methodologies have been used to set rates in Michigan. The Michigan PSC rejected the use of marginal-cost pricing in developing rates, stating "[Marginal cost] determinations are replete with uncertainty and... can accomplish little more in the way of providing correct price signals to the consumer than the current... method."[28] However, the Michigan PSC is currently examining the potential usefulness of marginal costs in rate design. The approved industrial TOD rates for both Detroit Edison and Consumers Power feature a 2-mil differential between on-peak and off-peak energy charges. Detroit Edison's customers are billed for the maximum demand measured during on-peak hours (9 a.m. through 9 p.m. weekdays) plus a capacity charge for the maximum 60-minute demand at any time during the month. Consumers Power's large industrial customers are billed only for the 15-minute maximum demand measured during the on-peak period (5 p.m. through 9 p.m., October through February, and 10 a.m. to 5 p.m., the rest of the year) unless off-peak demand is at least 3 times greater than on-peak demand.[29]

New York. On August 10, 1976, in an opinion and order examining the merits of applying marginal-cost concepts to electric rates, the New York Public Service Commission ordered: "Each electric Utility shall proceed to develop marginal cost data and other pertinent studies in accordance with this Opinion... and advise the Commission within 90 days of a schedule for doing so."[30] A final order was issued within four months, in December 1976, approving mandatory time-of-day rates for 175 Long Island Lighting Company (LILCO) customers, each with maximum monthly demands exceeding 750 kW.

Collectively, these 175 customers account for 8.8 percent of coincident LILCO peak load. The rate structure has three pricing periods. The ratio of peak–off-peak charges varies from 1.68:1 (3.37 ¢/kWh to 2.01 ¢/kWh) to 1.73:1. The peak-period demand charge varies from $7.17/kW to $9.81/kW, and the ratio between the peak- and intermediate-demand charges is 4:1. A report on the impact of TOD rates is being prepared by LILCO staff.

In the Central Hudson Gas and Electricity Company service area, 49 customers are on mandatory TOD rates. These customers face no price

Time-of-Day Pricing of Electricity 161

differential in the energy charge between the peak and off-peak periods. Peak-period demand is charged at $13.7/kW; off-peak demand, at $1.40/kW.

In the Consolidated Edison service area, 224 customers, each with maximum demands exceeding 3,000 kW, were put on mandatory TOD rates on January 1, 1980. Collectively they account for 12.3 percent of the system peak load. The rate structure has two pricing periods. The peak–off-peak ratio is 1.41:1 (3.87 ¢/kWh to 2.74 ¢/kWh). The peak-period demand charge varies from $6.39/kW to $10.70/kW. The rates do not vary seasonally.[31]

Residential Customers

For residential customers TOD pricing activities are divided into two categories: pricing and experiments and nonexperimental implementation.

Pricing Experiments. With funding from the U.S. Federal Energy Administration, Department of Energy, fourteen pricing experiments have been conducted between 1975 and 1979 in order to examine the impact of TOD rates on residential patterns of electricity consumption. As of this writing, seven experiments had been completed, and seven were still continuing. A recently published Electric Power Research Institute (EPRI) report prepared by the University of Michigan examines the sample design characteristics of the fourteen experiments.[32] The report is cautious about the suitability of many of the experiments for generating "transferable" elasticity estimates. This conclusion is based primarily on the lack of scientific sampling techniques in the design and implementation phases of many of the pricing experiments.

Work is currently underway at the Research Triangle Institute to analyze the data generated from these pricing experiments. Promising results are expected from the Wisconsin and North Carolina experiments, as well as from the two California experiments pertaining to the LASWP and SCE/SDG&E. These experiments are characterized by relatively sound statistical design and considerable price variation, which should enable statistically significant detection of price effects.

Nonexperimental Implementation. For large residential customers, TOD rates have been approved in California, Wisconsin, and New York. In the LADWP service area, 1,000 customers were placed on TOD rates in November 1979. These rates are voluntary. It is expected that ultimately 5,000 customers will utilize the TOD rate.[33] In the WEPCO service area, 577 customers, each with an annual consumption exceeding approximately

40,000 kWh, were put on mandatory TOD rates in July 1978. The rates are based on marginal costs. The rate structure has two pricing periods. The ratio of peak–off-peak energy charges is 6.3:1 (8.2 ¢/kWh to 1.3 ¢/kWh) otherwise. There is no demand charge.[34]

In early 1980, LILCO plans to implement approved mandatory TOD rates for 950 residential customers, each consuming more than 45,000 kWh annually. The approved tariff establishes five periods: day and night, winter and summer, and a temperature-controlled (81°F or higher) portion of summer days. Associated energy charges presently range from 2.9 ¢/kWh during the winter night period to as much as 30.4 ¢/kWh on a summer day when the temperature reaches 81°F or warmer (a ratio of 10.5:1).[35]

In the Virginia Electric Power service area, it is possible that approximately 20,000 customers, each of whom consumed more than 3,500 kWh during a summer month in 1976 to 1978, will be placed on mandatory or voluntary TOD rates. The proposed rate structure features two pricing periods: the ratio of peak–off-peak energy charges will be 1.59:1 (2.39 ¢/kWh to 1.50 ¢/kWh). Demand charge will be $3.16/kW during summer peak hours and $2.39/kWh during winter peak hours.[36] A formal hearing will be scheduled during 1980.

Summary and Conclusions

We hope that the information provided in this chapter will be of use to researchers, regulatory agencies, and utilities concerned with the application of TOD pricing of electricity. By drawing on the experience of those programs that have already made significant progress in designing, applying, and analyzing these tariffs, much delay and duplicated effort can be avoided. Of course, additional research and information are certainly needed, particularly in the areas of cost/benefit analysis and load-shape modifications associated with TOD pricing. The presence of risk and uncertainty associated with TOD pricing justifies moving with some caution. However, this should not be confused with immobility.

Notes

1. For a discussion concerning electricity costs, see Malko and Uhler (1979, pp. 11–17).

2. For information on regulatory activities concerning electricity rate-structure reform, see Electric Utility Rate Design Study (1979*d*).

3. See Wisconsin Public Service Commission (1974). For an analysis of the major issues in this case, consult Cudahy and Malko (1976, pp 47–73).

Time-of-Day Pricing of Electricity 163

4. See PURPA, sections 111 and 115.

5. See U.S. Department of Energy (1978), sections 1 and 2.

6. See U.S. Department of Energy (1979).

7. See PURPA, sections 111 and 115.

8. Ibid., section 111d. For a detailed discussion of rate-making standards and related matters in PURPA, see Electric Utility Rate Design Study (1979e).

9. See Public Utility Regulatory Policies Act of 1978 (1978), sections 115a to c.

10. Ibid., section 112b.

11. Ibid.

12. For a detailed discussion of these activities for the consideration and implementation of time-of-day tariffs, see Malko, Ray, and Hassig (1979), Malko and Simpson (1978), and Electric Utility Rate Design Study (1979c).

13. See Samuelson (1976, pp. 125–126).

14. See Aigner (1979, p. 1).

15. For a generic discussion on the usefulness of electricity measures, consult Faruqui (1979) and Electric Utility Rate Design Study (1980).

16. See California Legislature (1974).

17. California Public Utilities Commission (1976). Jackalyne Smith of the CPUC, personal communication. For all California utilities, the energy-price ratios exclude the energy-cost adjustment charge (ECAC), which applies uniformly to peak and off-peak kilowatt hours. Inclusion of ECAC would move the ratios closer to unity.

18. Pacific Gas and Electric Company (1979). Steve P. Reynolds of PG&E, personal communication.

19. Southern California Edison Company (1979); San Diego Gas & Electric Company (1979).

20. California Public Utilities Commission (1977b). Jackalyne Smith of the CPUC: personal communication.

21. See Southern California Edison Company (1979) and San Diego Gas & Electric Company (1979).

22. California Public Utilities Commission (1977b). John Asmus of San Diego Gas & Electric Company: personal communication.

23. Dennis Whitney of LADWP: personal communication. A small demand charge of $0.25/kW is used to collect distribution costs.

24. Wisconsin Public Service Commission, "Madison Gas and Electric: Docket No. 2-U-7423," and "Policy Statement and Notice of Proposed Rules, Docket No. 01-ER-1."

25. John L. Walker of WP&L: personal communication; Wisconsin Public Service Commission, "Status of Time-of-Day Pricing in Wisconsin"; Malko, Ray, and Hasig (1979).

26. Ibid.

27. Ibid.

28. Michigan Public Service Commission, "Consumers' Power: Order, Case No. U-4840."

29. Consumers Power Company and Detroit Edison. For an analysis of the Michigan experience, see Malko, Ray, and Hassig (1979).

30. New York Public Service Commission (1976, p. 33).

31. Ronald J. Liberty of the New York Public Service Commission; personal communication.

32. Electric Power Research Institute (1979).

33. Dennis Whitney of LADWP: personal communication.

34. Wisconsin Public Service Commission (1977). Consult Malko (1978).

35. Refer to New York Public Service Commission (1977). Consult Malko (1978).

36. Consult Malko (1978).

10 Demand for Electricity by Time of Day: An Evaluation of Experimental Results

Wallace Hendricks and
Roger Koenker

In the last six years, there has been a tremendous growth in interest in the implementation of time-differentiated rates in electric utilities. At the beginning of this period, almost all the information which was available on customer response to these rates came from Europe.[1] However, most economists and industry experts felt that the European experience was not directly applicable to the United States because of substantial differences in both system characteristics and customer uses of electricity. The Federal Energy Administration, now the Department of Energy (DOE), attempted to fill this gap by sponsoring a number of "demonstration projects" which were designed to gather information on customer responses to time-differentiated rates. By 1978 Congress was sufficiently convinced about the value of time-of-day (TOD) rates to include a provision in the Public Utilities Regulatory Policies Act (PURPA) of 1978 that TOD rates should be charged to each class of customers "unless such rates are not cost-effective with respect to each class...."[2]

According to a recent survey, between July 1977 and January 1979 some form of TOD or seasonal rates was adopted by thirty-two states, of which sixteen states adopted some TOD rate for at least one customer class.[3] However, only seven of forty-five commissions had actually published a report on the cost-effectiveness of TOD rates. Unfortunately, these seven reports were largely made without any real evidence about customer response to these rates. Thus, while there has been a substantial amount of federal and state pressure for utilities to initiate TOD rates, as yet there has been very little evaluation of the cost-effectiveness of these rates (whether they have been adopted or not).

This chapter is a survey of the evidence on TOD rates as applied to residential consumers.[4] The focus is on the evidence now becoming available from the DOE-sponsored demonstration projects. Obviously many mportant issues arise in the evaluation of this evidence. Since we cannot possibly discuss all these issues in this short chapter, we focus on only a few. Specifically, we have purposely not chosen to focus on either experiment-specific problems with the data or specific criticisms of individual analyses. Readers interested in these two areas should consult Research Triangle

Institute (1978) in the former case and Aigner and Poirier (1980) in the latter.

The chapter is divided into four sections. The first considers the potential benefits from the demonstration project data. The second analyzes the advantages and disadvantages of various methods of analysis of the data. The third section reviews some of the preliminary results from the projects. The fourth section gives our conclusions.

Potential Benefits from Experimental Results

The primary goal of the current research in TOD rates is to provide information which can be used to evaluate the costs and benefits of alternative rate designs. Some observers have suggested that TOD rates should simply be implemented without experimentation, and we have some sympathy for this viewpoint for some classes of customers. However, there are good reasons why utilities and regulatory commissions are somewhat reluctant to institute TOD rates without some evidence on consumer response. First, the capital expenditure involved with changing meters and increasing customer service may be substantial. Second, the transition costs of moving from one rate schedule to another may be very large. Since the cost/benefit ratio will vary among pricing policies, one possible way of finding the optimum combination of prices would be simply to iterate across the various possibilities. As the French have discovered, this iteration is not always politically feasible. What is more, there may be a substantial loss in benefits depending on which "path" is chosen to the optimum price combination. These arguments suggest that some experimentation may be fruitful before full implementation occurs.

Experiments are not without drawbacks. Decisions on TOD pricing are delayed until the experimental data can be evaluated. The experiments, by their very nature, can provide information on only short-run changes in consumer behavior. The response to TOD pricing and therefore its benefits will typically be understated by experimental results. However, it is reasonable to assume that these results will provide a lower bound on the potential gains from TOD pricing. Finally, the results of these experiments, like those of all experiments, depend on how well the experiments were designed. A whole host of problems, including experimental ("Hawthorne") effects, nonrandom exclusions, participation biases, and incentive payments, may make it very difficult to generalize from experimental results.[5]

Given that an experiment has been done and that it has been well designed, how do we evaluate the costs and benefits of TOD pricing? Well, PURPA indicates that TOD rates should be implemented where they are "cost-effective." In turn, *cost-effective* is defined as when "the long run benefits... are likely to exceed the metering costs and other costs associated

Demand for Electricity by Time-of-Day

with the use of such rates" (PURPA, section 115b). Estimates of the additional costs of TOD rates, including metering costs, replacement of distribution-system equipment, control-system costs, and customer-service costs, typically can be made without experimental data (although the experiments will provide some experience in this area).[6]

The "long-run benefits" are another matter. There appear to be two polar extremes on how long-run benefits should be evaluated. At one extreme, these benefits are equated with cost reductions which will occur when consumers shift their consumption from peak to off-peak hours of the day.[7] The major cost savings would be due to more efficient use of low-incremental-cost generating units and to forestalling future additions to capacity. Experimental results can be used to predict load shapes under various TOD rate schedules. These predicted load shapes can then be combined with engineering cost data to yield predicted cost changes of moving between rate schedules. It is clear that rate schedules could be designed which would be cost-effective by using this definition of long-run benefits, but they may be totally unacceptable to consumers because this definition does not consider the value consumers give to alternative consumption paths. Thus, the "cost savings" approach to long-run benefits yields results which can be either over- or underestimates of the true benefits. At the other extreme, these benefits are equated with changes in welfare of the customers, and cost savings are ignored.[8] In this case, experimental results can be used to estimate demand functions, which in turn are input to standard welfare-theory calculations of welfare gains (or losses) of different pricing policies. On the assumption that cost savings are not negative, this approach will yield an underestimate of long-run benefits.

The correct aproach to calculating long-run benefits is obviously to consider both the cost savings and the welfare changes associated with changes in prices. Thus an analysis of experimental results should have two key features. First, it should allow for estimation of demand paths (and therefore load curves) in sufficient detail that cost savings of alternative price sets may be estimated. Second, the functional relationship between prices and quantities should be consistent with utility maximization by consumers so that standard welfare theory can be applied. If one or both of these features are lacking, calculation of long-run benefits may be very difficult. Thus, one of the potential benefits of conducting the experiment depends heavily on the method of analysis.

Methods of Analysis

The DOE-sponsored demonstration projects are of two kinds. The first consists of projects which have a test group, who all face the same time-of-day prices, and a control group, who have no change in their price schedules from the current rate (for example, Connecticut and Ohio). Since there is no variation in prices within the test group, it is not possible to predict customers' responses for alternative time-of-day schedules without very restrictive assumptions.[9] The problem posed here is effectively one of estimating a multicommodity demand system with only two observed price regimes; or, in statistical parlance, a multidimensional response surface must be estimated with only two design points. The methods of analysis of data from projects in this set are fairly straightforward exercises in analysis of covariance, although the econometric techniques may become quite complicated. Basically, these methods involve a comparison of consumption between two groups; tests versus controls during the test period, the test group during the test period versus this same group in some "base-line period," or change between base-line and test period for the test group versus the control group.[10]

The second set of projects includes experiments which have several pricing policies within the test group. Obviously the same kind of comparisons can be made with the data from these projects as those made in projects included in the first set (although measurement errors in comparing groups may be larger as a result of the smaller number of customers under each test rate). However, if a functional relationship between prices and quantities can be convincingly demonstrated, these experiments also allow researchers to generalize to pricing policies which were not actually included in the experimental rates; that is, price elasticities can be computed.

In the discussion which follows we have grouped methods of analysis under two broad headings: analysis of covariance (ANCOVA), in which no functional relationship between quantities and prices is assumed, and demand analysis, in which the parameters of the hypothesized functional relationship are estimated.

The problem of handling the large amount of data generated by time-of-day experiments is common to all methods of analysis. This necessitates some preprocessing of the data which is often accomplished by some form of temporal averaging. For example, if 15-minute data are analyzed for a single year, there are over 35,000 different observations on consumption for every household unit. A convenient way of representing these data is the linear regression framework

$$Y_n = X_n B_n + \varepsilon_n \qquad (10.1)$$

where the Y_n are T-dimensional column vectors of consumed quantities for each of the individual households and T time periods for the time frame being analyzed (for example, the summer months), the $\{X_n\}$ are $T \times K$ matrices of independent variables, the $\{B_n\}$ are K-dimensional coefficient vectors, and the $\{\varepsilon_n\}$ are T-dimensional disturbance vectors with null means and block-

Demand for Electricity by Time-of-Day

diagonal covariance matrix $\Sigma = [\Sigma_{ii}]$. If the $\{X_n\}$ are simply matrices of dummy variables representing time periods, then the $\{B_n\}$ will simply be mean consumption during these periods.

This first step in the analysis of the data (whether explicit or implicit) is common to all ANCOVA and demand analysis methods. The second step is to relate the underlying parameters from the first step to some exogenous variables Z_n by

$$B_n = Z_n \gamma + u_n \qquad (10.2)$$

where γ represents a J-dimensional column vector of "metaparameters" of primary interest. If the $\{Z_n\}$ are simply indicator variables for pricing groups and the $\{B_n\}$ are estimated means, this simply reduces to difference-of-means tests for the K grouped time periods and the J pricing groups.

ANCOVA Methods

By definition, ANCOVA methods are not constrained by a choice of a particular functional relationship between quantities demanded and prices. It is therefore not surprising that almost all work on alternative specifications of the first stage of the analysis has been done in ANCOVA studies. The two major examples of attempts to parameterize the entire load curve, instead of simply calculating means for long periods of the day, occur in studies of the Connecticut Demonstration Project Data. Hendricks, Koenker and Poirier (1979a, 1979b) use a smooth, periodic, cubic spline function while Granger et al. (1979) use a step function defined over the hours of the day. The major advantage of these specifications is that they produce a parsimonious representation of the entire load curve. Thus, results from the second stage of the analysis allow the forecasting of entire load curves for the price sets being compared. These load curves can then be combined with cost data to yield changes in costs between price sets. This represents a major advantage over studies which aggregate usage during the day into only a few periods because these later studies make cost calculations very difficult.

A second advantage of these explicit specifications of the first stage is that they make it clear that some assumptions about the error structure must be made. The $\{B_n\}$ cannot be observed, but must be estimated by the $\{\hat{B}_n\}$ from the first stage. These estimated and actual values are related by

$$\hat{B}_n = B_n + h_n \qquad (10.3)$$

where $E(h_n) = 0$ and $E(h_n h'_n) = (X_n \Sigma_n X_n)$. Substituting equation 10.3 into 10.2 yields

$$\hat{B}_n = Z_n\gamma + u_n + h_n \qquad (10.4)$$

Thus errors in the second stage of the analysis will have two components: errors in estimating the $\{B_n\}$ in the first stage and random deviations in the second stage. Best estimates of the metaparameters in the second stage therefore require use of this knowledge about the error structure. This issue is explicitly dealt with in the above studies, but is largely ignored in all others.

Specification of the second stage in ANCOVA studies is fairly straightforward. The independent variables typically include the indicator variable(s) for different pricing groups, control variables for different demographic characteristics of the households, and sometimes interactions between the control variables and the indicator variables. The control variables are usually included to avoid problems associated with imbalanced sample designs. The interaction variables allow different predicted responses within pricing groups. These may be of considerable policy interest in answering questions about the differential impact of rates by income class.

Unfortunately, the flexibility of ANCOVA studies also leads to a major problem. To do any cost/benefit analysis of the results from the TOD experiments, it is necessary to evaluate the welfare gains (or losses) to consumers for various pricing policies. This requires some assumptions about the functional relationship between prices and quantities demanded. It therefore seems reasonable to impose these assumptions during the analysis rather than after it is completed.

Demand Analysis Methods

Analysis of covariance is admirably suited to most of the early peak-load pricing experiments which have only two or three different pricing-policy "treatments." It is possible in these experiments to make a rather precise estimate of the "test effect" of moving from, say, a specified flat-rate pricing policy to the specified peak-load policy administered during the experiment.[11] However, it is extremely difficult to infer anything about the effects of pricing policies which were not experimental "treatments" from such an analysis. We may have estimated quite accurately two or three points on a demand surface, but so little is known about the shape of that surface that further inference is extremely hazardous. The early experiments with only a few distinct pricing treatments established that consumers were responsive to TOD pricing. This finding is obviously a precondition to further experimentation designed to reveal more detailed information about consumer preferences.

As we increase the number of experimental treatments and thus the number of different pricing policies facing experiment participants, we

Demand for Electricity by Time-of-Day

dramatically improve our ability to predict the consequences of a wide variety of pricing policies. Of course, we will always be best able to predict the effect of policies which are "close" in some reasonable sense to ones for which we have direct experimental evidence. As the number of experimental treatments increases, it becomes advantageous to turn attention from estimating isolated points on a demand surface to estimating some parametric representation of the surface itself.

As noted above, studies which have used demand analysis methods typically have not experimented with alternative specifications of the first stage in the analysis. In every case, the regressor matrix X_n has consisted of dummy variables for aggregates of hours during the day. The estimated coefficients $\hat{B}_n$ are then simply means for each of the daily subperiods. Thus all the "action" in studies of demand analysis methods is in the specification of the second stage and the dependent variables in this second stage. Typically the stochastic consequences of this step are ignored.

These methods require some assumptions about the functional relationship between prices and quantities demanded in the second stage. It seems logical to use the economic theory of demand to select the appropriate functional forms and the restrictions which should be placed on these relations. Some researchers, however, have been reluctant to impose any a priori restrictions on this functional relationship. In this case, a functional form should be chosen which is able to approximate a wide variety of underlying "true" demand functions. This can be accomplished by doing a Taylor expansion in prices around some arbitrary demand function. We have chosen to label this approach as "simple" demand analysis and approaches which impose these restrictions as "neoclassical" demand analysis.

"Simple" Demand Analysis

Ignoring for the moment the impact of nonprice variables and all third-order and higher price effects, we can write out a discrete time version of the second stage of the typical simple analysis as

$$B_n^k = \gamma^k + \sum_{j=1}^{J} \gamma_j^k P_{nj} + \sum_{j=1}^{J} \sum_{l \geq j} \partial_{jl}^k P_{nj} P_{nl} + u_n \qquad n = 1, \ldots, N \quad (10.5)$$

where B_n^k = kth coefficient estimate from first stage for nth customer
N = number of customers
J = total number of prices which influence B^k

In principle, the total number of prices which influence the quantity demanded is very large. That is, demand at 10 a.m. is influenced by prices at all other times of the day and perhaps by prices during other days as well. In practice, the actual number of price coefficients that can be estimated is severely limited by the lack of price variation in the data set. Thus most "simple" demand studies estimate only a limited number of first-order coefficients and very often ignore the second-order coefficients altogether.

The most common formulation of simple demand models involves entering all variables in logarithmic form so that the coefficients can be interpreted as price elasticities. Since the expenditure for electricity is allowed to vary in these models, these elasticities are *full* price elasticities.

The attractive features of this simple approach are that it is computationally quite easy and that it is relatively free from untested assumptions. Unfortunately, this latter advantage is probably only illusionary.

The linear-in-logs demand function yields an implied utility function which is more, rather than less, restrictive than is typically assumed in neo classical studies. What is more, the estimated demand function is not necessarily consistent with utility maximization. Since the utility-maximization hypothesis is necessary for any welfare analysis, the usefulness of price elasticities from simple studies may be quite limited.

Neoclassical Demand Analysis

The choice of parametric forms for systems of neoclassical demand equations has spawned an enormous economic literature. The dominant strain of this literature has produced several "plausible" parametric models of demand, that is, models which arise from constrained maximization of a specified parametric utility function. This feature is particularly useful in demand applications in which the welfare consequences of pricing policies must be investigated. While consumer-surplus computations can be made with arbitrary (implausible) demand models, it is extremely convenient to have explicit indirect utility and expenditure functions available for welfare (benefit) analysis. We return to this point later.

Demand for electricity under peak-load pricing poses one serious new problem of specifying empirical models of demand. Since time is, in principle, infinitely divisible, the commodity space is infinite-dimensional. Unlike the demand for citrus fruit of which there are only a few varieties with distinct costs, the demand for nonstorable goods such as electricity has distinguishable costs depending on when they are produced. Therefore demand must be disaggregated by time of day, week, year, and so on. In principle, this temporal disaggregation could proceed until we distinguish consumption at each instant as a distinct commodity. Should such an approach be taken, some further assumptions would be necessary or we would be left with a problem of estimating an infinite-dimensional taste parameter. Some assumption of smoothness of preferences is essential. Two approaches have been suggested. The first approach (which characterizes virtually all the existing empirical work in this field) maintains that preferences are essentially constant within large blocks of time, but abrupt changes in preferences occur at a few critical instants. This view permits temporal aggregation of demands into a few discrete time periods, and then these aggregate demands can be treated as distinct commodities in the conventional framework of demand analysis. Although the positioning of these hypothesized discontinuities in preferences could be chosen quite arbitrarily, in empirical applications it is universally true that locations are chosen to coincide with points of time at which pricing policies take their discrete jumps. *Thus experimental design determines in an essential way the maintained model of consumer demand.* Models of consumer demand with almost-always-constant preferences have several serious defects in our view. They must choose an a priori periodization. Within periods tastes are constant. Thus if periods are long, important details concerning the time path of preferences may be obscured. If periods are short, the number of parameters of the demand system may quickly get out of hand, and precision will be lost in estimation of a plethora of parameters. Another disturbing feature of such models is the implication that demand may take discrete jumps during periods of constant price. Positioning of taste jumps at price jumps obscures this feature but does not eliminate it.

The alternative to discrete, almost-always-constant taste models lies in the formulation of continuous-time models in which preference parameters change smoothly with time. Smoothness plays an essential role in these models by permitting a finite-dimensional parametric representation of tastes. The notion that tastes change *gradually* with time is substituted for the hypothesis that tastes change abruptly at only a few points. This approach is presented in detail for a continuous-time version of the linear expenditure system in Hendricks and Koenker (1980). We should emphasize that the choice between discrete-time and continuous-time versions of neoclassical demand models may rest on empirical results. Discrete-time versions may yield good approximations to the underlying preference pattern, and they are considerably easier to estimate than continuous-time models. Our criticism should not be viewed as a condemnation of their results, but rather as an alternative specification which we believe is theoretically more appealing. There are a number of parametric forms for a utility function, including linear expenditure system (LES), constant elasticity of substitution (CES), translog, and generalized Leontief forms, which lead to "plausible" parametric models of demand. The CES formulation is reasonable only when there are only two "commodities" in the electricity branch of the utility function. However, the translog and generalized Leontief can also be formulated in continuous time.[12] Both are more flexible than the

LES form, but they are also much more difficult to estimate. Since neither can yield a satisfactory representation of consumer behavior over the entire range of possible data points, the choice between the two ultimately rests on the characteristics of the data set being investigated.[13]

A second assumption frequently made in empirical research using one of these parametric forms is that preferences over demand at various times of day are *homothetic*. This assumption ensures that quantity ratios and budget shares are invariant to the level of income. This is an extremely powerful assumption and often considerably simplifies problems of estimation because it frequently changes what would otherwise be a nonlinear estimation problem into one which is linear in parameters. However, we would like to stress that there exists strong empirical evidence against the hypothesis of homotheticity. (See below.) Since homotheticity implies budget shares invariant to income, it in turn implies unitary income elasticities by time of day. Several studies which have estimated the time pattern of income elasticities for electricity all reject this pattern. Despite its tempting appeal, the maintained hypothesis of homothetic preferences should be approached with great caution.

Once we discard the assumption of homotheticity, we are faced with the problem of introducing some dependence of budget shares on income. One approach is to specify preferences within an "electricity branch" of a utility tree and to make total expenditure on electricity serve as an income variable with that branch. This approach has some apparent advantages. It is obvious that such an expenditure variable is much more precisely measured than the household-income variables which are typically produced by survey questionnaires. However, and again we must stress this point, within-branch expenditure variables in demand models are *endogenous* and therefore may introduce serious bias unless they are properly treated. Total expenditure on electricity is clearly a function of the existing shape and level of the pricing policy, and ignoring this dependence can be potentially disastrous. If models of this type are estimated, then household income, value of domicile, and/or other variables should be used as instruments for the expenditure variable in any estimation scheme.

One sometimes hears the view expressed that peak-load pricing policies should be revenue-neutral, and therefore at least for some hypothetical "average consumer," expenditure on electricity will be invariant along a locus of revenue-neutral pricing policies. The first point to emphasize is that this is emphatically false in the specific cases of the rates implemented in the several DOE demonstration projects; consumers on different rates in Wisconsin, for example, have highly significant differences in aggregate expenditures on electricity.

The second methodological consequence of the notion of revenue neutrality is an emphasis in the empirical literature on what we will call partial elasticities of demand.[14] Rather than holding nominal *income* fixed when demand elasticities are defined, the tendency to treat aggregate expenditure on electricity as an exogenous variable (playing the role of income) has led to definitions of price elasticities which hold this expenditure variable constant.

There are several problems with these elasticities. First, they are often produced by models which treat an endogenous expenditure variable as exogenous. Second, since experimental peak-load pricing policies typically do not achieve revenue neutrality, it is somewhat misleading to employ elasticity notions which impose revenue-neutrality assumptions to measure price responses. In particular, we find that a large component of the impact of the test rates is the aggregate-expenditure effect. This effect typically temporizes the "pure price effect," and hence "revenue-neutral" elasticities are often considerably larger than classical nominal-income constant elasticities.

There are several advantages of specifying demand models which are theoretically plausible in the sense that they arise from a proper parametric utility function. Restrictions on parameters arising, for example, from symmetry conditions on the substitution matrix or homogeneity conditions are often useful. Further, a direct estimate of the expenditure (or cost-of-utility) function which is typically available from plausible demand models is of enormous value in any subsequent welfare analysis. In the multicommodity setting, it is extremely convenient to be able to compute compensating variations directly rather than relying on surplus calculations from an ad hoc specification of demands. There are two serious disadvantages to adhering to plausible demand models in empirical work. First, such models are often very restrictive and may be unsuitable in some applications. Second, the restrictions imposed on parametric models needed to ensure plausibility often create rather nasty nonlinear estimation problems. Thus we are placed in the unfortunate position of having to balance several desiderata. We may choose an ad hoc demand specification which is quite flexible, capable of approximating a very general substitution structure, and quite easily estimable; but we do so at the risk of making subsequent welfare comparisons much more difficult and fraught with ambiguous approximations. Or we may endure the difficulties of somewhat more restrictive demand specifications, which are probably more difficult to estimate, and thus reap the advantages of relatively straightforward welfare comparisons of alternative pricing policies.

Review of Results

Analysis of Covariance

Our primary motivation for this short review of the ANCOVA results to date is to provide some background for the demand analysis results in the next section. Individual ANCOVA results are of only limited interest mainly because the price sets faced by test and control customers are not likely to be duplicated in other utilities. In fact, the test prices are often even unrealistic for the utility itself. However, these ANCOVA results do provide some common themes which are helpful in the evaluation of elasticity results.

To date, ANCOVA results are available for five of the demonstration projects (Connecticut, Ohio, Wisconsin, Arizona, and Arkansas).[15] In most cases, these results are still highly tentative. Peak-period electricity use declined in all cases, although this decline was relatively small for Arizona customers and small users in Arkansas. Changes in usage for other periods (both off-peak and intermediate for Arizona and Connecticut and off-peak for Ohio, Wisconsin, and Arkansas) were less dramatic. The evidence for shifting of consumption from peak periods to these periods is mixed. On the one hand, there is evidence of increased usage in the late night hours and early morning hours to avoid peak hours. On the other hand, this increased usage generally does not make up for the total decrease during peak hours. That is, total consumption generally falls or remains approximately constant.

Contrary to some experts' expectations, declines in peak usage are generally as large during system peak days as for other days of the year. Thus. studies which focus on relatively long time frames (for example, summer months) find similar declines in peak usages as those that use only peak days. There is also very little evidence of "needle peaking" during hours directly before or after peak periods. However, there is evidence which indicates that the residential class peak (measured in kilowatts) may shift to off-peak hours and may be almost as large as the peak for non-TOD customers. Thus, studies which aggregate all off-peak hours into a single average may miss this shifting phenomenon entirely.

ANCOVA studies yield relatively good information about the impact of control variables (especially large appliances) on the load curve. In general, these studies do not support the homotheticity hypothesis. Users with electric space heating (winter) and/or air conditioning (summer) have different load profiles from customers without these systems. Since large users typically have these systems, their load profiles are different from those for smaller users. Income elasticity also appears to vary by time of day. Unfortunately, results of control-variable-indicator–variable interactions are not as clear-cut. Significant interactions have been found, but they differ from study to study. In particular, income does not appear to explain differences in price impacts, although this might be explained by poor measurement of income in most studies.

Two other results of ANCOVA studies deserve note. First, consumption relative to some base period (for example, night hours) appears to be much easier to fit than absolute consumption.[16] Unfortunately, this approach requires another step to predict consumption, and this step yields relatively poor results. Thus the advantages of a relative approach may be only illusionary. Second, errors in the first stage of the statistical model outlined above appear to be an order of magnitude less than errors in the second stage. Thus, studies which ignore the error structure in the first stage probably yield similar results to those which would be found if knowledge of the error structure were explicitly introduced into the estimation scheme.

Demand Analysis

Before we review the results from demand analysis studies, it is appropriate to ask what kind of results we might expect. The only study which attempted to estimate elasticities by time of day prior to the current experiments was done by Cargill and Meyer (1971). Unfortunately, this study used total consumption by all users (industrial, commercial, residential, and purchased power). Since the price elasticities of these groups appear to be substantially different in aggregate studies (see Taylor 1975), this study sheds little light on what we might expect from the TOD data. Aggregate studies of residential electricity use typically find short-run aggregate elasticities of approximately −0.1. As a first approximation, we might expect full (uncompensated) price elasticities for large aggregates of hours to be around this figure. Since simple demand studies yield these full-price elasticities, we should expect fairly low elasticity estimates.

Neoclassical demand studies are another matter. Most neoclassical studies which have been done to date have estimated discrete-time "partial" (either compensated or uncompensated) elasticities. The discrete-time link between partial uncompensated and full uncompensated elasticities is

$$\eta_{ij} = \eta_{ij}^e + Z_j \frac{dE}{dP_E} \frac{PE}{E} \qquad (10.6)$$

$$= \eta_{ij}^e + Z_j(1 + \eta)$$

where η is the aggregate price elasticity, Z_j is the share of total electricity expenditure in the jth period, η_{ij}^e is the partial uncompensated elasticity, and η_{ij} is the full uncompensated elasticity.[17] With $\eta > -1$, the partial elasticity will always be more elastic than the full elasticity. For a given aggregate-demand elasticity, this difference will depend on the expenditure share of the period being used. Thus, *ceteris paribus*, we expect higher partial elasticities for longer periods and periods with relatively high prices *even if* the underlying full-price elasticities are identical.

We can also guess at the relative magnitude of two other elasticities which are quoted in the literature, the partial compensated elasticity and the full compensated elasticity n^*_{ij}. The discrete-time definitions of these elasticities are

$$\eta^e_{ij} = \eta^{e*}_{ij} - Z_j \, \eta_{iE} \tag{10.7}$$

and
$$\eta_{ij} = \eta^*_{ij} - w_j \eta^M_j \tag{10.8}$$

where η_{iE} is the electricity-expenditure elasticity with respect to i, w_j is the share of good j in the total budget, and η^M_j is the income elasticity. The electricity-expenditure elasticity η_{iE} is often assumed to be equal to 1. Thus, if the aggregate-demand elasticity is near zero, the full uncompensated and partial compensated elasticities are approximately equal. As the aggregate-demand elasticity increases, the compensated partial will be more elastic than the uncompensated full elasticity. Finally, the uncompensated and compensated full elasticities should be very similar since the income elasticity is probably in the range of 0.3 and the share of the total budget is typically a small number. In summary, discrete-time measurements of compensated and uncompensated full elasticities and compensated partial elasticities are likely to lead to similar results (although the uncompensated partials may be slightly more elastic), while measurements of partial uncompensated elasticities will yield estimates which are much more elastic.

Several authors have tried to explain the different elasticities which are found in neoclassical and simple studies (using the same data base) as primarily due to the restrictions of neoclassical theory. This may be true, but a simpler and apparently more important explanation is that the two types of studies *have measured different concepts*.

To make the various estimates of elasticities more comparable, we have computed full uncompensated elasticities under the asumption that the aggregate-demand elasticity is −0.1 for all the neoclassical studies.[18] These can be compared to the elasticities found by using simple methods. Of course, it should be remembered that these full uncompensated elasticities would be more elastic if the aggregate-demand elasticity were more elastic. For example, if the aggregate-demand elasticity were −0.5, this would decrease the full uncompensated elasticities by approximately 0.1 to 0.2.

The three studies which have estimated full elasticities directly (Miedema et al. 1978; Taylor 1978; and Manning and Action 1978) yield elasticities which are very close to zero. The Miedema et al. and Taylor results give estimates which are often insignificant, while the results of Manning and Acton yield own full elasticities around −0.1.[19] The remainder of the studies have measured (either explicitly or implicitly) partial elasticities. There is a much wider variance (between studies) in the point estimates of these partial elasticities than in the full elasticities in the three studies above. This variance may be attributed to a number of factors, including choice of a priori restrictions, functional form, and level of aggregation as well as "real" factors which differ between experiments such as weather, appliance profile of customers, and length and spacing of pricing periods. However, the full elasticities which are implied by these partial elasticities have a much smaller range of approximately −0.1 to −0.3.

Which of these sets of elasticities is appropriate for public policy considerations? Some experts have argued that the partial elasticities are appropriate since revenue considerations would suggest that utility commissions require total expenditure after the introduction of TOD prices to be equal to expenditures under the current rate structures. Besides the methodological considerations noted earlier, there are two other reasons for believing that these partials are inappropriate. First, costs will change if the introduction of TOD prices shifts the load curve. These changing costs will alter revenue requirements. Second, the restriction of a particular revenue requirement should be used not in the estimation of elasticities, but in the choice of rate structures once the elasticities are known. For example, a given revenue requirement might be achieved by altering the fixed charge associated with TOD prices, altering the marginal prices, changing the timing of the prices, or some combination of these choices. The actual choice should depend on cost/benefit calculations. Thus, we believe that full elasticities are most important in setting public policy.

These considerations leave us in a delicate situation. On the one hand, neoclassical studies have the appropriate theoretical base to do cost/benefit analysis, and on this dimension alone they should be considered superior to the simple studies. On the other hand, problems with functional forms, questionable assumptions, and the partial nature of the results from these studies may tilt the case in favor of the results from simple studies. These problems become crucial because the range of estimated elasticities includes values which are likely to yield ambiguous results in most cost/benefit analyses. Thus, refinement of our methods of analysis of TOD data is not simply an "ivory tower" exercise for economists.

Conclusions

At this point it is apparent that the experimental results from the DOE demonstration projects are of only limited use in attempting to follow PURPA guidelines on decisons about TOD pricing. In fact, the DOE itself has chosen to ignore experimental results in Connecticut in its analysis of the cost and benefits of TOD pricing in that state.[20] In part, this limited use stems from the poor design of early experiments and the tentative nature of the results from later experiments. It also comes from a misunderstanding of the results of using the various methods of analysis which we have outlined above. Hopefully we have clarified some of these misunderstandings.

It is our opinion, based on tentative results in Wisconsin and Los

Angeles,[21] that it is very important to perform careful analysis of the data because the welfare implications of TOD pricing are not unambiguously positive or negative either for all sets of residential customers or for all pricing policies. Analysis of the results from these experiments should therefore include both analysis within the neoclassical model which we have outlined above *and* serious cost analysis, as is currently done in the EPRI rate-design study. Only then can we have serious cost/benefit analysis for the individual utilities, let alone attempt to transfer the results to other utilities who have not done any experimentation.

Notes

1. See Mitchell, Manning, and Acton (1978), Boggis (1974), and Cicchetti and Foell (1975).
2. PURPA, section 111d.
3. Electric Utility Rate Design Study (1979*a*).
4. The initiation of TOD rates for commercial and industrial customers seems to be considerably less controversial as a result of the relatively small additional metering costs. For a discussion see Chapter 9.
5. See Research Triangle Institute (1978) and Aigner and Hausman (1978).
6. Electric Utility Rate Design Study (1977).
7. Electric Utility Rate Design Study (1977); a, b, c, and d.
8. For example, Levin, Taylor, and Wenders (1979), and Wenders and Lyman (1979).
9. For two possible approaches see Lawrence and Braithwaite (1979) and Hausman and McFadden (1978).
10. See Hendricks, Koenker, and Poirier (1979*b*), Hausman and McFadden (1978), and Granger et al. (1979) for details of these methods.
11. See Hendricks, Koenker, and Poirier (1979*a*, 1979*b*) for such an analysis of the Connecticut experiment.
12. See Koenker (1978).
13. See Caves and Christensen (forthcoming) for a comparison of the global properties of the translog and generalized Leontief.
14. The first paper to systematically investigate the relationship between these partial and full elasticities is Caves and Christensen (1978).
15. For Connecticut results see Burbank (1977); Hendricks, Koenker, and Poirier (1979*a*, 1979*b*): Granger et al. (1979); White et al. (1978); and Hausman and McFadden (1978). For Ohio, see White, Alexander, and Duncan (1978). For Wisconsin, see Miedema et al. (1978). For Arkansas results, see Arkansas Public Service Commission (undated).
16. See Hausman and McFadden (1978).

17. These relationships were first worked out in Caves and Christensen (1978). Much of this discussion derives from their work.
18. These results are presented in Hendricks and Koenker (1980).
19. The insignificant Arizona results are probably a result of very small sample sizes as well as design problems in the experiment. See Miedema et al. (1978).
20. See Miller and Reed (1979).
21. See Acton and Mitchell (1980) and Hendricks and Koenker (1980).

11

Measuring the Potential Impacts from Lifeline Pricing of Electricity and Natural-Gas Services

Dennis Ray and
Rodney Stevenson

Rapidly rising energy prices are placing a severe economic burden on the consuming public. In response, legislators and regulators are examining possible methods of relief for those segments of the population most severely affected. Lifeline pricing, a method of utility-service pricing in which low prices are charged for minimum "human needs" consumption levels, is one such method. Other methods include increased welfare and income-transfer payments, direct grants, and energy stamps. Selection of appropriate methods to provide aid should be based on criteria such as coverage of the legitimate-needs population, timing of benefits and needs, administrative ease, administrative costs, and general acceptability of the program.

In this chapter we present a method for analyzing some of the economic effects of lifeline pricing. The analysis is limited in scope, being concerned mainly with the effects on all consumers' bills resulting from lifeline rates. In the first section, alternative forms of lifeline pricing are discussed. An economic model for calculating the revenue burden generated by implementing any particular lifeline option and the price adjustments needed to offset that burden are presented in the second section. Test-year results from applying the economic model to an electricity and a natural-gas utility are provided in the third and final section.

Lifeline-Pricing Options

Welfare Needs and Lifeline Pricing

Energy prices have increased at a significantly higher rate than prices for other goods and services. Since 1967, consumer prices, as indicated by the

---

The authors acknowledge with appreciation the assistance provided by the following individuals in making this chapter possible: Larry Adcock, Dail Miller, and John Meyers, of Larry Adcock and Associates, Albuquerque, New Mexico; Lawrence G. Williams, of the New Mexico Public Service Commission; Merle Benson, of the New Mexico Energy Institute; and David Reifschneider and Jeffrey Small, of the University of Wisconsin.

consumer price index, have risen by over 120 percent while the prices for natural gas and electricity have grown by more than 170 percent. While consumer prices rose steadily over the last decade, most of the natural-gas and electricity price increase occurred in the last five years.

The economic effects of raising energy prices are not distributed evenly over the population. Table 11–1 shows that average low-income households spend a much larger percentage of income on natural gas, electricity, and other forms of energy than households with higher incomes. As a result, energy price increases are more severe for low-income households and rapidly undermine the economic well-being of those with fixed incomes.

Lifeline pricing of utility services has been suggested as a way of offsetting the adverse economic effects of rising energy prices on low- and fixed-income households. The basic intent of the lifeline concept is to provide aid to specific customer groups by maintaining a relatively low price for some minimum amount of utility service. With lifeline pricing, the utility rate structure is used to achieve the equivalent of an income transfer.

Approaches to Lifeline Pricing

The lifeline concept may be applied in many different ways, in terms of both the customers covered by the lifeline rate and the manner in which the lifeline rate is constructed. In this chapter we examine the application of lifeline pricing to four customer groups:

1. Across the board to all residential customers
2. Targeted to low-income residential customers only
3. Targeted to elderly residential customers only
4. Targeted to low-income elderly residential customers only

With across-the-board lifeline pricing, all residential customers face a low rate for the lineline consumption block; thus, benefits would be provided to low-volume consumers regardless of age or income. As nonlifeline rates rise to compensate for the lifeline benefits, the size of the benefit will first dwindle to zero and then become an increasing burden for progressively larger levels of consumption. Consequently, with across-the-board lineline pricing, it is likely that low-income households which are large consumers will subsidize other low-income consumers as well as some consumers who are not economically disadvantaged. Targeted lifeline pricing seeks to avoid the anomalous cross-subsidization problems of the across-the-board approach by limiting benefits to the targeted socioeconomic class and shifting the responsibility for revenue recoupment outside the targeted population.

Several state public-utility regulatory agencies have already implemented across-the-board or targeted lifeline rates.[1] An across-the-board lifeline rate

Table 11-1
Annual Electricity and Natural-Gas Use and Expenditures by Various Residential Groups

Group	Electricity[a] Average Use (kWh)	Average Expenditure ($)	Average Expenditure as percent of Average Income	Natural Gas[b] Average Use (therms)	Average Expenditure ($)	Average Expenditure as percent of Average Income
Overall	6,613	336	1.8	1,285	285	1.6
< 65 yr[c]	6,948	351	1.8	1,312	291	1.5
≥ 65 yr	4,902	256	2.1	1,160	260	2.1
> $7,000[d]	6,992	353	1.6	1,317	291	1.3
≤ $7,000	5,084	264	6.6	1,161	261	6.5
≥ 65 and $7,000	5,583	288	1.7	1,267	281	1.5
≥ 65 and $7,000	3,668	199	4.6	996	227	5.3

Source: New Mexico Public Service Commission, *Lifeline Rates: A Study of the Possibility of Lifeline Rates for Gas and Electric Utility Service in New Mexico*, January 1980.

[a] Statistics reported for sampled customers of the Public Service Company of New Mexico (period: January to December 1978).
[b] Statistics reported for sampled cusotmers of the Gas Company of New Mexico (period: August 1978 to July 1979).
[c] One or more household members reported as being over 65 years of age.
[d] Adjusted (or modified) gross income as reported on the 1978 state income tax return.

went into effect in 1975 for California residential customers.[2] The California lifeline rates apply to both electricity and natural gas. The Masschusetts[3] and Michigan[4] regulatory agencies and the Los Angeles Department of Water and Power have authorized electricity lifeline rates targeted for elderly customers.

Effect of Lifeline Pricing on Residential Rates

Any of the various lifeline approaches requires the setting of new prices for utility service. Lifeline prices for a minimum amount of utility service will depend on the amount of assistance to be provided. New nonlifeline price levels will depend on a number of factors, including the size of the revenue burden arising from the establishment of the lifeline process, the allocation of the lifeline revenue burden over the utility's various customer classes, the consumption patterns of existing customers, the extent to which consumption is price-elastic, and, assuming price-elastic consumption, the utility's marginal cost of operation.

To determine the nonlifeline prices under the various lifeline options, we construct a price-generation model (PGM). Using the model, first we calculate the revenue burden associated with a particular lifeline option. Then we determine the nonlifeline prices consistent with the revenue-burden requirements. We assume within the model that the utility's profits will remain unchanged, even though total revenues might fluctuate.

Economic Analysis of Consumer Behavior

The price-generation model enables the systematic consideration of customer response to price changes. Our treatment of price responsiveness is built on the economic theory of consumption. Electricity or natural-gas prices can be represented as a vector

$$P = \{P_1, \ldots, P_n\}$$

where P_k is the price of consumption per unit of service for all consumption which occurs in the kth block only. Total consumption for customers whose last or marginal unit of consumption is in the kth rate block may be stated as

$$Q_k = q_k + \sum_{j=1}^{k-1} V_j$$

where q_k is the consumer's consumption in the kth block only and the V_j are the number of units in the inframarginal blocks.

Measuring the Potential Impacts

For a customer consuming in the kth block, the effects of price changes in inframarginal and marginal blocks (assuming that the customer does not shift to a new block) may be stated as

$$\frac{\partial Q_k}{\partial P_j} = \begin{cases} \dfrac{\partial I}{\partial P_j}\dfrac{\partial Q_k}{\partial I} & \text{for } j = k \quad (11.1) \\[1em] \left.\dfrac{\partial Q_k}{\partial P_j}\right|_I + \dfrac{\partial I}{\partial P_j}\dfrac{\partial Q_j}{\partial I} & \text{for } j = k \quad (11.2) \end{cases}$$

where I is the customer's income. With a block-pricing system, the budget constraint for the utility service and all other goods and services is piecewise linear. Under our assumption that the price changes would not induce the typical customer to shift from one rate block to another, the change in an inframarginal block price would be interpreted by the consumer as a change in his or her real income and hence induce the income response specified in equation 11.1. For a change in the marginal block price, the consumer's response would reflect both a substitution response (due to the change in relative prices for the relevant section of the budget constraint) and an income response. Noting the Hicksian compensating-variation relationship

$$\frac{\partial I}{\partial P_j} = -V_j \qquad \text{for } j < k$$

$$\frac{\partial I}{\partial P_k} = -q_k \qquad \text{for } j = k$$

we can reformulate equations 11.1 and 11.2 as

$$\frac{\partial Q_k}{\partial P_j} = \begin{cases} -V_j \dfrac{\partial Q_k}{\partial I} & \text{for } j < k \quad (11.3) \\[1em] \left.\dfrac{\partial Q_k}{\partial P_j}\right|_I - q_k \dfrac{\partial Q_k}{\partial I} & \text{for } j = k \quad (11.4) \end{cases}$$

Cross-multiplying equations 11.3 and 11.4 by p_1/Q_k, we have the basic Slutsky relationships:

$$\frac{\partial Q_k}{\partial P_k}\frac{P_j}{Q_k} = \begin{cases} -\dfrac{P_i V_j}{I}\dfrac{I}{Q_k}\dfrac{\partial Q_k}{\partial I} & \text{for } j < k \quad (11.5) \\[1em] \left.\dfrac{\partial Q_k}{\partial P_j}\dfrac{P_i}{Q_k}\right|_I - \dfrac{P_i q_k}{I}\dfrac{I}{Q_k}\dfrac{\partial Q_k}{\partial I} & \text{for } j = k \quad (11.6) \end{cases}$$

Equations 11.5 and 11.6 are the total price elasticity of demand for changes in the inframarginal and marginal rate-block prices, respectively. For a change in the inframarginal price, the price elasticity is equal to the income elasticity of demand times the "share" or proportion of total income which goes for purchasing an intramarginal block V_j of usage.

Defining η_s as the "income-compensated" price elasticity of demand and η_I as the income elasticity of demand, we can compute ∂Q_k, the change in Q_k, arising from a rate-block price change as

$$\partial Q_k = -Q_k \frac{\partial P_j + P_j V_j}{P_j \quad I} \eta_I \qquad \text{for } j < k \qquad (11.7)$$

$$Q_k \frac{\partial P_j}{P_j} \left(\eta_s - \frac{P_j q_k}{I} \eta_I \right) \qquad \text{for } j = k \qquad (11.8)$$

Equations 11.7 and 11.8 constitute the basis for incorporating the income and substitution effects, attendant with rate-block price changes, into our price-generation model.

Revenue-Burden Determination

The revenue for a given lifeline rate has two components. The first is the difference in the lifeline customers' revenues generated under the old rates and the revenues produced by the new lifeline rates for the consumption falling within the lifeline rate blocks. This component of the revenue burden is calculated as if customers do not change their consumption of electricity or natural gas in response to a price change. If consumption is price-responsive, then the second component must be considered.

The second component of the revenue-burden equation is the increase in consumption times the difference in the incremental cost of providing an additional unit of service and the price the customer would pay for that unit of service. Since lifeline prices would be lower than existing prices, and since electric and natural-gas services are considered to be "normal goods," we would expect the consumers who could take advantage of the lifeline rates to increase their consumption to the extent that their consumption is price-responsive. As the lifeline customers consume more service, additional costs will be incurred by the utility; however, the additional costs will be offset by the additional revenue generated from increased consumption. If marginal cost lies below the relevant price in the block in which the increase in consumption occurs, the second component reduces the total revenue burden. Conversely, if the marginal cost is greater than the respective price, the second component increases the burden.

Measuring the Potential Impacts

In general, we can state the revenue-burden (RB) components as

$$RB = \Delta PQ + (MC - P)\Delta Q$$

where ΔP = absolute price change after lifeline rate is implemented
Q = consumption before lifeline rates
MC = marginal cost
P = prelifeline price
ΔQ = change in consumption due to price change

More formally, the across-the-board lifeline-rate revenue burden is calculated as

$$RB = \sum_{i=1}^{12} \sum_{c=1}^{4} \sum_{k=1}^{l_i} [(1-\alpha)P_{ki}\tilde{Q}_{ki}^c + (MC_i - \alpha P_{ki})N_{ki}^c Q_{ki}^c (\alpha - 1) Y_{ki}^c] \quad (11.9)$$

and the revenue burden arising from a targeted lifeline can be specified as

$$RB_{C(T)} = \sum_{i=1}^{12} \sum_{C(T)} \sum_{k=1}^{l_i} [(1-\alpha)P_{ki}\tilde{Q}_{ki}^c + (MC - \alpha P_{ki})N_{ki}^c Q_{ki}^c (\alpha - 1) Y_{ki}^c]$$

$$+ \sum_{i=1}^{12} \sum_{C(T)} \sum_{k=l_i+1}^{S} [(MC - P_{ki})N_{ki}^c Q_{ki}^c (\alpha - 1) \sum_{j=1}^{l_i} W_{ki}^{cj}] \quad (11.10)$$

where, for the subscripts and superscripts,
i = month
j = inframarginal rate block
k = marginal rate block (block in which last unit of consumption falls)
l_i = number of lifeline rate blocks
s = total number of rate blocks
c = class, where 1 = elderly nonpoor, 2 = nonelderly nonpoor, 3 = elderly poor, and 4 = nonelderly poor
$C(T)$ = classes affected by specific targeted lifeline rate

and for the variables,
α = lifeline price-adjustment factor ($0 < \alpha < 1$)
P_{ki} = existing price
V_{ki} = width of the existing rate block ($k = 1, \ldots, s-1$)
MC_i = marginal cost
N_{ki}^c = total residential customers in class c whose consumption terminates in the kth block
N_i = total residential customers
Q_{ki}^c = average consumption of the N_{ki}^c group

q_{ki}^c = average consumption in the kth block only of the N_{ki}^c group
$\hat{Q}_{ki}^c$ = total consumption priced at P_{ki}
I_{ki}^c = average monthly income of N_{ki}^c group
η_s = income-compensated price elasticity of demand
η_I = income elasticity of demand
Z_{ki}^c = total price elasticity for a change in kth marginal block price only
W_{ki}^c = income effect of a change in jth inframarginal block price for residential customers whose consumption terminates in kth block

and the equation definitions are

$$Q_{ki}^c = q_{ki}^c + \sum_{j=1}^{k-1} V_{ji}$$

$$\hat{Q}_{ki}^c = N_{ki}^c q_{ki}^c + V_{ki} \sum_{m=k+1}^{S} N_{mi}^c$$

$$Z_{ki}^c = \eta_s - \frac{P_{ki} c_{ki}^c}{I_{ki}^c} \eta_I$$

$$W_{ki}^{cj} = \frac{-P_{ji} V_{ji}}{I_{ki}^c} \eta_I \quad j < k$$

$$Y_{ki}^c = Z_{ki}^c + \sum_{j=1}^{k-1} W_{ki}^{cj} \quad (= Z_{ki}^c \text{ for } k = 1)$$

The first term of equation 11.9 accounts for the revenue loss from repricing the lifeline blocks. The second term, $MC_i - \alpha P_{ki}$ times the change in consumption resulting from a change in price for the lifeline blocks, determines the addition to (subtraction from) the revenue function due to increased consumption when the marginal cost is greater (less) than the marginal price.

In equation 11.10, the targeted lifeline revenue burden is calculated in the same general fashion as the revenue burden for the across-the-board lifeline case; however, there are some differences. The first difference is that with the targeted lifeline rate, the burden is calculated for the target group only, that is, only for the poor, elderly, or elderly poor. The second difference is that in the targeted lifeline case, none of the revenue burden is assumed to be pased onto targeted-class customers who consume above the lineline level. The implication of the second difference is that the revenue-burden calculation should include a net revenue factor equaling the difference in marginal cost and price times the change in consumption for those targeted customers who

Measuring the Potential Impacts 191

consume above the lifeline level. The last expression in equation 11.10 is that factor.

Determining the Level of Nonlifeline-Rate Adjustments

Once the revenue-burden assessment is made, it is necessary to determine the new nonlifeline rates. The adjusted nonlifeline rates should be sufficient to yield revenues covering the assessed lifeline revenue burden, the revenues which would have come from the nonlifeline customer class had there not been lifeline pricing, and the change in costs arising from any change in nonlifeline consumption in response to the new rates.

There are several ways of adjusting the nonlifeline rates. In this chapter, two methods of rate adjustment are considered. The first method is to increase all nonlifeline rates by an equal percentage. This method maintains the same relative relationship among the nonlifeline rate-block prices as existed previously, but increases the absolute differences. The second approach is to add an equal per-unit-of-service surcharge to existing nonlifeline prices. This second rate-adjustment method keeps the same absolute difference between nonlifeline rate-block prices, but reduces the relative difference. For a system of declining block pricing, the second approach (an equal unit-of-service surcharge) places slightly more of the additional revenue burden on the larger nonlifeline users than the first approach does. The general formulation of the problem is

$$P^*Q^* = \delta RB + PQ + MC \, \Delta Q$$

where P^* = new nonlifeline price
Q^* = nonlifeline consumption at price P^*
P = existing nonlifeline price
P = nonlifeline consumption at price P
ΔQ = $Q^* - Q$
MC = marginal cost
δ = allocation factor (portion of lifeline revenue burden allocated to specific nonlifeline rate class)

For the equal-proportional increase, we define P^* as βP, where β is the equal-proportional price-adjustment factor. For the equal per-unit surcharge, we define P^* as $P + \pi$, where π is the surcharge value. Using the economic theory of consumption given above, given information on existing prices and quantities and given assumed values for the income and income-compensated price elasticities, we can calculate β and π. The solution takes the form of a quadratic equation. By incorporating the definitions provided above, the equations used to determine the nonlifeline residential rates for the different lifeline forms are as follows:

Equal-proportional increase

Across the board

$$\sum_{i=1}^{12}\sum_{c=1}^{4}\sum_{k=1}^{S}(\beta^2(P_{ki}N^c_{ki}Q^c_{ki}Y_{ki})+\beta\{P_{ki}\tilde{Q}^c_{ki}-N^c_{ki}Q^c_{ki}[P_{ki}(Y^c_{ki}-X^c_{ki})$$
$$+MC_iY^c_{ki}]\}+MC_iN^c_{ki}Q^c_{ki}(Y^c_{ki}-X^c_{ki})-P_{ki}\tilde{Q}^c_{ki})-\delta RB=0$$

Targeted

$$\sum_{i=1}^{12}\sum_{C(NT)}\sum_{k=1}^{S}\{\beta^2(P_{ki}N^c_{ki}Q^c_{ki}ZZ^c_{ki})+\beta[P_{ki}\tilde{Q}^c_{ki}$$
$$-N^c_{ki}Q^c_{ki}ZZ^c_{ki}(P_{ki}+MC)]+MC_iN^c_{ki}Q^c_{ki}ZZ^c_{ki}-P_{ki}Q^c_{ki}]$$
$$-\delta RB=0$$

Equal per-unit surcharge

Across the board

$$\sum_{i=1}^{12}\sum_{c=1}^{4}\sum_{k=l_i+1}^{l_i}\{\Pi^2(N^c_{ki}Q^c_{ki}G^c_{ki})+\Pi[\tilde{Q}^c_{ki}+N^c_{ki}Q^c_{ki}X^c_{ki}$$
$$+(P_{ki}-MC_i)N^c_{ki}Q^c_{ki}G^c_{ki}]+N^c_{ki}Q^c_{ki}X^c_{ki}(P_{ki}-MC_i)\}-\delta RE=0$$

Targeted

$$\sum_{i=1}^{12}\sum_{C(NT)}\sum_{k=1}^{S}\{\Pi^2(\tilde{Q}^c_{ki}H^c_{ki})+\Pi[\tilde{Q}^c_{ki}+N^c_{ki}Q^c_{ki}H^c_{ki}(P_{ki}-MC_i)[\}$$
$$-\delta RB=0$$

where $C(NT)$ = nonlifeline target classes

$$X^c_{ki}=(\alpha-1)\sum_{j=1}^{l_i}W^{cj}_{ki}$$

$$ZZ^c_{ki}=Z^c_{ki}+\sum_{j=1}^{k-1}W^{cj}_{ki}$$

$$G_{ki}^c = \begin{cases} \dfrac{Z_{ki}^c}{P_{ki}} + \sum_{j=1}^{k-1} \dfrac{W_{ki}^{cj}}{P_{ji}} & \text{for } j < k-1 \\[1em] \dfrac{Z_{ki}^c}{P_{ki}} & \text{for } j = k-1 \end{cases}$$

$$H_{ki}^c = \begin{cases} \dfrac{Z_{ki}^c}{P_{ki}} + \sum_{j=1}^{k-1} \dfrac{W_{ki}^{cj}}{P_{ji}} & \text{for } j < k-1 \\[1em] \dfrac{Z_{ki}^c}{P_{ki}} & \text{for } j = k-1 \end{cases}$$

In summary, the price-generation model estimates the revenue burden and the associated price change for nonlifeline consumption under any lifeline pricing approach. Next we present the results from a lifeline-rate economic analysis in which the model was applied.

An Assessment of the Economic Effects of Lifeline Pricing

Overview of New Mexico Study

The price-generation model was used in the analysis of the economic effects of implementing lifeline rates in several New Mexico utilities. A detailed study of residential energy-use patterns and of the feasibility of lifeline pricing was conducted under the auspices of the New Mexico Public Service Commission.[5] Data was gathered from participating utilities on monthly household electricity and natural-gas consumption and expenditures. Sufficient data were obtained to permit a test-year analysis of the revenue ramifications of lifeline pricing. Only data from customers with a full year's record were used in the PGM analysis. Income data were obtained from the New Mexico Taxation and Revenue Department (TRD). A match between a customer named and address on a utility's billing record and a 1978 income tax filer's name and address provided the means for estimating household income. To ensure confidentiality, no names or addresses were included in any file released from TRD. All utility and TRD record-matching operations were accomplished on TRD premises.

The household-income measure is either the reported adjusted gross income (AGI) on the state income tax form or the modified gross income (MGI) figure available for filers seeking a low-income tax credit. The modified gross income figure includes the AGI plus various taxable and nontaxable items such as social security benefits, unemployment-compensation benefits, pensions and annuities, and an estimate of in-kind benefits such a free gifts and room and board. Adjusted gross income differs from the TGI figure reported on federal forms, but not available on New Mexico income tax forms, in that business expenses, moving expenses, capital gain and loss, business income or loss, alimony, and other miscellaneous incomes and deductions are not included. The age of household members was determined based on whether an exemption was claimed for the filer or spouse being 65 or older.

Using the AGI or MGI as the household-income measure tends to result in overestimating the revenue burden for income-based, targeted lifeline approaches. The household-income measure is probably lower than the actual total household income because of various deductions and because it does not include nontaxable income such as veteran's or social security benefits. The measure also does not include incomes from all household members, although if the husband and wife filed jointly, their joint income is counted. As a result of understating actual household income, more households are estimated as being eligible for a targeted lifeline than would actually be the case, thus causing the revenue-burden projection to be too liberal.

Sampling was done randomly, stratified based on geographical area. Stratification by geographical area was necessary because the minimum-need lifeline levels included heating-energy requirements which were geographically dependent on climatic variations. Large sample sizes were necessary in order to give more statistical power to analyses on small socioeconomic groups within the population. In this chapter, we present the results of our analyses of data from the Public Service Corporation of New Mexico (PNM) and the Gas Company of New Mexico (GASCO). The PNM sample size was 11,000, or about 6 percent of all its residential customers. About 17 percent of all GASCO residential customers were in that utility's sample.

Tables 11–2 and 11–3 give the residential rate structures existing during the test period. The PNM rate structure is a traditional declining block, whereas GASCO's rates change from a declining block to an inverted rate in about the middle of the test period. Both include price adjustments on either a monthly or quarterly basis which pass through the cost-of-fuel or cost-of-service changes.

The lifeline consumption levels for which lifeline prices apply were selected by studying the energy requirements for lighting, refrigeration, water heating, cooking, and space-heating in New Mexico and by examining appliance saturations. For PNM, 200 kilowatthours per month was the

Table 11-2
Gas Company of New Mexico: Residential Natural-Gas Prices

| Rate Schedule, August 1978–February 1979 || Rate Schedule, March–July 1979 ||
Usage Block (Therms)	Price[a] (Cents per Therm)	Usage Block (Therms)	Price[b] (Cents per Therm)
0–40	22.3	0–165	24.03
Over 40	22.84	166–340	24.26
		Over 340	25.66

[a]Price includes a representative cost of gas adjustment of 16 cents per therm.
[b]Bill includes a $1.25 service charge and 4 percent sales tax.

Table 11-3
Public Service Company of New Mexico: Residential Electricity Prices

| For Customers with Overhead Service || For Customers with Underground Service ||
Usage Block (kWh)	Price[a] (¢/kWh)	Block (kWh)	Price[b] (¢/kWh)
0–200	5.0	0–200	5.3
201–650	4.6	200–800	4.8
Over 650	4.1 (June–Oct.)	Over 800	4.1 (June–Oct.)
	3.9 (Nov.–May)		3.9 (Nov.–May)

[a]Price includes a representative fuel and cost-of-service adjustment of 2.1 ¢/kWh.
[b]Bill includes a $1.60 and $2.60 service charge plus 4 percent sales tax for overhead and underground customers, respectively.

lifeline level. GASCO lifeline levels were 25 therms per month plus 85, 115, 120, and 140 therms per winter month for GASCO's low, moderate, high, and very high heating requirement regions, respectively. The definition of winter months varied by region depending on seasonal temperature patterns.

*Calculation of the Revenue Burden
for Two New Mexico Utilities*

The revenue-burden calculations were made by using monthly utility data including prices, total number of residential customers, and rate-block widths. Sample data were used for consumption and income variables for each of four classes; these classes were low income under 65, low income over 65, high income under 65, and high income over 65.

Each utility provided at least twelve months of data, though the twelve-month periods were not the same. The PNM data were for January 1978 through December 1978. For GASCO, the data covered August 1978 through July 1979. In both cases, income data were for calendar year 1978.

The PNM and GASCO revenue burdens were computed under various assumptions about income elasticity, income-compensated price elasticity, and marginal cost. Marginal costs were assumed to be unit short-run variable costs at current prices. Although the model accommodates varying price and income elasticities by class and rate-block group, the revenue burdens were calculated under an assumption of equal elasticities across groups and use levels. The chosen elasticities assume a short-run response. For all cases, revenue burdens were computed with lifeline prices at 65, 50, and 35 percent of the existing prices; that is, the lifeline price-adjustment factors were 0.65, 0.5, and 0.35.

The computed revenue burdens are presented in tables 11–4 and 11–5. As expected, the burdens are lower for the smaller than for the larger target populations. Although the burdens were computed under various elasticity assumptions, our calculations show that they are fairly insensitive to changes in η_s and η_I.

Table 11–4
PNM Revenue Burden
Price Elasticity = 0.2
Income elasticity = 0.6
Marginal cost = $0.0207/kWh

Lifeline Implementation Scenario	Lifeline Price-Adjustment Factor	Revenue Burden ($)	Percentage of Total Company Revenue
Across the board	0.65	7,043,674	4.8
	0.50	10,086,966	6.8
	0.35	13,145,004	8.9
Low income	0.65	2,555,133	1.7
	0.50	3,666,046	2.5
	0.35	4,786,473	3.2
Elderly	0.65	865,264	0.6
	0.50	1,241,636	0.8
	0.35	1,621,334	1.1
Low-income elderly	0.65	392,730	0.3
	0.50	564,949	0.4
	0.35	739,511	0.5

Measuring the Potential Impacts

Table 11–5
GASCO Revenue Burden
Price elasticity = 0.2
Income elasticity = 0.6
Marginal cost = $0.2096/therm

Lifeline Implementation Scenario	Lifeline Price-Adjustment Factor	Revenue Burden ($)	Percentage of Total Company Revenue
Across the board	0.65	16,036,362	7.9
	0.50	23,123,635	11.4
	0.35	30,339,634	14.9
Low income	0.65	6,302,971	3.1
	0.50	9,076,295	4.5
	0.35	11,892,851	5.8
Elderly	0.65	2,275,814	1.1
	0.50	3,281,078	1.6
	0.35	4,304,291	2.1
Low-income elderly	0.65	1,222,092	0.6
	0.50	1,761,738	0.9
	0.35	2,310,920	1.1

Calculation of the Rate Adjustments for Nonlifeline Consumption for the Two New Mexico Utilities

The rate adjustments for nonlifeline residential consumption were computed for each of the New Mexico utilities. Similar analytical procedures and price- and income-elasticity assumptions were used for these calculations as were employed in the revenue-burden calculations.

We selected three different values for the revenue-burden proportion allocated to nonresidential service classes. The percentage allocations are 0, 25, and 50.

To compute the equal-proportional (β) and equal-surcharge (π) rate adjustment, we assume the adjustment is unchanged throughout the twelve-month period. With GASCO, computations were first made for each heating area and then aggregated for the calculation of β and π. The computed rate adjustments are presented in tables 11–6 and 11–7. Comparing the two tables shows that the β and π results for PNM and GASCO are quite similar.

To determine the sensitivity of the rate adjustments to the price- and income-elasticity assumptions, we calculated rate-adjustment factors for several cases, varying the elasticity values. This sensitivity analysis indicates that β and π increase for higher price elasticities, but are generally unaffected by the size of the income elasticity. For a lifeline price-adjustment factor of

Table 11-6
PNM Nonlifeline Residential Consumption-Rate Increases

Price elasticity = 0.2
Income elasticity = 0.6
Marginal cost = $0.0207/kWh
β = proportional increase[a]
Π = incremental dollar increase[b]

Lifeline Implementation Scenario	Lifeline Price-Adjustment Factor	100 β	100 Π	75 β	75 Π	50 β	50 Π
Across the board	0.65	1.2878	0.0134	1.2094	0.0097	1.1358	0.0063
	0.50	1.4374	0.0205	1.3118	0.0145	1.1990	0.0092
	0.35	1.6147	0.0293	1.4251	0.0199	1.2659	0.0123
Low income	0.65	1.0809	0.0039	1.0604	0.0029	1.0019	
	0.50	1.1169	0.0056	1.0871	0.0042	1.0577	0.0028
	0.35	1.1538	0.0074	1.1144	0.0055	1.0757	0.0036
Elderly	0.65	1.0204	0.0010	1.0152	0.0007	1.0102	0.0005
	0.50	1.0293	0.0014	1.0219	0.0010	1.0146	0.0007
	0.35	1.0383	0.0018	1.0287	0.0014	1.0191	0.0009
Low-income elderly	0.65	1.0087	0.0004	1.0065	0.0003	1.0043	0.0002
	0.50	1.0125	0.0006	1.0093	0.0004	1.0062	0.0003
	0.35	1.0163	0.0008	1.0122	0.0006	1.0081	0.0004

Percentage of Revenue-Burden Allocation to Residential Customers

[a]The proportional increase β, when multiplied by the existing price, equals the new price to be paid for nonlifeline residential quantities of consumption.
[b]Π is in units of dollars per kilowatthour.

Table 11-7
GASCO Nonlifeline Residential Consumption-Rate Increases

Price elasticity = 0.2
Income elasticity = 0.6
Marginal cost = $0.2096/therm
β = proportional increase[a]
Π = incremental dollar increase[b]

Percentage of Revenue-Burden Allocation to Residential Customers

Lifeline Implementation Scenario	Lifeline Price-Adjustment Factor	100 β	100 Π	75 β	75 Π	50 β	50 Π
Across the board	0.65	1.2316	0.0571	1.1721	0.0424	1.1137	0.0280
	0.50	1.3399	0.0841	1.2513	0.0624	1.1652	0.0407
	0.35	1.4545	0.1129	1.3342	0.0827	1.2187	0.0539
Low income	0.65	1.0880	0.0213	1.0658	0.0159	1.0438	0.0106
	0.50	1.1274	0.0309	1.0952	0.0231	1.0632	0.0153
	0.35	1.1677	0.0407	1.1252	0.0303	1.0830	0.0201
Elderly	0.65	1.0224	0.0054	1.0168	0.0041	1.0112	0.0027
	0.50	1.0324	0.0078	1.0243	0.0059	1.0162	0.0039
	0.35	1.0425	0.0103	1.0319	0.0077	1.0212	0.0051
Low-income elderly	0.65	1.0112	0.0027	1.0084	0.0020	1.0056	0.0014
	0.50	1.0162	0.0039	1.0121	0.0029	1.0081	0.0020
	0.35	1.0213	0.0051	1.0159	0.0039	1.0106	0.0026

[a] The proportional increase β, when multiplied by the existing price, equals the new price to be paid for nonlifeline residential quantities of consumption.
[b] Π is in units of dollars per therm.

0.65 and a 75 percent revenue-burden allocation to the residential class, the computed β for PNM ranged from 1.16 to 1.33, 1.054 to 1.069, 1.014 to 1.017, and 1.006 to 1.008 for across-the-board, targeted, low-income, elderly, and low-income elderly for price elasticities varying between 0 and -0.4. Over a price elasticity range of 0 to -0.6 and with the same lifeline price-adjustment factor and revenue-burden allocation as above, the β for GASCO were from 1.163 to 1.195, 1.064 to 1.071, 1.016 to 1.018, and 1.008 to 1.009 for the four lifeline approaches, respectively.

Effect of Lifeline Pricing on Residential Customer Bills

Of basic interest with lifeline pricing is its effect on the bills of the residential customers. In the last section, we presented the residential nonlifeline rate-adjustment factors β and π. Those factors were used as input to a bill impact analysis model (BIAM). BIAM computes the new prices, customer bills under existing prices, customer bills under lifeline prices, and the percentage change in the bill for any given consumption level.

BIAM computations show that lifeline benefits accrue to customers in varying amounts, depending on the consumption level and the particular method of lifeline pricing. Tables 11–8 and 11–9 present the maximum dollar benefits for the eligible customer of PNM and GASCO. Maximum benefits for PNM customers with overhead and underground service and for GASCO customers in each region are given for a summer month, a winter month, and the year. The lifeline price was determined by multiplying the lifeline price-adjustment factor times the existing price; thus the maximum dollar benefit varies among utilities becaue of differing initial price and lifeline block size. During the winter months, the maximum dollar benefit changes with the size of the heating lifeline block in the four GASCO heating regions. Annual benefits vary as a result of differences in initial price, lifeline block size, and length of heating season.

Unless specified otherwise, the following results were based on PGM calculations using a lifeline price-adjustment factor of 0.65, a 100 percent revenue-burden allocation to the residential class, and a price elasticity of -0.2 and an income elasticity of 0.6.

Under the across-the-board lifeline approach, the maximum dollar benefit accrues to a consumer only if consumption occurs exactly at the maximum lifeline level and not beyond. Tables 11–10 and 11–11 present the percentage change and absolute dollar benefits for various quantities of consumption under an across-the-board lifeline-pricing approach. If we recall the previously mentioned lifeline levels, tables 11–9 and 11–10 show that benefits decline as use goes beyond the lifeline level.

Major costs of lifeline rates are the increases in customers' bills they

Table 11-8
Maximum Lifeline Benefits
(lifeline price = 65% of existing price)

	Summer Month ($)	Winter Month ($)	Annual ($)
PNM, overhead	3.73	4.00	44.02
PNM, underground	3.95	4.22	46.64
GASCO, very high	2.19	14.46	120.74
GASCO, high	2.19	12.71	96.86
GASCO, moderate	2.19	12.28	83.88
GASCO, low	2.19	9.66	61.54

Table 11-9
Maximum Lifeline Benefits
(lifeline price = 35% of existing price)

	Summer Month ($)	Winter Month ($)	Annual ($)
PNM, overhead	6.94	7.44	81.74
PNM, underground	7.34	7.84	86.61
GASCO, very high	4.07	26.85	224.24
GASCO, high	4.07	23.61	179.88
GASCO, moderate	4.07	22.80	155.77
GASCO, low	4.07	17.94	114.29

Table 11-10
Absolute Dollar and Percentage Changes in Customer Bills for Across-the-Board Lifeline Pricing
(based on August 1978 rates)

Monthly Consumption (kWh)	Absolute Dollar Change	Percentage Change
100	−1.87	−26.7
200	−3.73	−30.3
300	−2.32	−13.4
400	−0.90	−4.1
500	0.51	1.9
600	1.93	6.0
800	4.54	11.0
1,500	13.40	18.6

cause. Tables 11-12 to 11-14 give the percentage increase to nonlifeline residential customers' bills needed to pay for the lifeline benefits to specific target groups. The percentages fall as the lifeline price-adjustment factor and the nonresidential revenue-burden allocation rise.

Table 11-11
GASCO Absolute Dollar and Percentage Changes in Customer Bills for Across-the-Board Lifeline Pricing

Summer

Monthly Comsumption (Therms)	Absolute Dollar Change	Percentage Change
15	−1.32	−26.0
20	−1.75	−27.8
25	−2.19	−29.0
30	−1.90	−21.6
35	−1.61	−16.0
40	−1.32	−11.7
45	−1.04	− 8.3
50	−0.75	− 5.5
75	0.67	3.4
100	2.09	8.0

Winter

Monthly Consumption (Therms)	Very High		High		Moderate		Low	
110	−9.66	−33.4	−9.66	−33.4	−9.66	−33.4	−9.66	−33.4
140	−12.28	−33.7	−12.28	−33.7	−12.28	−33.7	−7.75	−21.3
160	−14.02	−33.9	−11.76	−28.4	−11.0	−26.6	−6.48	−15.7
180	−13.50	−29.1	−10.49	−22.6	−9.73	−21.0	−5.21	−11.2
200	−12.23	−23.8	−9.21	−18.0	−8.46	−16.5	−3.94	−7.7
220	−10.96	−19.5	−7.94	−14.1	−7.19	−12.8	−2.66	−4.7
240	−9.69	−15.8	−6.67	−10.9	−5.92	−9.7	−1.39	−2.3
300	−5.87	−7.7	−2.85	−3.7	−2.10	−2.8	2.42	3.2
350	−2.69	−3.0	0.33	0.4	1.08	1.2	5.60	6.3
400	0.49	0.05	3.51	3.5	4.26	4.2	8.78	8.7

Table 11-12
Percentage Increase in Nonlifeline Rates Required for Targeted Lifeline Aid to Low-Income Customers

Utility	Lifeline Price-Adjustment Factor	Percentage of Revenue Burden Allocated to Residential Customers		
		50	75	100
PNM	0.65	4.01	6.04	8.09
	0.50	5.77	8.71	11.69
	0.35	7.57	11.44	15.38
GASCO	0.65	4.38	6.58	8.80
	0.50	6.32	9.52	12.74
	0.35	8.30	12.52	16.77

Table 11-13
Percentage Increase in Nonlifeline Rates Required for Targeted Lifeline Aid to the Elderly

Utility	Lifeline Price-Adjustment Factor	\multicolumn{3}{c}{Percentage of Revenue Burden Allocated to Residential Customers}		
		50	*75*	*100*
PNM	0.65	1.02	1.52	2.04
	0.50	1.46	2.19	2.93
	0.35	1.91	2.87	3.83
GASCO	0.65	1.12	1.68	2.24
	0.50	1.62	2.43	3.24
	0.35	2.12	3.19	4.25

Table 11-14
Percentage Increase in Nonlifeline Rates Required for Targeted Lifeline Aid for Low-Income Elderly

Utility	Lifeline Price-Adjustment Factor	\multicolumn{3}{c}{Percentage of Revenue Burden Allocated to Residential Customers}		
		50	*75*	*100*
PNM	0.65	0.43	0.65	0.87
	0.50	0.62	0.93	1.25
	0.35	0.81	1.22	1.63
GASCO	0.65	0.56	0.84	1.12
	0.50	0.81	1.21	1.62
	0.35	1.06	1.59	2.13

For across-the-board lifeline, there is a consumption level beyond which customer bills increase. This point of consumption is called the breakeven level. The computed breakeven levels are 430 kWh for PNM, 60 therms in the summer, and from 260 to 400 therms for the low to the very high GASCO regions in the winter. The winter-month breakeven levels differ between GASCO's heating regions because of the different lifeline block sizes for each one.

The distribution of benefits and costs from lifeline pricing among the four socioeconomic groups can be seen through analyzing the electricity and natural-gas consumption distributions given in tables 11-15 and 11-16. For the sake of conciseness, but without loss of generality, only the natural-gas consumption distributions for the moderate GASCO heating region are given. The distributions suggest that the average benefit for poor and elderly customers is lower under across-the-board than the targeted lifeline approach, assuming that all eligible customers take the lifeline rates. The average benefit is lower because target-group customers do not pay a higher

Table 11-15
Percentage Distribution of Residential Consumers by Age and Income Class, PNM[a]

Consumption Level (kWh)	August Under 65 Under $7,000	August Under 65 Over $7,000	August 65 and over Under $7,000	August 65 and over Over $7,000	December Under 65 Under $7,000	December Under 65 Over $7,000	December 65 and over Under $7,000	December 65 and over Over $7,000
To 100	5.3	1.2	9.1	2.5	4.3	0.9	8.1	1.8
101–200	12.2	3.9	20.2	8.0	9.6	2.7	16.3	4.8
201–300	13.8	8.7	25.2	16.1	13.1	6.4	24.2	12.1
301–400	14.8	12.9	16.5	18.2	13.3	10.2	17.5	17.6
401–500	14.9	15.7	11.8	16.4	13.2	13.3	15.8	16.9
501–600	10.2	14.6	7.0	13.0	10.6	14.2	6.9	14.9
601–700	8.2	12.7	4.2	8.3	8.8	12.6	4.6	11.8
701–800	6.4	9.3	3.1	4.7	7.3	11.3	2.9	6.9
801–900	4.1	6.1	1.2	2.8	6.5	8.8	1.6	4.9
901–1,500	7.7	11.4	1.4	7.1	10.5	15.8	1.7	5.9
Over 1,500	2.4	3.5	0.3	2.9	2.8	3.8	0.5	2.5

[a]Percentages may not sum to 100 percent because of rounding.

Measuring the Potential Impacts

price for consumption above the lifeline block under a targeted lifeline whereas they do under an across-the-board lifeline.

Some poor and elderly customers could also face a significant bill increase under an across-the-board lifeline. By referring to tables 11–10 and 11–15, it can be seen that in August 1978, approximately 14 percent of the under-65, low-income households and 3 percent of the over-65, low-income households would have received electricity-bill increases exceeding 11 percent. In reference to tables 11–11 and 11–16, about 4 percent of the under-65, low-income households and 1 percent of the over-65, low-income households would have seen more than a 4 percent gas-bill increase. Under the targeted lifeline approach, this problem does not occur; all targeted customers consuming at or above the lifeline level receive the maximum benefit.

Table 11–16
Percentage Distributions of Residential Consumers by Age and Income Class, GASCO Moderate[a]

Consumption Level (Therms)	August			
	Under $7,000	Over $7,000	Under $7,000	Over $7,000
To 15	9.9	7.8	21.7	16.6
16–20	8.8	9.1	17.0	15.9
21–25	11.8	12.1	17.6	16.0
26–30	14.2	13.5	14.4	13.3
31–35	10.9	13.6	8.6	11.0
36–40	10.9	11.8	6.4	6.9
41–45	8.5	8.9	4.8	6.5
46–50	6.7	6.5	2.7	4.2
51–75	14.4	12.5	5.5	6.9
76–100	2.2	2.0	0.5	1.3
Over 100	1.7	2.2	0.7	1.5

Consumption Level (Therms)	December			
	Under 65		65 and over	
	Under $7,000	Over $7,000	Under $7,000	Over $7,000
0–110	15.3	8.8	24.2	11.6
111–140	12.2	9.4	18.2	11.8
141–160	9.6	8.7	11.7	7.9
161–180	9.8	8.9	12.2	11.1
181–200	9.8	9.5	8.2	10.1
201–220	7.9	9.4	7.3	9.0
221–240	7.5	9.0	5.7	7.2
241–300	14.1	19.3	8.6	16.7
301–350	6.7	8.5	1.8	7.6
351–400	3.5	4.4	0.7	3.6
Over 400	3.5	4.2	1.2	3.5

[a]Percentages may not sum to 100 percent because of rounding.

Effect of Lifeline Pricing on Nonresidential Customers

Lifeline pricing affects nonresidential (industrial, commercial) customers to the extent that a portion of the revenue burden generated by lifeline pricing is allocated to the nonresidential classes of service. Three possibilities for allocating the revenue burden among the nonlifeline customers were considered. The first scenario limits the assessment of the lifeline revenue burden to the residential class. The other two scenarios assume a 25 and a 50 percent allocation, respectively, to the nonresidential customers. If a portion of the revenue burden is allocated to the nonresidential class, their rates will increase.

The impact of the alternative allocations to the nonresidential classes can be seen in tables 11–17 and 11–18. They give the percentage increase in nonresidential revenues, assuming existing levels of consumption for differing lifeline price-adjustment factors and revenue-burden allocations. The likely impact of those increases can be estimated by considering the portion of total industrial and commercial costs which goes for electricity or natural-gas consumption. The portion is very low, usually less than 2 percent.[6] The impact on the prices of the goods sold by manufacturers or other firms, assuming all the increase is passed on to the customers, can be estimated by multiplying the percentage of revenue increase by the percentage of total costs of the firm which goes for natural-gas and electricity service. For example, with a 10 percent increase in rates and a natural-gas and electricity expenditure share of 1 percent, the total costs of the firm would rise by only 0.1 percent.

Final Comments

We have presented a methodology for assessing the economic effects of implementing any one of several lifeline pricing approaches and have given the results of analyses of the rate and revenue implications of lifeline pricing as applied to two New Mexico utilities. The results suggest that lifeline pricing can be a viable method for supplying aid to needy households.

Several important issues remain to be addressed in future research. One issue pertains to economic welfare costs and optimal pricing. We have neither undertaken to quantify the economic welfare costs of establishing a set of prices which diverge from either the existing prices or an optimal set of utility prices, nor attempted to structure the nonlifeline prices in an optimal fashion, given the levels of lifeline benefit selected. Thus we note that the price results we show may be Pareto-superior to the existing prices, but are most likely Pareto-inferior to an alternative set of nonlinear prices. Other important issues are:

Table 11-17
Allocated GASCO Revenue Burden as a Percentage of Nonresidential Revenue

Lifeline Implemntation Scenario	Lifeline Price-Adujstment Factor	Percentage Allocated to Nonresidential Classes 25	50
Across the board	0.65	2.69	5.38
	0.50	3.88	7.76
	0.35	5.09	10.18
Low income	0.65	1.06	2.12
	0.50	1.52	3.05
	0.35	2.00	3.99
Elderly	0.65	0.38	0.76
	0.50	0.55	1.10
	0.35	0.72	1.44
Low-income elderly	0.65	0.21	0.41
	0.50	0.30	0.59
	0.35	0.39	0.78

Table 11-18
Allocated PNM Revenue Burden as a Percentage of Nonresidential Revenue

Lifeline Implementation Scenario	Lifeline Price-Adjustment Factor	Percentage Allocated to Nonresidential Classes 25	50
Across the board	0.65	1.83	3.67
	0.50	2.63	5.25
	0.35	3.42	6.84
Low income	0.65	0.67	1.33
	0.50	0.95	1.91
	0.35	1.25	2.49
Elderly	0.65	0.23	0.45
	0.50	0.32	0.65
	0.35	0.42	0.84
Low-income elderly	0.65	0.10	0.20
	0.50	0.15	0.29
	0.35	0.19	0.39

1. What are the administrative costs and coverage benefits of alternative forms of welfare?
2. How could aid be provided to that portion of the population which does not pay utility bills directly?
3. What portion of the population would avail itself of the targeted lifeline benefits?

4. What would the administrative costs of a targeted lifeline scenario be?

Consideration of these issues along with the type of economic analysis given in this chapter should help legislators and regulators as they examine methods to ease the unequally distributed burden of rising energy costs.

Notes

1. New Mexico Public Service Commission (1980).
2. Public Utilities Commission of California (1976).
3. Massachusetts Department of Public Utilities, Order No. 19376.
4. Michigan Public Service Commission, Order Nos. U-5331 and U-6020, for the Consumers Power Company, January 29, 1979, and No. U-6006 for the Detroit Edison Company, May 22, 1979.
5. New Mexico Public Service Commission (1980).
6. Ibid., p. V42.

References

Acton, J.P., and Mitchell, B.M., 1980. Evaluating time-of-day electricity rates for residential customers. R-2509-DWP, Rand Corporation, October. Forthcoming in *Regulated Industries and Public Enterprise: European and United States Perspectives*, eds. B.M. Mitchell and P.R. Kleindorfer. Lexington, Mass.: Lexington Books, D.C. Heath.

Aigner, D.J. 1979. Price elasticities by time-of-use. Draft manuscript prepared for the Electric Power Research Institute.

Aigner, D.J., and Hausman, J.A., 1978*a*. Correcting for selection bias in the analysis of volunteer experiments in time-of-day pricing of electricity. In *Proceedings of EPRI Workshop on Modeling and Analysis of Electricity Demand by Time-of-Day*, ed. D. Aigner, pp. 9-1 to 9-20, San Diego, Calif., June 11-14.

──────. 1978*b*. Correcting for truncation bias in the analysis of experiments in time-of-day pricing of electricity. Presented at the EPRI Workshop on Modeling and Analysis of Electricity Demand by Time-of-Day. San Diego, Calif., June 12-14.

Aigner, D. J., and Poirier, D.J., 1980. *Electricity Demand and Consumption by Time-of-Use: A Survey*. Palo Alto, Calif.: Electric Power Research Institute, forthcoming.

Arkansas Public Service Commission, Final report—Arkansas demand management demonstration study. Processed by the Department of Energy (undated).

Artle, R., and Averous, C. 1973. The telephone system as a public good: Static and dynamic aspects. *The Bell Journal of Economics and Management Science* 4 (Spring).

Atkinson, S. 1977. Responsiveness to time-of-day electricity pricing: First empirical results. In *Forecasting and Modeling Time-of-Day and Seasonal Electricity Demands*, ed. A. Lawrence, Palo Alto, Calif.: EPRI report EA-578-SR.

──────. A comparative analysis of consumer response to time-of-use electricity pricing: Arizona and Wisconsin. In *Proceedings of EPRI Workshop on Modeling and Analysis of Electricity Demand by Time-of-day*, ed. D. J. Aigner, pp. 8-1 to 8-33. San Diego, Calif., June 11-14.

Averch, H., and Johnson, L.L. 1962. Behavior of the firm under regulatory constraint. *American Economic Review* 52 (December): 1052-1069.

Bailey, E.E. 1973. *Economic Theory of Regulatory Constraint*. Lexington, Mass.: Lexington Books, D.C. Heath.

Bailey, E.E., and Coleman, R.D. 1971. The effect of lagged regulation in an Averch-Johnson model. *Bell Journal of Economics and Management Science* 2 (Spring): 278-292

Bailey, E.E., and Malone, J.C. 1970. Resource allocation and the regulated firm. *Bell Journal of Economics* 1 (Spring): 129–142.

Baron, D.P. 1980. Regulatory strategies under assymetric information. Working Paper, Northwestern University. Evanston, Ill.

Baron, D.P., and De Bondt, R.R. 1979. Fuel adjustment mechanisms and economic efficiency. *Journal of Industrial Economics* 27 (March): 243–261.

Baron, D.P., and De Bondt, R.R., 1980. "Factor price changes, technical efficiency and revenue requirements. Working Paper, Northwestern University, Evanston, Ill.

Baron, D.P., and Myerson, R.B. 1979. Regulating a monopolist with uncertain costs. Working Paper, Northwestern University. Evanston, Ill.

Baron, D.P., and Taggart, R.A. 1977. A model of regulation under uncertainty and a test for regulatory bias. *Bell Journal of Economics* 8, no. 1 (Spring): 151–167.

_____. 1978. Regulatory pricing policies and input choices. Discussion Paper, Graduate School of Management, Northwestern University, Evanston, Ill.

Bauer, J. 1925. *Effective Regulation of Public Utilities*. New York: Macmillan.

_____. 1966. *Updating Public Utility Regulation*. Washington: Public Administration Publishers.

Baumol, W.J., and Bradford, D.F. 1970. Optimal departures from marginal cost pricing. *American Economic Review* 60 (January): 265–283.

Baumol, W.J., and Klevorick, A.K. 1970. Input choices and rate-of-return regulation: An overview of the discussion. *Bell Journal of Economics* Fall, pp. 162–190.

Baumol, W.J.; Fischer, D.; Raa, T. 1979. The Price–iso return locus and rational rate regulation. *Bell Journal of Economics* 10(Autumn): 648–658.

Beauvais, E.C. 1977. The demand for residential telephone service under non-metered tariffs: Implications for alternative pricing policies. General Telephone & Electronics, Stamford, Conn.: Paper presented at the Western Economic Association Meetings, Anaheim, Calif., June.

Becker, G.S. 1965. A theory of the allocation of time. *Economic Journal* 75(September): 493–517.

Berkowitz, M.K. 1977. Power grid economics in a peak load pricing framework. *Canadian Journal of Economics* 10, no. 4 (November): 621–636.

Billinton, R. 1970. *Power System Reliability Evaluation*. New York: Gordon & Breach.

Blattenberger, G.R. 1977. The residential demand for electricity. Unpublished Ph.D. dissertation. Department of Economics, University of Michigan, Ann Arbor.

References

Boggis, J.G. 1974. Domestic tariffs experiment. *Load and Market Research Report.* No. 121. London: The Electricity Council.

Bonbright, J.C. 1948. Utility rate cases considered in light of the *Hope* natural gas case. *American Economic Review* 38 (May): 465–482.

Braeutigam, R.R. 1979. An analysis of fully distributed cost pricing in regulated industries. Working Paper, Northwestern University. Evanston, Ill.

Brooks, J. 1976. *Telephone: The First Hundred Years*, New York: Harper & Row.

Buchanan, J.M. 1952–1953. The theory of monopolistic discount pricing. *Review of Economic Studies* 20.

Burbank, H.D. 1977. The Connecticut peak load pricing experiment. In *Forecasting and Modeling Time-of-Day and Seasonal Electricity Demands*, ed. A. Lawrence. Palo Alto, Calif.: Electric Power Research Institute, EA 578-SR.

California Legislature. 1974. Assembly Concurrent Resolution No. 192. August 31.

California Public Utilities Commission. 1976. Pacific Gas and Electric Company: Decision No. 86632. November 16.

———. 1977a. San Diego Gas and Electric Company: Decision No. 87445. August 23.

———. 1977b. Southern California Edison Company: Decision No. 87444. August 23.

———. California's lifeline energy rate reform program. November 2.

Cargill, T.E., and Meyer, R.A. 1971. Estimating the demand for electricity by time-of-day. *Applied Economics* 3: 233–246.

Caves, D.W., and Christensen, L.R. 1978. Econometric analysis of the Wisconsin residential time-of-use electricity pricing experiment. In *Proceedings of the EPRI Workshop on Modeling and Analysis of Electricity Demand by Time-of-Day*, ed. D. Aigner, pp. 7-1 to 7-26. San Diego, Calif., June 11–14.

———. 1979. Residential substitution of off peak for peak electricity usage under time-of-use pricing: An analysis of 1976 and 1977 summer dat from the Wisconsin experiment. Manuscript.

———. 1980. Global properties of flexible functional forms. *American Economic Review* (forthcoming).

Cicchetti, C.J., and Foell, W.K. eds. 1975. *Energy Systems Forecasting Planning and Pricing: Proceedings of a French-American Conference.* Madison, Wisc.: Institute for Environmental Studies.

Clemens, E. 1954. Some aspects of the rate of return problem. *Land Economics* 30 (February): 32–43.

Consumers Power Company. Electric Department. Summary of the time-of-day study ordered by MPSC Order U-4840.

Cosgrove, J.G., and Linhart, P.B. 1979. Customer choices under local measured telephone service. *Public Utilities Fortnightly* 17 (August 30) and 104, no. 5 (August): 27–31.

Crain, W.M., and Ekelund, R.B., Jr. 1976. Chadwick and Demsetz on competition and regulation. *The Journal of Law and Economics* 19 (April): 149–162.

Crew, M.A., ed. 1979. *Problems in Public Utility Economics and Regulations.* Lexington, Mass.: Lexington Books, D.C. Heath.

Crew, M.A., and P.R. Kleindorfer. 1975. Optimal plant mix in peak load pricing. *Scottish Journal of Political Economy* 22, no. 3 (November): 277–291.

_____. 1976. Peak load pricing with a diverse technology. *Bell Journal of Economics* 7(Spring).

_____. 1978. Reliability and public utility pricing. *American Economic Review* 68(March).

_____. 1979a. Some elementary considerations of reliability and regulation. In Problems in Public Utility Economics and Regulations, ed. M.A. Crew. Lexington, Mass.: Lexington Books, D.C. Heath.

_____. 1979b. Managerial discretion and public utility regulation. *Southern Economic Journal* 45(January): 696–709.

_____. 1979c. *Public Utility Economics.* New York: St. Martin's Press.

_____. 1980. Rate-of-return regulation with a diverse technology. Unpublished manuscript.

Cudahy, R.D., and Malko, J.R. 1976. Electric peak-load pricing: Madison Gas and beyond. *Wisconsin Law Review* 1: 47–73.

Davis, E.G. 1973. A dynamic model of the regulated firm with a price adjustment mechanism. *Bell Journal of Economics* 4(Spring): 270–282.

Demsetz, H. 1968. Why regulate utilities? *The Journal of Law and Economics* 11(April): 55–65.

De Muth, L.W., Jr. 1979. The shapes and shadows of the regulators' economic dilemma. In *Pricing in Regulated Industries: Theory and Practice*, ed. J.T. Wenders. Denver, Colo.: Mountain Bell Telephone and Telegraph Co.

Detroit Edison. 1978. *Effect of Time-Of-Use Rates on Load Characteristics for Primary Rate Customers, 1975–1978,* (November), Detroit.

Dordick, H.S. 1979. *Proceedings of the 6th Annual Telecommunications Policy Research Conference.* Lexington, Mass.: Lexington Books, D.C. Heath.

Electric Power Research Institute. 1979. Evaluation of the Federal Energy Administration's load management and rate design demonstration projects. Palo Alto, Calif.: EPRI report EA-1152.

Electric Utility Rate Design Study. 1977a. Potential cost advantages of peak load pricing: Topic 6 Report 16. Prepared by Power Technologies, Inc.

_____. 1977b. Estimating the benefits of peak-load pricing for utilities:

References

Topic 6. Report 17. Prepared by Systems Control, Inc.

———. 1977c. Measuring the potential cost advantages of peak-load pricing: Topic 6. Report 17. Prepared by Systems Control, Inc.

———. 1977d. Potential cost advantages of load management: Topic 6. Prepared by Task Force No. 6.

———. 1979a. Reference Manual and Procedures for Implementing PURPA. Report to National Association of Regulatory Utility Commissioners, p. 82. Palo Alto, Calif.

———. 1979b. An evaluation of four marginal costing methodologies, Report no. 66. Prepared by Temple Barker and Sloane, Inc.

———. 1979c. Equipment for load management: Communications, metering, and equipment for using off-peak energy, Topic Paper 4. Report 87. Palo Alto, Calif.: Electric Power Research Institute.

———. 1979d. 1979 survey: State and federal regulatory commissions: Electric utility rate design and load management activities. Report 80. Palo Alto, Calif.: Electric Power Research Institute.

———. 1979e. Reference manual and procedures for implementing PURPA, electric utility rate design study. Report 82. Palo Alto, Calif.: Electric Power Research Institute.

———. 1980. Elasticities by time-of-use. Topic Paper 1. Palo Alto, Calif.: Electric Power Research Institute (forthcoming).

Endrenyi, J. 1978. *Reliability Modeling in Electric Power Systems.* New York: John Wiley & Sons.

Faruqui, A. 1979. The dynamics of energy substitution in California manufacturing: 1958–1976. Unpublished Ph.D. dissertation. University of California at Davis.

Faulhaber, R., and Panzar, J.C. 1977. Optimal two-part tariffs with self-selection. *Bell Laboratories Economic Discussion Paper* 74.

Federal Communications Commission. 1976. *Docket No. 18128 Memorandum Opinion and Order.*

Gabor, A. 1966. Further comment (on peak loads and efficient pricing). *Quarterly Journal of Economics* 80(August): 472–480.

Garfinkel, L., and Linhart, P.B. 1979. The transition to local measured telephone service. *Public Utilities Fortnightly* 17(August 16) and 104(4): 17–21.

Gelhaus, R.J., and Wilson, G.D. 1968. An earnings-price approach to fair rate of return in regulated industries. *Stanford Law Review* 58 (December): 975–1005.

Gordon, M.J. 1977. Comparison of historical cost and general price level adjusted cost rate base regulation. *Journal of Finance* 32 (December): 1501–1513.

Gordon, M.J., and McCallum, J.S. 1972. Valuation and the cost of capital for regulated industries: Comment. *Journal of Finance* 27(December): 1141–1146.

Granger, C.W.J.; Engle, R.; Ramanathan, R.; Anderson, A. 1979. Residential load curves and time-of-day pricing: An econometric analysis. *Journal of Econometrics* 9, nos. 1 and 2 (January): 13–32.

Greenhut, M.L., and Ohta, H. 1975. Theory of spatial pricing and market areas. Durham, N.C.: Duke University Press.

Gronau, R. 1976. Leisure, home production, and work—the theory of the allocation of time revisited. *Journal of Political Economy* 35, no. 6 (December 1977).

Hausman, J.A., and McFadden, D. 1978. A two-level electricity demand model: Evaluation of the Connecticut time-of-day pricing test. In *Proceedings of EPRI Workshop on Modeling and Analysis of Electricity Demand by Time-of-Day*, ed. D. Aigner. pp. 12–1 to 12–30, San Diego, Calif., June 11–14.

Hendricks, W., and Koenker, R. 1980. Demand for electricity by time-of-day: An evaluation of experimental results. *Bell Laboratories Working Paper*.

Hendricks, W.; Koenker, R.; Poirier, D. 1979a. Residential demand for electricity by time-of-day, An econometric approach. *Journal of Econometrics* 19, nos. 1, 2 (January): 33–57.

———. 1979b. Stochastic parameter models for panel data: An application to the Connecticut peak load pricing experiment. *International Economic Review* 20, no. 3 (October): 121–138.

Hieronymus, W.H., and Hughes, W.R. 1977. Residential load forecasting with time-of-day rates. In *Forecasting and Modeling Time-of-Day and Seasonal Electricity Demands*, ed. A. Lawrence. Palo Alto, Calif.: Electric Power Research Institute.

Infosino, W.J. 1980. Class of service choice among residence telephone customers. Report. Murray Hill, N.J.: Bell Laboratories.

Jones, F. 1978. An empirical test of input efficiency in the regulated electric utility. Ph.D. dissertation. New York: Garland Pub. Co. (forthcoming).

Joskow, P. 1974. Inflation and environmental concern: Structural changes in the process of public utility price regulation. *Journal of Law and Economics* 17 (October): 291–327.

Kahn, A.E., and Zielinski, C.A. 1976. New rate structures in communications. *Public Utilities Fortnightly* 101(March 25): 19–24.

Keeler, E.; Newhouse, J.; Phelps, C. 1977. Deductibles and the demand for medical services: The theory of the consumer facing a variable price schedule under uncertainty. *Econometrica* 45, no. 3 (April): 641–655.

Keran, M. 1976. Inflation, regulation, and utility stock prices. *Bell Journal of Economics* 7(Spring): 268–280.

Klevorick, A.K. The behavior of a firm subject to stochastic regulatory review. *Bell Journal of Economics* 4(Spring): 57–88.

Koenker, R. 1978. Econometric models of periodic demand in continuous

References

time. In *Proceedings of EPRI Workshop on Modeling and Analysis of Electricity Demand by Time-of-Day*, ed. D. Aigner, San Diego, Calif.: pp. 11-1 to 11-17. June 11-14.

Krutilla, J.V. 1967. Conservation reconsidered. *American Economic Review* 57 (September).

Lau, L.J., and Lilliard, L.A. 1978. A random response model of the demand for electricity by time-of-day. In *Proceedings of EPRI Workshop on Modeling and Analysis of Electricity Demand by Time-of-Day*, ed. D. Aigner, pp. 10-1 to 10-26. San Diego, Calif.: June 11-14.

Lawrence, A., and Braithwaite, S. 1977. The residential demand for electricity by time-of-day: An econometric analysis. In *Forecasting and Modeling Time-of-Day and Seasonal Electricity Demands*, ed. A. Lawrence. Palo Alto, Calif.: Electric Power Research Institute.

──────. 1979. The residential demand for electricity by time-of-day: An econometric analysis. *Journal of Econometrics* 9, nos. 1, 2 (January): 59-77.

Leibenstein, H. 1966. Allocative vs. X-efficiency. *American Economic Review* 56(June): 392-415.

Leland, H.E. 1974. Regulation of natural monopolies and the fair rate of return. *Bell Journal of Economics* 5(Spring): 3-15.

Leventhal, H. 1965. Vitality of the comparable earnings standard for regulation of utilities in a growth economy. *Yale Law Journal* 74(May): 989-1018.

Levin, S.; Taylor, L.D.; Wenders, J.T. 1979. *The Impact of Marginal Cost Electricity Pricing in the State of Maryland*. Washington: Data Resources, Inc.

Linder, S.B. 1970. *The Harried Leisure Class*. New York: Columbia University Press.

Lintner, J. 1965. The valuation of risk assets and the selection of risky investments in stock portfolios and capital budgets. *Review of Economics and Statistics*, February.

Littlechild, S.C. 1972. A state preference approach to public utility pricing and investment under risk. *Bell Journal of Economics* 3, no. 1 (Spring): 340-345.

──────. 1975b. Two-part tariffs and consumption externalities. *Bell Journal of Economics* 6(Autumn): 661-670.

Litzenberger, R.H., and Sosin, H.B. 1979. A comparison of capital structure decisions of regulated and non-regulated firms. *Financial Management* 8(Autumn): 17-21.

Maddala, G.S. 1977. *Econometrics*. New York: McGraw-Hill.

Malko, J.R. 1978. Implementing time-of-use pricing. Presented at *Engineering Economy for Public Utilities*, Seventeenth Annual Program, Stanford University. Palo Alto, Calif.

Malko, J.R.; Ray, D.J.; Hassig, N.L. 1979. Time-of-day pricing of electricity activities in some Midwestern states. Presented at the Midwest Economics Association annual meeting. Chicago, Ill., April.

Malko, J.R., and Simpson, J. 1978. Time-of-use pricing in practice: Some recent regulatory actions. In *Assessing New Pricing Concepts in Public Utilities*, ed. H.M. Trebing. Presented at the ninth annual conference, Institute of Public Utilities. Williamsburg, Va., December 1977.

Malko, J.R., and Uhler, R.G. 1979. The rate design study: Helping evaluate load management. *Public Utilities Fortnightly*, October 11, pp. 11–17.

Manning, W.G., Jr., and Acton, J.P., 1978. Residential energy demand under time-of-day pricing: Preliminary results from the Los Angeles rate study. Preliminary draft. Rand Corporation, Santa Monica, Calif.

Marino, A. 1978. Peak-load pricing in a neoclassical technology with bounds on variable input utilization. *Bell Journal of Economics* 9(Spring): 249–259.

Massachusetts Department of Public Utilities. Order No. 19376.

McKie, J.W. 1970. Regulation and the free market: The problem of boundaries. *Bell Journal of Economics* 1(Spring): 6–26.

Meyer, J.R.; Wilson, R.W.; Baughcum, M.A.; Barton, E.; Caouette, L. 1979. *The Economics of Competition in the Telecommunications Industry*. Boston: Charles River Associates, Inc.

Michigan Public Service Commission. 1976. Consumers' power: Order, case no. U-4840, p. 71. (April 12).

──────. 1976. Opinion and order determining relevance of marginal costs to electric rate structures. Opinion no. 76–15, case 26806. August 10, p. 33.

──────. 1979. Order nos. U-5331 and U-6020 for the Consumers Power Company and U-6006 for the Detroit Edison Company.

Miedama, A.K.; Olson, J.A.; Lifson, D.P.; Krakauer, B. 1978. Analysis of the effects of time-of-use electricity rates in the Arizona electric utility demonstration project. Final draft report. North Carolina: Research Triangle Institute.

Miedema, A.K.; Lifson, D.P.; Reid, P.A. Time-of-use electricity prices, Wisconsin—Interim Report. Research Triangle Institute.

Miller, R.E., and Reed, H.J. 1979. Testimony on behalf of the United States Department of Energy before the State of Connecticut Department of Business Regulation. Docket nos. 790521, 790522.

Mitchell, B.M. 1976. Optimal pricing of local telephone service. Rand Corporation R-1962-MF.

──────. 1978. Optimal pricing of local telephone service. *American Economic Review* 68(September): 517–537.

──────. 1979*a*. Economic aspects of measured-service telephone pricing. Rand Corporation Report P-632kL.

References

———. 1979b. Economic issues in local measured service. In *Perspectives on Local Measured Service*, ed. J.A. Baruk, pp. 41–56. Telecommunications Industry Workshop Organizing Committee.

———. 1979c. Pricing policies in selected European telephone systems. In *Proceeding of the Sixth Annual Telecommunications Policy Research Conference*, ed. H.S. Dordick, p. 437–475. Lexington, Mass.: Lexington Books, D.C. Heath.

———. 1979d. Telephone call pricing in Europe: Localizing the pulse. In *Pricing in Regulated Industries: II*, ed. J.T. Wenders, pp. 19–50. Denver, Colo.: Mountain States Telephone and Telegraph Co.

Mitchell, B.M., and Kleindorfer, P.R., eds. 1980. *Regulated Industries and Public Enterprise*. Lexington, Mass.: Lexington Books, D.C. Heath.

Mitchell, B.M.; Manning, W.G., Jr.; Acton, J.P. 1978. *Peak Load Pricing: European Lessons for U.S. Energy Policy*. Cambridge, Mass.: Ballinger.

Modigliani, F., and Miller, M.H. 1958. The cost of capital, corporation finance, and the theory of investment. *American Economic Review* 48(June): 261–297.

Morehouse, E.W. 1955. Comment on the rate of return problem and cost of capital in public utilities. *Land Economics* 31(Feburary): 75–77.

Morton, W.A. 1952. Rate of return and value of money in public utilities. *Land Economics* 28(May): 91–131.

Mossin, J. 1966. Equilibrium in a capital asset market. *Econometrica*, October.

Myers, S.C. 1973. A simple model of firm behavior under regulation and uncertainty. *Bell Journal of Economics* 4(Spring): 304–315.

New Mexico Public Service Commission. 1975. Public Service Company of New Mexico. Case no. 1196. *Public Utility Reports 8 4th*: (April 22): 113–139.

———. 1980. Lifeline rates: A study of the possibility of lifeline rates for gas and electric utility service in New Mexico, Washington, D.C.

New York Public Service Commission, 1976. Opinion and order determining relevance of marginal costs to electric rate structures. Opinion no. 76-15 Case 26806, Albany, N.Y.

Ng, Y.-K, and Weisser, M. 1974. Optimal pricing with a budget constraint: The case of the two-part tariff. *Review of Economic Studies* 41 (July): 337–345.

Nichols, E. 1955. *Ruling Principles of Utility Regulation: Rate of Return*. Washington: Public Utilities Reports.

Oi, W.Y. 1971. A Disneyland dilemma: Two-part tariffs for a Mickey Mouse monopoly. *Quarterly Journal of Economics* 85(Feburary): 77–96.

Owen, B.M., and Braeutigam, R. 1978. *The Regulation Game: Strategic*

Use of the Administrative Process. Cambridge, Mass.: Ballinger.

Pacific Gas and Electric Company. 1979. Time-of-use rates for very large customers. Second annual report, Rate Department, Load Management Section. San Francisco, March 31.

Panzar, J.C. 1976. A neoclassical approach to peak load pricing. *Bell Journal of Economics* 7, no. 2 (Autumn): 521–530.

_____. 1979. The Pareto domination of usage insensitive pricing. In *Proceedings of the Sixth Annual Telecommunications Policy Research,* ed. H. Dordick, pp. 425–436. Lexington, Mass.: Lexington Books, D.C. Heath.

Panzar, J.C., and Faulhaber, G.R. 1977. Optimal two-part tariffs with self-selection. *Bell Laboratories Discussion Paper* 74(January).

Park, R.E.; Mitchell, B.M.; Wetzel, B.M.; 1980. Demographic effects of local calling under measured vs. flat rate service: Analysis of data from GTE Illinois experiment. In *Pacific Telecommunications Conference Proceedings*. Honolulu, Hawaii.

Pavarini, C. 1978. The effect of flat-to-measured rate conversions on local telephone usage. *Proceedings of Mountain Bell Economics Seminar.* Keystone, Colo., August.

Peles, Y.C., and Stein, J.L. 1976. The effect of rate of return regulation is highly sensitive to the nature of uncertainty. *American Economic Review* 66(June): 278–289.

Perrakis, S. 1976*a*. Rate of return regulation of a monopoly firm with random demand. *International Economic Review* 17(Feburary): 149–162.

_____. 1976*b*. On the regulated price-setting monopoly firm with a random demand curve. *American Economic Review* 66(June): 410–416.

Petersen, H.C. 1975. An empirical test of regulation effects. *Bell Journal of Economics* 6(Spring): 111–126.

_____. 1976. The effect of "fair value" rate base valuation in electric utility regulation. *Journal of Finance* 31(December): 1487–1490.

Pickett, J.C., and Herden, J.P. 1977. National electric rate design policies. Written statements prepared for House Subcommittee on Energy and Power, May 23.

Poirier, D.J. 1978. Econometric issues in load forecasting. In *Proceedings of EPRI Workshop on Modeling and Analysis of Electricity Demand by Time-of-Day*, ed. D. Aigner, pp. 3-1 to 3-54. San Diego, Calif.: June 11–14.

Public Uility Regulatory Policies Act of 1978. 1978. *Public Law 9S-617, Title I.* Sections 111–115.

Ramsey, F. 1927. A contribution to the theory of taxation. *The Economic Journal* 37(March): 47–61.

Rau, N.L. On regulation and uncertainty: Comment. *American Economic Review* 69(March): 190–194.

References

Rees, R. 1980. Consumer choice and non-price rationing in public utility pricing. In *Regulated Industries and Public Enterprise*, eds. B.M. Mitchell and P.R. Kleindorfer. Lexington, Mass.: Lexington Books, D.C. Heath.

Research Triangle Institute. 1978. Analytical master plan for the analysis of the data from the elective utility rate demonstration projects I and II. June. Research Triangle Park, N.C.

Robeson, F.E.; Norland, D.L.; Gannon, M. 1978. Economic and social costs of over-supply *versus* under-supply of electric generating capacity. *Edison Electric Institute Publication No. 78–50*. Washington.

Robicheck, A.A. 1978. Regulation and modern finance theory. *Journal of Finance* 33(June): 693–705.

Rohlfs, J. 1974. A theory of interdependent demand for a communications service. *Bell Journal of Economics and Management Science* 5(Spring).

———. 1978. Economically efficient Bell-System pricing. Unpublished Bell Laboratories memorandum, Attachment H. Transmitted by R.L. McGuire of AT&T to Congressman Lionel Van Deerlin. October 31.

———. 1979. Economically-efficient Bell-System pricing. *Economics Discussion Paper* 138. Murray Hill, N.J.: Bell Laboratories.

Salomon Brothers (Members of NYSE). 1973. Fuel mix data and fuel adjustment clause survey. July 30. In U.S. House of Representatives, 94th Cong., October 1975. Washington, D.C.

Samuelson, P.A. 1976. *Foundations of Economic Analysis*. New York: Atheneum, pp. 125–126.

San Diego Gas and Electric Company. 1979. Annual report for 1978. San Diego, Calif., Rates and Valuation.

Schmalensee, R. 1978. A note on economics of scale and natural monopoly in the distribution of public utility services. *Bell Journal of Economics* 9, no. 1 (Spring): 270–276.

Schmidt, L.W. 1979. A telephone industry perspective. In *Perspectives on Local Measured Service*, ed. J.A. Baruk, pp. 179–200. Proceedings of Telecommunications Industry Workshop. Kansas City, Mo., March 13–14.

Schramm, R., and Sherman, R. 1977. A rationale for administered pricing. *Southern Economic Journal*, July, pp. 125–135.

Scott, F.A. 1979. An economic analysis of fuel adjustment clauses. Ph.D. dissertation, University of Virginia.

Sharpe, W. 1964. Capital asset prices: A theory of market equilibrium under conditions of risk. *Journal of Finance*, September.

Sherman, R. 1974. *The Economics of Industry*. Boston: Little, Brown.

———. 1977a. *Ex ante* rates of return for regulated utilities. *Land Economics* 53(May): 172–184.

———. 1977b. Financial aspects of the regulated firm. *Southern Economic Journal* 44(October): 240–248.

Sherman, R., and Visscher, M.L. 1979. Rate-of-return regulation and price structure. In *Problems in Public Utility Economics and Regulation*, ed. M.A. Crew. Lexington, Mass.: D.C. Heath.

Sheshinski, E. 1971. Welfare aspects of a regulatory constraint: Note. *American Economic Review* 61, no. 1 (March): 175–178.

Southern California Edison Company. 1979. Time-of-use study for very large power commercial and industrial customers. Rosemead, Calif.: Revenue Requirements Department, Load Research Division. May.

Squire, L. 1973. Some aspects of optimal pricing for telecommunications. *Bell Journal of Economics and Management Science* 4(Autumn).

Stewart, J.F. 1979. Plant size, plant factor, and the shape of the average cost function in electric power generation, a nonhomogeneous capital approach. *Bell Journal of Economics and Management Science* 10 (Autumn): 549–565.

Taylor, L.D. 1975. The demand for electricity: A survey. *Bell Journal of Economics and Management Science* 6(Autumn) 74–110 and 6, no. 1 (Spring).

_____. 1978. The demand for telephone service: A survey and critique of the literature. Monograph. University of Arizona. November.

_____. 1979. On modeling the residential demand for electricity by time of day. *Journal of Econometrics* 9, nos. 1, 2 (January): 97–115.

_____. 1980. *Telecommunications Demand: A Survey and Critique*. Cambridge, Mass.: Ballinger Publishing Co.

Taylor, L.D.; Blattenberger, G.R.; Rennhack, R. 1980. The residential demand for energy. Report to the Electric Power Research Institute on RP1098. Lexington, Mass.: Data Resources, Inc.

Telson, M.L. 1973. The economics of reliability for electric generation systems. Report MIT-EL 73-016. Cambridge, Mass.: Energy Laboratory, Massachusetts Institute of Technology.

_____. 1975. The economics of alternative levels of reliability for electric power generation systems. *Bell Journal of Economics* 6(Autumn): 679–694.

Thatcher, L.W. 1954. Cost-of-capital techniques employed in determining the rate of return for public utilities. *Land Economics* 30(May): 85–111.

Thompson, H.E., and Thatcher, L.W. 1973. Required rate of return for equity capital under conditions of growth and consideration of regulatory lag. *Land Economics* 49 (May): 148–162.

Trebing, H.M., ed. 1978. Assessing new pricing concepts in public utilities. Public Utilities papers, Michigan State University.

Tschirhart, J., and Jen, F. 1979. Behavior of a monopoly offering interruptible service. *Bell Journal of Economics and Management Science* 10, no. 1 (Spring): 244–258.

U.S. Department of Energy (formerly FPC). *Statistics of Privately-Owned Electric Utilities in the United States*. Annual.

References

_____. 1978. *The National Energy Act (NEA), General Information* 2 (November).

_____. 1979. Office of Public Affairs. *A New Start, The National Energy Act* 1.

U.S. House of Representatives. 1975. Electric utility automatic fuel adjustment clauses. Report by the Subcommittee on Oversight and Investigations of the Committee on Interstate and Foreign Commerce, 94th Cong. (October).

Vogelsang, I., and Finsinger, J. 1979. A regulatory adjustment process for optimal pricing by multiproduct monopoly firms. *Bell Journal of Economics and Management Science* 10(Spring): 157–171.

Vogelsang, I., and Neuefeind, W. 1979. The impact of uncertainty on the effects of rate of return regulation remains highly uncertain. *Energy Laboratory, Massachusetts Institute of Technology, Working Paper* MIT-EL 79-011 WP. February.

Von Rabenau, B., and Stahl, K. 1974. Dynamic aspects of public goods: A further analysis of the telephone system. *Bell Journal of Economics and Management Science* 5(Autumn).

Weisbrod, B.A. 1964. Collective-consumption of individual consumption goods. *Quarterly Journal of Economics* 78(August).

Wenders, J.T., and Lyman, A. R. 1977. A benefit cost analysis of the peak load pricing of electricity to residential users. In *Forecasting and Modeling Time-of-Day and Seasonal Electricity Demands*, ed. A. Lawrence. EA 578–SR. Palo Alto, Calif.: Electric Power Research Institute.

_____. 1979. An analysis of the benefits and costs of seasonal time-of-day electricity rates. In *Problems in Public Utility Economics and Regulation*, ed. M.A. Crew. Lexington, Mass.: Lexington Books, D.C. Heath.

White, S.B.; Alexander, B.V.; Duncan, D.P. 1978. Analysis of the effects of the time-of-use electricity rate in the Ohio electric utility demonstration project. Draft final report. Research Triangle Institute. August. Research Triangle Park, N.C.

White, S.B.; Clayton, C.A.; Alexander, B.V.; Duncan, D.P. 1978. Analysis of the effects of the time-of-use electricity rate in the Connecticut electric utility demonstration project. Draft final report. Research Triangle Institute. July. Research Triangle Park, N.C.

Williamson, O.E. 1966. Peak load pricing and optimal capacity. *American Economic Review* 56(September): 810–827.

_____. 1968. Economies as an antitrust defense: The welfare tradeoffs. *American Economic Review* 58(March): 18–36.

_____. 1976. Franchise bidding for natural monopolies-in-general and with respect to CATV. *Bell Journal of Economics and Management Science* 7(Spring): 73–104.

Willig, R.D. 1978. Pareto-superior nonlinear outlay schedules. *Bell Journal of Economics and Management Science* 9(Spring): 56–59.

———. 1980. The theory of network access pricing. Paper presented at the Illinois Bell/Northwestern University Conference on the Economics of Telecommunications: Current Research on Demand, Pricing, and Regulation. Evanston, Ill.: James L. Allen Center, Northwestern University. January 17–18.

Wisconsin Public Service Commission. 1974. Madison Gas and Electric Company: Docket no. 2-U-7423. (August 8).

———. 1975. Policy Statement and Notice of Proposed Rules, Docket No. 01-ER-1.

———. 1977. Wisconsin Electric Power Company: Findings of fact and Order nos. 6630-ER-2 and 6630-ER-5 (December).

———. Status of time-of-day pricing in Wisconsin. Mimeographed.

Zajac, E.E. 1970. A geometric treatment of Averch-Johnson's behavior of the firm model. *American Economic Review* 60(March): 117–125.

Seminar Speakers and Discussants

James Alleman
Manager, Policy Research
General Telephone and Electronics

David P. Baron
Morrison Professor of Decision Sciences
North Western University

Biff Bentley
Supervisor, Forecasting
Florida Power and Light Company

Sanford V. Berg
Associate Professor of Economics and Executive Director of Public Utility Research Center
University of Florida

Gary Bowman
Associate Professor of Economics
Temple University

Frank Cassidy
Manager, Engineering Economics
Public Service Electric and Gas Company

Tom Cowing
Associate Professor of Economics
State University of New York at Binghamton

Michael A. Crew
Professor, Graduate School of Management, and Director of the Business Research Center
Rutgers University

Robert E. Dansby
Member of Technical Staff
Bell Laboratories
Adjunct Associate Professor
Graduate School of Management
Rutgers University

Horace J. De Podwin
Dean, Graduate School of Management
Rutgers University

Catherine C. Eckel
Assistant Professor of Policy Analysis
University of British Columbia

Fred S. Grygiel
Chief Public Utility Economist
New Jersey Board of Public Utilities

H.E. Harvey, Jr.
Director
American Telephone & Telegraph

Wallace Hendricks
Associate Professor of Economics
University of Illinois

Duncan M. Holthausen
Associate Professor of Economics
North Carolina State University

Paul R. Kleindorfer
Professor of Decision Sciences
University of Pennsylvania

Roger Koenker
Member of Technical Staff
Bell Laboratories

J. Robert Malko
Program Manager
Electric Utility Rate Design Study
Electric Power Research Institute

Pat Marfisi
Supervisor
American Telephone and Telegraph Company

Bridger M. Mitchell
Senior Research Fellow
The Rand Corporation

Michael M. Murphy
Staff Economist
United Telecommunications

John C. Panzar
Manager, Economic Analysis
Bell Laboratories

Frank A. Scott
Assistant Professor of Economics
Auburn University

Roger Sherman
Professor of Economics
University of Virginia

Rodney Stevenson
Assistant Professor of Business
University of Wisconsin

Robert A. Taggart
Assistant Professor of Finance
Northwestern University

Lester Taylor
Professor of Economics
University of Arizona

Ingo Vogelsang
Assistant Professor of Economics
Rheinische Friedrich-Wilhelms
 University, Bonn

David K. Whitcomb
Professor, Graduate School of
 Management
Rutgers University

About the Editor

Michael A. Crew was educated in England, receiving the B. Com. and Ph.D. degrees from the University of Birmingham and the University of Bradford, respectively. He has taught economics at universities in the United Kingdom and the United States. He has published five books and several articles on public-utility economics, monopoly, and antitrust in the leading professional journals. Two of his recent books in the field of public utilities are *Problems in Public-Utility Economics and Regulation* (Lexington Books, D.C. Heath, 1979) and, with P.R. Kleindorfer, *Public Utility Economics* (St. Martin's Press, 1979). He has been a consultant to state and federal regulators and utility companies. He is professor and director of the Business Research Center, Graduate School of Management, Rutgers University.